ALSO BY MICHELE WEINER-DAVIS

In Search of Solutions (with William O'Hanlon)
Divorce Busting

Change Your Life and Everyone In It

HOW TO:

Transform Difficult Relationships
Overcome Anxiety and Depression
Break Free from Self-Defeating Ways of
Thinking, Feeling, and Acting
In One Month or Less

Michele Weiner-Davis

Simon & Schuster Paperbacks
New York   London   Toronto   Sydney

Simon & Schuster Paperbacks
Rockefeller Center
1230 Avenue of the Americas
New York, NY 10020

First paperback edition 1996

Simon & Schuster Paperbacks and colophon are registered
trademarks of Simon & Schuster, Inc.

Designed by Irving Perkins Associates

Manufactured in the United States of America

10   9   8   7

Library of Congress Cataloging-in-Publication Data is available.

ISBN-13: 978-0-671-86755-3

ISBN-13: 978-0-684-82469-7 (Pbk)

Previously published as *Fire Your Shrink!*

Acknowledgments

BEHIND EVERY GOOD manuscript, there's a good woman . . . and a good man. Actually, there are quite a few of them. I am truly grateful to those who have helped and inspired me.

First, there are my dear family members, Byll, Leah, and Lila, who politely kept asking, "How's the book going?" Now I can finally say, "Swell." Thanks for your love and support. Next in line are the close friends whose emotional support has kept me centered. Arnold Woodruff deserves special mention for being such a great friend for so long and for all his help with the manuscript. Noble Golden, Cathy Pidek, Diane Sollee, thanks for being you.

I want to thank the colleagues who have shared information, cases and time with me: Lorraine Adam, Mary Andrews, Rich Simon, David Weir, and Frank Pittman. In particular, I want to thank Steve de Shazer for helping me to become "simple-minded," and Michael Yapko and Mike Nichols for being so generous with their time. My assistant, Virginia Peeples, deserves special appreciation for her dedication to making my life simpler and for her extensive help in preparing the manuscript for publication. Mindy "Mary Poppins" Baker, who won't have to keep the kids quiet anymore, deserves my gratitude.

I want to thank Suzanne Gluck, my agent, for encouraging me to write this book and for moving us out of title hell; and Becky Saletan, my editor, whose enthusiasm, accessibility, superb editorial skills, and compulsive thoroughness have made this collaboration an extremely productive and enjoyable one.

I'd like to thank the American Association of Marriage and Family Therapy for its incredible support of my work and for the opportunities it has given me to spread the word. I am also grateful to the groups who have sponsored my workshops and the people who have attended them. I have learned a great deal from you.

These acknowledgments would not be complete without mention of my clients, who have trusted me enough to share their lives with me and, in so doing, have taught me the greatest lesson about how people change. Thank you so very much.

The case examples presented in this book are based on real people and their experiences, but I have changed names and other details to protect the anonymity of the people and their families.

To my wonderful families, the one that created me and the one that sustains me. I am very lucky.

To my mother, who has given me the gift of a lifetime—unconditional and unending love and support. I'm forever grateful.

To my father, whose "I can do anything" philosophy has lit an ever-burning fire beneath me.

To Danielle, who blossomed into a loving and incredibly beautiful young woman during the writing of this book.

To Zach, whose presence brings unbelievable joy to my life.

Finally, to my husband and best friend, Jim, without whose love and support none of this would have been possible. I love you more than you'll ever know.

Contents

"The self-help tradition has always been covertly authoritarian and conformist, relying as it does on a mystique of expertise, encouraging people to look outside themselves for standardized instruction on how to be, teaching us that different people with different problems can easily be saved by the same techniques. It is anathema to independent thought. . . . The best self-help books are like good parents, dispensing common sense."

—*Wendy Kaminer*, I'm Dysfunctional, You're Dysfunctional

Chapter One

Why Ask Why?

By VIRTUE OF the fact that you picked up this book, I know something about you. You're ready for a change in your life. You may want to change something about yourself—you might want to lose weight, free yourself from depression, or improve your self-esteem. On the other hand, perhaps you feel fine about yourself, it's the people around you who need to shape up—you might feel your partner is overly critical or inattentive, your kids are driving you nuts, or your coworkers are making your life miserable. Or all of the above.

I also know that when I say, "You're ready for a change in your life," it doesn't mean that you weren't ready to make this change yesterday, last month, or even last year. Chances are, your thirst for change didn't just happen. You've been thinking and dreaming about it for some time now. You've probably even tried to make things better. But, you're still not where you want to be. Real change, it seems, has been extremely difficult and frustratingly elusive.

I know because that's exactly what I used to think—and that's really scary because I'm an "expert," a psychotherapist, a shrink—the person whose job it is to help people change their lives. But I confess. There was a time when I was stumbling in the dark, when my thinking about truly helping people was just wishful thinking.

Thankfully, those days are long gone. Through a process of trial and error I figured out what works. I have learned that change isn't nearly as complicated or involved as I once thought.

I want you to know that there is a new way to find solutions—immediate solutions—to chronic problems that doesn't require you to analyze the problem to death. In fact, it doesn't require painful re-hashing of the problem at all. Although there's a widespread belief that understanding *why* you are having a problem will help you to solve the problem, you know in your heart that it simply isn't so. Knowing *why* you overeat or are depressed doesn't help you control your eating or make you feel better. Understanding how you were raised doesn't help you stop fighting with your spouse or get along better with your kids. Recognizing what's at the root of the friction in the office doesn't make it go away. Perhaps you've secretly suspected this all along but were afraid to acknowledge it because, *in theory*, analyzing a problem is supposed to help. But you and I both know it doesn't! It only makes you an expert on why you're stuck. By now, you probably have an advanced degree in understanding how the problems in your life came into being, but take it from me, there's no future in it.

For the past ten years, I have been observing miracles. An eight-year-old girl, described by her teacher as "the most insecure little girl I've ever seen," experiences perpetual urinary problems and a cough so wrenching that she vomits nightly, problems her doctors diagnose as psychosomatic and stress-related. Within weeks, she is symptom-free and is transformed into a well-adjusted, happy, loving, healthy child, leaving her parents, doctors, and teacher amazed. A woman in her mid-twenties, depressed beyond words over the loss of a boyfriend six months before, regains her zest for life within days. A middle-aged salesman at risk of losing his job attacks his work with an enthusiasm he hasn't felt for years and doubles his accounts within weeks. On the brink of divorce, a couple with years of emotional distance between them put a halt to the legal process and successfully regenerate their love.

If you're thinking that all this sounds too good to be true, I couldn't agree more. After ten years of witnessing countless transformations such as these, I still find them unbelievable. I am in awe of how quickly people find solutions to complex problems or make momentous deci-sions that radically improve their lives. After all, conventional wisdom suggests that change of any kind is painful and slow. The miracles I see simply defy common sense. They also defy everything I had ever been taught about how people change.

Seventeen years ago, I hung out my shingle as a professional therapist. My training had been fairly traditional. I had learned to be an empathetic listener, to watch closely for telling body language, to explore people's childhoods to unravel the causes of current problems, to encourage the expression of intense feelings of anger or hurt. I had been taught that people really can't escape the stranglehold of the past until they relive sometimes excruciating memories and glean the appropriate insights or "truths" about their lives. I conscientiously and religiously put these principles into practice but soon discovered a shocking fact. They simply didn't work.

For example, a couple I was seeing complained of frequent arguments over the handling of money. Each time one of them wished to make a purchase, the other balked and an argument ensued: "You tell me that I shouldn't spend money on new work clothes, but you go to every sporting event imaginable," and so on. Soon, the arguing about money spilled over into other areas of their lives. They now fought about housework, child care, and how free time was spent.

I had been trained to believe that, in order to overcome problems such as these, people must first gain insight into the ways in which their childhood has influenced them. The theory is that problems are symptoms of underlying issues that stem from childhood experiences and cannot be resolved until the root of the problem is identified and "worked through."

Accordingly, I determined that this couple's arguments were a symptom of underlying issues of power and control in their marriage. We were very thorough in our search for clues about the origins of these problems. They discussed how each of them was raised and examined their own parents' marriages for telltale signs of similar struggles. Painstakingly, we assembled all the pieces of the puzzle, until it was clear to all three of us how their respective upbringings had affected them. Whereupon the couple turned to me and said, "Michele, now we understand *why* we are having arguments about money, but we still don't have a clue as to what to do differently." Unfortunately, it wasn't the last time I heard that objection.

It slowly became apparent to me that understanding *why* someone has a particular problem has absolutely nothing to do with solving it. All the insight in the world didn't help most of my clients improve the quality of their lives. Those who were overweight knew exactly *why* they were overeating—to fill an emotional void, to hide, to repel intimacy, and so on—but they continued to overeat. Quarrelsome spouses recognized how the divergent expectations they brought to marriage were often at the root of their clashes, but this awareness didn't make one bit of difference: the fighting persisted. People plagued with low self-esteem realized how derogatory and belittling messages given to them as children made them feel insecure and inadequate, but nothing changed: they still felt lousy. Overly permissive parents acknowledged after long soul-searching that their permissiveness was an extreme reaction to their own restrictive upbringings, but this insight failed to assist them in setting limits for their children. In short, the people with whom I worked all had the usual "aha!" revelations—flashes of tremendous insight—but when they returned for subsequent sessions their misery persisted, the only difference being that they were now experts on why they were unhappy.

The fact that the majority of my clients left therapy enlightened but unchanged confused me. According to my training, the process of gaining insight should have been more helpful. Eager to make sense of my experiences, I asked other therapists about their "therapy failures" and learned that I was not alone. My colleagues, however, concluded that clients who didn't solve their problems during therapy had only them-

"Well, I do have this recurring dream that one day I might see some results."

selves to blame. "They're just resistant," I was told. "She is not ready to change." "He is only window-shopping—not really motivated." It was tempting simply to agree, but at heart I was not convinced. My instincts told me that most people seek professional help because they are in pain and really do want to change. I resolved to find a better way.

My urgency to find an effective problem-solving method was fueled by other unsettling discoveries about what really goes on behind therapists' closed doors. No longer confident that insight into the past would provide the vehicle for change, I fell back on the other techniques I had been taught to help my clients beyond impasses. One such method is based on the notion that people feel better when they "get their pain and anger out." So, whenever I noticed a wince cross a client's face, indicating fertile emotional ground, I'd faithfully urge, "Let it out, it's okay." I placed boxes of tissues within handy arm's length as an unspoken reminder that tears are good. In no time at all, many of my clients were "letting it out," and when they sobbed I felt proud that I was able to help them do such "intense work." The intensity of the sessions convinced me that I was doing "real therapy."

But I soon became aware that, instead of feeling relief when they spent the majority of a session discussing painful memories or uncomfortable feelings, my clients felt terrible when they walked out the door. I consoled them (and myself) by reminding them that people must feel their pain in order to get beyond it. But the truth of the matter was that, despite their so-called catharsis, most of my clients didn't get to the other side. Session after session they returned, the dour expression on their faces indicating that nothing had changed.

It became clear to me that, although "getting it out" was cathartic for some people under certain circumstances, the relief it gave them was short-lived. For others, it brought no relief at all. Some of my more honest clients eventually admitted that they looked forward to therapy sessions about as much as they looked forward to going to the dentist. I couldn't keep from pondering the irony that a tool that is supposed to help people feel better seemed to leave many people feeling worse.

My faith in conventional therapy methods was running thin, but at least I thought I could rely on a principle I'd learned in Psychology 101, that relationship problems can be resolved when people become aware of their "inner feelings" and express them to others. Therefore, I routinely chanted my therapist mantra—"Look at her and tell her how you feel inside"—assuming that it would magically bring about a solution. But once again I was disappointed. I discovered that by the time most people come for therapy they are already acutely aware of and have expressed their feelings to others, yet their problems still remain. Exploring these feelings in therapy did nothing to resolve the differences between people.

For example, even when a parent told his child how her irresponsible behavior in school and at home disappointed and hurt him, she continued cutting classes and being fresh at home. Soon after a woman told her husband that she wanted him to spend more quality time with the family, he informed her that he had signed up for a new golf league. A week after a woman confessed to a friend her irritation at the friend's habitual lateness, her friend showed up a half-hour late for lunch. A husband told his wife that he needed more intimacy in their marriage, yet she continued to use every imaginable excuse to avoid his company. Unfortunately, all of these divulgences seemed to fall on deaf ears. No one changed his or her behavior as a result of hearing how it displeased others, even when the feedback was sincere and sensitively stated.

Gradually, and reluctantly, I concluded that the effectiveness of understanding and expressing feelings about relationship problems is drastically overrated. In fact, I noticed that rehashing each party's discordant feelings ad nauseam tends to exaggerate differences, making them more difficult to reconcile.

I was at a loss. It seemed that nothing I had been taught about helping people to change worked. That's when I encountered a radically different therapy approach, solution-oriented brief therapy (SBT). At the time, brief therapy was in its infancy. Scattered about were small revolutionary think tanks, pioneers courageous enough to question traditional psychotherapy gospel. Upon discovering these forward thinkers and their unorthodox methods, I sensed immediately that I had "come home."

As its name implies, SBT works quickly, enabling most people to resolve their problems in three to six sessions. The secret to its brevity is that, instead of taking a long introspective journey into the past, SBT helps people to envision a positive future and to identify fail-safe strategies for getting there. Instead of channeling people's efforts into understanding *why* they are experiencing problems, SBT helps them figure out how to resolve problems. Instead of identifying the causes of problems, SBT identifies the causes of solutions. It is a technology for change, not introspection, allowing most people to feel better about their lives within days, not months or years.

This approach is based on a very simple formula: do more of what works and less of what doesn't. No matter what type of problem people are experiencing or how bad the situation seems at the moment, there are times when things go more smoothly. First, SBT reminds people to recognize *what they already know about what works* so that they can repeat successful solutions. Second, SBT helps people to identify and eliminate the repetitive, unproductive patterns that lead to failure. The most common complaint I used to hear from clients was, "I still don't know have a clue about what *to do* to change my situation." I don't hear that anymore. Now my clients leave armed with a plan they can implement the moment they walk out the door.

As I began practicing SBT, several advantages of this focused approach quickly became apparent. Most people felt some relief from their problems immediately. The emphasis on solutions showed people light at the end of the tunnel, which had a powerfully reassuring effect, especially after months or years of brooding about their problems. Often they had become so immersed in their difficulties that they had come to believe that nothing would or could ever change. SBT got them to question that premise. Many told me as they left the initial meeting that for the first time in months they felt hope.

It became clear that, the more hopeful people became, the more they expected good things to happen, and therefore the more energy they put into making good things happen—hence, many more good things did in fact happen. More than ever before, I began to appreciate the power of optimism and the toxicity of pessimism about the future. Pessimism saps people's energies and prevents them from taking—or noticing—baby steps forward. I realized that the traditional methods I had been using, by not offering some instant relief, actually increased pessimism, making positive outcomes less likely. The sixties saying "If you're not part of the solution, you're part of the problem" took on new meaning for me. Part of the magic of SBT, I began to see, is that it immediately became part of the solution, instilling hopefulness and helping people to reverse downward spirals swiftly. Here is a message a woman recently left on my answering machine:

I called you last week and I wrote you a letter and I was desperate. I was going to commit suicide. You will never know what you have done with my life. One week ago I had written my goodbyes to everyone. This week, it's 5 A.M. this morning, and I am going to a gym to work out. You have changed my whole life. I just can't tell you. I can't believe that through two years of counseling and thousands of dollars all I ever got was, "You have to change your past," and the patterns in our marriage never changed, not one bit, until I saw you on television. It gave me hope and I just can't believe the person I am this week. Thank you so much.

Nor did SBT require me to drag people through the past, eliciting uncomfortable memories and feelings. It always seemed absurd to me to rub people's faces in the failures of their parents and then expect them to feel resourceful enough to change their lives! Even on those rare occasions when it worked, I felt as if I were pulling people into the middle of a lake so I could save them from drowning.

Instead of probing the past, which is often painful and always unchangeable, SBT helps people envision a future without the problem and to focus on how it will be possible to get there. As a result, clients feel tremendously empowered, a far more useful frame of mind for solving problems.

But here's the most interesting part. Shortly after I began practicing this method, I made a startling observation. It became apparent to me that the vast majority of clients who consulted me had already begun to resolve their problems on their own before they even got to the initial session! Without my help, they had taken important steps to improve their lives. All along I had been attributing the sudden changes in people's lives to the power of SBT in my "expert" hands, but it began to dawn on me that most people were capable of getting the ball rolling without therapy of any sort.

Though feeling some trepidation, I discussed my observations with my colleagues. We wondered if I had just opened the lid to Pandora's box. "What will other therapists think of this?" one colleague fretted. Another said, "Boy, Michele, you really have the tiger by the tail." Intrigued by my discovery, I suggested that we research the prevalence of "pretherapy changes." As I will explain in greater detail later, my own research demonstrated that two-thirds of the people who come for therapy begin to change as soon as they make their first appointment—that is, before the appointment itself! This suggests that *the decision to change is itself change.* It also clearly shows that people are considerably more resourceful than they give themselves credit for.

Oddly enough, few of my clients ever mentioned the positive changes they had initiated on their own unless I specifically asked about them. But once they heard themselves tell me, "Yes, things have been better since I called," the journey to empowerment had begun. I began to see that, for people to overcome the hurdles in their lives, they need to ask themselves the right questions. I became determined to teach people the powerful questions that could help them discover within themselves the answers for which they are searching.

The more I saw my clients change, the more strongly I believed in every person's ability to create his or her own destiny. No matter how serious or how deeply entrenched their problems were, I felt certain that my clients would be able to find solutions. This faith led to astonishing rates of incredibly positive outcomes. Eventually, I became aware that I approached my practice with a sense that every problem is solvable. There were, needless to say, a few exceptions, but my enthusiasm, together with my clients' newfound optimism and resourcefulness—and the powerful technology that guided us both—dramatically increased the positive outcomes.

I know that you are probably thinking, "How is it possible that problems, particularly long-standing ones, can be resolved so quickly?" Believe me, I asked myself that same question many, many times, but in case after case, the results spoke for themselves. Without dissecting the past, my clients were feeling better about themselves and their loved ones and getting more out of their lives in a remarkably short period of time. Still, I worried whether these improvements would last. I asked myself, "Is it possible that this is just a quick fix?" and "If we don't get to the bottom of things, won't other problems develop down the road?" Here's what I learned: In follow-up surveys, people have reported that the gains they made in therapy have continued, and that there has been additional progress over time. [1]

I knew I had in my possession compelling information about how people change, and it wasn't long before I felt a strong need to share what I was learning with my colleagues. I began to offer professional training seminars and co-authored a professional book, *In Search of Solutions*, to disseminate the information. From the enormous popularity of the seminars and the book, it was clear that thousands of therapists had become equally dissatisfied with their out-dated tools and were looking for alternatives.

Gratifying as it was (and is) to teach my peers, an undeniable frustration began to creep in. I desperately wanted to reach more people. I was well aware that not everybody goes to a therapist (except in Manhattan!), and therefore the vast majority of people had no chance to learn of this amazingly simple but effective method for creating change. I wanted to share my passion about the transformations I had been observing in people's lives with the general public.

Given the astronomical divorce rate in the United States, I decided to focus my energies on what was clearly a problem for so many people. In *Divorce Busting*, I presented readers with a radically different approach to resolving marital problems and the equally radical notion that most marriages can be saved, if even one partner so chooses. I was deluged with phone calls and letters testifying that the book had restored hope and resurrected marriage vows. Countless people told me how they had made dramatic changes, finding creative solutions to long-standing problems, *without the help of a therapist.* "My dear Ms. Weiner-Davis," one woman wrote:

I'd like to take this time to thank you from the bottom of my heart. My husband and I were living like brother and sister, sleeping in separate rooms and just waiting to get the money together to hire a lawyer for the divorce. I was totally devastated. I wanted to work things out and he just wanted out. There had been more tears and fights than I care to count. I felt like a loser with no pride left to lose and then I saw you on the Oprah Winfrey Show and something made me tape it. My husband and I watched the tape together and he told me I could get the book "for all the good it would do." The next day I read the book like a woman possessed and I felt like you had gathered your research in my living room. I asked my husband if he wanted to read it and I got a very stern, "No!" Three days later he left for a two week cruise (he's in the navy) and I noticed my book was gone. When he returned, he put our six year old to bed in her own bed where he usually slept and this shocked me because she had been sleeping with me. We sat and talked and we laughed, something we haven't done in a year. He moved back into our room and just last night after making love he asked me to marry him all over again and I very happily agreed. Thank you again for your wonderful book and for saving my marriage.

I began to realize that I had only scratched the surface. If people could so readily learn a solution-oriented approach to marital problems from a book, there was no reason a book couldn't teach them to apply the same approach to *any* of the problems they might experience—depression, low self-esteem, lack of motivation, loneliness, grief, panic attacks, eating disorders, sexual dysfunction, lack of communication, financial difficulties, substance abuse, poor academic and job performance, juvenile delinquency, and so on. That's how I decided to write *Change Your Life and Everyone In It.*

So, whether you picked up this book because you feel depressed, your children are driving you crazy, your friendships are disappointing, your spouse refuses to see the error of his ways, enjoyment has gone out of your life, you wish you could lose weight, you want to feel more love, you feel overburdened at work, your relationship is no longer satisfying, or because therapy has lightened your pocket but not your load, you have come to the right place. The very fact that you have picked it up is evidence that you have made the decision to change. You have set the wheel of change in motion, which is the hardest part of the process. Congratulations! Now you just need to be pointed in the right direction.

But how? Unlike most self-help books, this one does not offer checklists and step-by-step routines for dealing with specific problems. Why not? Because real change doesn't work like that. What works for you may not work for your neighbor. What works one day may not work the next. What works with your oldest child might bomb with your youngest. What appeals to you might be unappealing to someone else. Out of enormous respect for the complexity of the human race, I believe that each person's path to solution is unique.

For example, if you have ever had trouble getting over the loss of a loved one to death, divorce, or a breakup, perhaps you have been advised to talk about your feelings with other people, to help yourself grieve. Although this is often a viable suggestion, it doesn't work for everyone. The fact is that we all grieve differently. Some people need to share feelings with friends and family, some need more private meditative time, whereas others just need to keep themselves busy. Some folks feel better after crying, others feel worse. Some people need a great deal of time before getting involved in another relationship, others want companionship sooner. No single method works for everyone in every instance.

What this book offers instead are powerful formulas that will enable you to assess *your* situation and what *you* need to do next to improve it. By applying these proven formulas to the dynamics of your situation, you will be able to devise a plan to change your life. If you've come to believe that you were raised in a dysfunctional family or that you're codependent, a woman who loves too much, a compulsive rescuer, an Adult Child of an Alcoholic, a food-, sex-, shop-, work-, or fill-in-the-blank-aholic, but that nagging little voice inside your head is still asking, "So what should I do about it?," read on. This book won't help make you an expert at diagnosing the causes of your problems, but it will certainly enable you to diagnose their solutions. Doesn't that make more sense anyway?

If you have ever found yourself saying (or thinking), "I'm so tired of talking about this situation," "I've told you a million times," or "I've analyzed this problem to death," it's time to stop living and breathing your problems and start solving them. Trust me, it will be a good deal less difficult. And I promise you, once you start thinking solutions, you will never want to go back.

I recognize that what I am suggesting may sound heretical or even outrageous, but the evidence I have seen is overwhelming: *it works.* I encourage and challenge you to let go of your old notions about change and open your mind to a completely different approach. If this is hard for you to do, consider this wise Zen saying: "In the beginner's mind there are many possibilities; in the expert's mind there are few." In other words, a beginner's mind is open to possibilities the expert can no longer see.

I heard a parable that may help to explain what I mean: A teacher went into a kindergarten classroom and drew a large dot on a chalkboard. Pointing to the dot, he asked the students, "What's this?" One little boy raised his hand. "That's a squashed bug." Another said, "That's the top of a telephone pole." A little girl disagreed: "It's a piece of candy." "Oh no," said her friend, "it's a bird flying way up in the sky."

The same teacher then went into a high-school classroom. Again he drew a large dot and asked, "What's this?" This time, though, he was met with dead silence. Moments passed before a girl finally raised her hand. "That is a dot on the chalkboard." The whole class seemed relieved that someone had finally stated the obvious.

It seems that we begin our lives with question marks but all too often end up with periods. That's unfortunate, because we learn so much more about ourselves and others when we approach life with an open mind. I've noticed that, when I embrace my work with a beginner's mind, people persistently teach me new and better ways to help them change. The day I start believing I've discovered the definitive answer to life's dilemmas is the day I stop doing what I do.

Perhaps solutions have escaped you because your expert mind has clouded your vision; you've seen only dots when you could have been seeing birds aloft in the sky. Maybe others have helped train you to think periods instead of question marks. That's why I'm inviting you to give your expert's mind a rest and rediscover the beginner in you as you read through this book. Once you do, you'll open the door to a world of possibilities. You'll discover commonsense solutions that will enable you to take expert control of your own life.

• • •

Seeing your way to solutions is a relatively easy endeavor once you give up on the idea that you must first know what caused your problem. I know that it's hard to relinquish that idea when practically everyone you know believes it's true. If you are someone who has been searching your past for clues about what's caused your dilemma, blaming the people in your life, reading self-help articles to diagnose your problem, or you've been chasing your tail in therapy, the next chapter will show you why you've been wasting your time. If you already know why "cause-hunting" isn't productive or you simply don't care, just fast forward to chapter three which will get you moving toward solutions immediately.

Chapter Two

Putting the Past Behind You

So WHAT'S THE problem with the usual problem-solving approach? If you're like most people, you assume that the first step to resolving any problem is to understand what caused it. Initially, you might look for immediate causes—"You started it." When that doesn't get you beyond a labyrinth of blame and counterblame, the search for causes intensifies. You delve into the distant past, blaming your spouse's irrational behavior on the way he or she was raised, or searching your memory for a childhood trauma that might explain a problem that plagues you as an adult.

This introspective process is so automatic—and universal—that you don't stop to question it. It may surprise you to know that it's evidence that you've subscribed to a Freudian way of thinking. In fact, even if you've never been to therapy, taken a psychology class, seen movies about therapy, listened to a psychologist, joined a self-help group, or even read another self-help book, you have been touched by Freudian ideas. The jargon associated with the theories of Sigmund Freud have become household words. Does your ego need boosting? How about your libido? Thinking of sex too much? Try sublimating. Repression, catharsis, unconscious, regression, defense mechanism, rationalize—these concepts are so much a part of our culture that the only way you could have avoided them is to have been brain-dead. A recent article in the *Washington Monthly* explained how this came to be.

A few decades ago, Freudian theory was only sold at expensive Central Park West psychoanalytic boutiques to customers like Mabel Dodge and Marshall Field III. Like most luxuries in America, however, it has been repackaged and is now available at McFreud outlets everywhere.

If you somehow made it through college without being exposed to the theories of Sigmund Freud, you will almost certainly be confronted with them shortly thereafter: You will be one, or you will know one, of the 10 million Americans who seek help from psychiatrists, psychologists, and psychiatric social workers every year.

. . . Although an increasing proportion of counseling and psychotherapy is not explicitly Freudian, most of it defers to the Viennese doctor indirectly. For the common denominator of virtually all counseling and psychotherapy is the Freudian assumption that intrapersonal and interpersonal problems—shyness, difficulty making a commitment, depression, anxiety, obsessiveness, slovenliness, substance abuse, eating disorders, loneliness, the inability to find meaning in life—originate in childhood experiences, especially in one's relations with parents. Thus solving those problems involves a painstaking, guided tour through one's childhood memories.[1]

Freud postulated that the key to unraveling emotional problems is hidden in a person's past, making it essential to retrieve childhood memories in order to comprehend the present. But as you may already have begun to discover, though analyzing the past can be interesting, it can also be a tremendous waste of time. The problem is, it doesn't provide answers about what to do next in the present if what you want to do is change. It only provides you with theories about *why* you are experiencing problems. In fact, the longer you analyze what's causing your problems, the longer you put off finding solutions.

Consider the following.

Milton Erickson, who many believe to be the father of SBT, was once asked to make a personal visit to an elderly woman who was depressed. He knew little about her or about the reason for her depression beforehand, except that she was an isolated woman whose only human contact was with her gardener and at church, which she attended regularly although she arrived late and left early.

When Erickson arrived at her home, he asked for a tour of her house. By and large, it was rather dingy, but she had a beautiful greenhouse and it appeared that she had a green thumb for African violets. Being a gardener himself, Erickson knew that African violets can be temperamental and was impressed with her skill.

Without inquiring about the reasons for her despair, he gave her a task. He told her to buy violets of every possible color, to take cuttings, and to nurture the cuttings into adult plants. He instructed her to get a list of the members of the congregation in her church and a church newsletter. Whenever there was an announcement of a christening, an engagement, an illness, or a death, she was to send one of her violets. Then he left.

The woman took the doctor's orders, and raised hundreds of plants. When she died, a headline in the local paper read: "African Violet Queen Dies, She Will be Missed by Thousands."

Without analyzing why she was depressed, without even talking about it, Erickson focused on the one bright spot in her life and helped it to grow. Who would ever have thought that the escape from this woman's despair was to become an African Violet Queen? Who would have ever believed it possible that she could be helped to feel better without knowing why she felt bad in the first place?

Before we get to what worked about this seemingly absurd approach, let's look at why the "logical" approach—analyzing what caused the problem in the first place—has such a poor track record.

To begin with, any trip down memory lane is fraught with inaccuracies, distortion, and blind alleys. That's because *memory is inherently unreliable*. No one, not even memory experts, knows exactly how it works, but some things are certain.[2] Contrary to popular belief, our minds are not like tape recorders or video cameras, objectively recording every incident and impression. Although millions of bits of information pass through our senses each day, we attend to only a minute fraction of these data; our perception is *selective*. Our memories represent only a tiny fraction of the total picture.

Perhaps you are saying to yourself, "Maybe I don't remember everything, but when something is important to me, I remember it." Research indicates that you are right, in part. For instance, when asked to recall a list of words that have been shown to them for several seconds, subjects are more likely to remember those that have meaning, such as "cat," "dog," "ball," "see," than nonsense syllables such as "biff," "mog," "fam," and so on.[3] If a situation holds great meaning for you— i.e., if it was emotionally charged—you are indeed more likely to remember it. But *how accurately* you remember is a different story, precisely because intense emotion can easily distort reality.

Many years ago, when I was in graduate school in Lawrence, Kansas, I invited some of my fellow students to my house for a party. One of them brought a friend with her. Being a gracious hostess, I introduced myself. I immediately noticed her New York accent and, a native New Yorker myself, asked where she'd grown up. To my amazement, it turned out she'd not only lived two blocks from my childhood home but had stood next to me in my first-grade class photo. Anyway, we got to reminiscing, and I mentioned that I thought our first-grade teacher was very mean. She thought otherwise and offered lots of detailed examples of what a caring, capable person our teacher had been. I had only one memory to offer, but it told quite a different story.

We were learning how to tell time. Mrs. Stevenson stood in front of the class with a cardboard clock and had each student say out loud what time it was, based on where she moved the hour and minute hands. If you were incorrect, you had to remain standing. I remember being one of the few students who erred. I recall the blood rushing to my face and not being able to resume my anonymity by sitting down. I never forgave her for this embarrassment, and the feeling has stayed with me all these years. The incident affected me so strongly that it tainted all other memories of first grade, both good and bad. It became the foreground, and everything else faded into the background.

Our beliefs, too, influence what we notice and what we remember. Anyone in a relationship knows the frustration of trying to convince your significant other what was *really* said during the argument on Saturday night. Two people, two completely different recollections. "I wish I had a tape recorder," are words regularly uttered in living rooms across the country.

She believes that she is a fair and reasonable person who is considerate of his feelings. Therefore, the details she remembers support her view. She recalls giving him ample time to share his views, not interrupting, and telling him several times that she could understand his feelings. He recalls nothing of the sort. He believes that she had made up her mind before they even began talking and that she just likes to hear herself talk. His memories of their argument support his · ʜ- recalls her interruptions, lengthy "lectures," and an unwillii quit fighting even after he requested a "time-out."

Each scans the interaction and focuses on events that substantiate his or her beliefs. There's an expression that "seeing is believing," but the opposite is also true: believing is seeing. Our beliefs about ourselves, others, and the world influence what we see, and therefore what we remember.

In addition to influencing *what* we remember, our current beliefs influence *how* we interpret memories. Were the kisses you received from your mother as a child "nurturing" or "smothering"? Did your older brother's perpetual teasing "toughen" you or make you "hypersensitive"? How you answer such questions depends heavily on how you feel about your mother and brother today, no matter how little these feelings have to do with the kisses or teasing itself.

A friend of mine told me that, when she and her siblings misbehaved, her father would throw a cupful of uncooked rice on the tile floor and make them kneel on it for hours at a time. Horrified, I asked her how she felt about her father. She said, "Oh, I adored him. He was extremely strict, but I always knew what to expect from him. With my mother, things were different. When we misbehaved, sometimes she would punish us, sometimes not. I always felt so safe with my dad. There were no surprises."

I was shocked by her response until I remembered how she had grieved when her father had died suddenly several years before. Had she evaluated his long-ago behavior as abusive, it would have been difficult to remember him with love. Her positive feelings about him were compounded by her feelings of loss, so she emphasized the positive aspects of his fathering.

Our current moods also affect our memory. Research shows that, if you ask people who describe themselves as depressed to tell you about their lives, what they talk about is depressing memories, one linked to another. Conversely, if you ask people who are happy to tell you about their lives, they relate a string of happy events and experiences.[4] We tend to sift the past for experiences that validate how we are feeling at the moment. A depressed person might dwell on the hardships of having grown up in poverty, whereas a happy person might fondly remember how having little money forced her to rely on her siblings for entertainment and drew them close.

Intense emotions can block as well as distort memories. Robert has attended several counseling sessions with his parents. For the most part, things have been going quite well, but today the family seem angry at each other as they enter my office. When I begin by asking about the good things that have happened since I've seen them last, they can't find much to say. Robert fails to recall that his parents have made an effort to allow him more freedom, nor do his parents recall the occasions on which he has acted more responsibly. Why? It turns out that they had an argument in the car about one of Robert's friends, whom his parents don't like very much. The unpleasant interaction has made it impossible for them to think clearly about their time together. Once we discuss the argument, their anger lifts, their mood changes, and positive memories come creeping back.

If nervousness has ever made you "draw a blank" during a performance or an exam for which you've rehearsed or studied long and hard, you know this phenomenon all too well. At the hospital to deliver my first baby, I was so nervous that, when the receptionist asked my address and telephone number, I had no idea what they were.

Memories are also subject to fading and distortion over time. The constant accumulation of experiences continually shapes and reshapes our beliefs, personalities, and outlooks on life, changing the lenses through which we view our memories. Unfortunately, many of the memories we seek when we are "trying to get at the root of things" are distant ones, which are likely to be hazy and incomplete. And when we have gaps in our memory, research shows that we tend to fill in the blanks. We make reasonable guesses about what happened, and over time, our conjectures pass as truths.

Finally, our memories are highly suggestible. A case in point: I feel most certain that I knew my grandfather well. I picture him easily and have a strong sense of what his presence was like. I can almost hear the sound of his voice and predict the things he would say. Yet he died several weeks before I was born. Why, then, do I feel so strongly as if he has been a part of my life? The answer is simple. Details I "remember" about my grandfather have been passed along to me by my mother, who was his "little sunshine" and loved him dearly in return. I've seen his face in old black-and-white photos and his wonderful oil paintings, and these, in combination with my mother's poignant memories, have brought him to life for me. The images that dance in my head feel like memories of him, not memories of stories about him.

In no place are memories of the past more suggestible than in the

TODAY'S SPECIAL GUEST

BRUNDAGE MORNALD, OF BATTLE CREEK, MONTANA
UNDER HYPNOSIS, MR. MORNALD RECOVERED LONG-BURIED MEMORIES OF A PERFECTLY NORMAL, HAPPY CHILDHOOD.

therapy room. Therapists of all varieties influence people; that's their job. Their methods vary with their ideologies, but all exert some form of influence. In traditional psychoanalytically oriented therapy, change is believed to come about through insight into the supposed roots of the problem in the client's past. Traditional therapists therefore exert their most powerful influence in conversations about clients' memories of the past.

Cathy, age forty-five, mother of three, married for twenty-seven years, has been struggling with anxiety attacks for two years. Several times throughout the day, her body begins to sweat profusely, her heart races, and she has an intense fear that she will either pass out or have a heart attack. Although she manages to go on with her life, volunteering in her daughters' school as well as on several community committees, she finds her anxiety attacks demoralizing and exhausting. She decides to seek therapy.

As it happens, Cathy finds a therapist with a Freudian background, a caring, gentle woman in her fifties named Dr. Adams. As soon as Cathy has described what is troubling her, Dr. Adams shifts the discussion to the past. She wants to know all about Cathy's parents, their marriage, their parenting style, her siblings, and all significant childhood events. Dr. Adams even draws a diagram of Cathy's family tree that traverses several generations and asks Cathy to share information about grandparents, great-grandparents, uncles, aunts, and cousins. At the end of the session, Cathy expresses relief that she has begun therapy, but uncertainty as to how the discussion of her family background will help. Dr. Adams asks Cathy to be patient, reminding her that change doesn't happen overnight.

For the next few sessions, they continue discussing Cathy's upbringing. The youngest of six children, she recalls her parents being rather strict and hardworking. The rules in the family were always clear, no exceptions. Though Cathy can't say she was incredibly close to her mother and father, she feels that she respected them greatly and loved them. Dr. Adams suggests that with so many siblings, Cathy might have felt neglected. She also wonders whether her parents' strictness thwarted her emotionally. "You were never really permitted to express feelings, were you?" she asks. "You were punished for speaking out."

Dr. Adams's theory about Cathy's personality and her problem with anxiety is crystallizing. She thinks that Cathy's parents never gave her the love she needed, and that Cathy harbored resentment toward them. Now, like a long-dormant volcano, that resentment is erupting in the form of panic attacks.

But that isn't how Cathy remembers feeling toward her parents. She always believed that, although they weren't perfect, they did the best they could given their own limitations. What she lacked in attention from them, she got from her siblings. Her oldest sister was very nurturing and maternal, and Cathy has always seen their relationship as a blessing. Dr. Adams insists that Cathy is "in denial" about her feelings, and that, until she allows herself to "get in touch" with her anger, she will not be able to relieve her anxiety.

Dr. Adams is not a bad person, nor is she malicious. In fact, she's merely doing what she is supposed to do based on the theory behind her approach. Theory is a therapist's guiding light, but it's a light that can also blind.

Cathy is lucky. She has enough faith in herself and her view of her life so that she is not convinced by Dr. Adams's theories, and she leaves Dr. Adams's practice with her own memories of her family intact. Other therapy seekers are less fortunate. In the same way that hearing stories about my grandfather eventually made him seem real to me, memories repeatedly cast in a bleak light, particularly by an "expert," can start to become three-dimensional, especially to those who are vulnerable and in pain. Before long, they start to see the past through their therapists' eyes, and memory readily furnishes further evidence to support this new perspective.

In my travels I have met many people who, upon discovering that I am a therapist, tell me with great excitement that therapists have helped them unravel the secret to what makes them tick. Amazingly, although these people come from different walks of life, family backgrounds, and regions, they all have discovered the same secret: the reason they are experiencing problems in their adult lives is that their parents didn't allow them to express their feelings. Each time they cried they were told, "Big boys don't cry," or "Stop crying or I'll give you something to cry about." As a result, they lack self-esteem or self-confidence and often have difficulty feeling or expressing emotions in intimate relationships. This, they are told, is what happens when your family is dysfunctional.

What makes these interpretations hard to discount is that they seem so specific. People don't realize that the assessment they received is a boilerplate diagnosis, so general that it could apply to almost anyone. It's like telling your fortune from a fortune cookie. In truth, "don't blame yourself, blame your parents" is a generic diagnosis.

As you can see, therapists are professional "spin doctors." In the same way that politicians cast their handling of controversial political issues in a favorable light to bolster their public image, therapists twist the meaning of events in people's lives to coincide with their own theories. Unfortunately, because they are seeking to explain current problems, not current successes, therapists who look to the past naturally give it a negative spin.

Consider Darlene's story. At twenty-five, Darlene has struggled for

much of her life with Tourette's syndrome, a neurological disorder causing both physical and vocal tics. It is generally considered physical
rather than emotional in nature, although, because of the unusual behavior associated with it, people who suffer from Tourette's syndrome
often experience emotional side effects. Darlene had various bodily
twitches and produced unusual vocal sounds in her throat. She was
ostracized by her peers as a child and shunned in public places.

Devastated by the effects of her condition, Darlene sought counseling. Unaware of the impact therapists' ideology has on their approach to
a problem, Darlene went to a psychoanalyst trained according to strict
Freudian theory. He told Darlene that

> the noises I made in my throat were attempts to duplicate the noises he
> was sure I had heard coming from my parents' bedroom sometime in early
> childhood. I had no such memory of ever hearing my parents having sex,
> but he felt sure that's what the noises were. He kept me on the couch for
> years talking about the usual bullshit, while I went on twitching my way
> through high school, work, marriage, motherhood . . . never knowing I
> had a real physical problem.

Recently, therapeutic approaches that depend on the weaving together of memories from the past have come under heavy scrutiny. For
example, increasing numbers of people are coming forward to accuse
their therapists of influencing them to believe they suffered sexual abuse
when in fact they did not. You can only begin to imagine how destructive such "discoveries" could be in the lives of the people who believe
them. "Victims" are usually encouraged to confront "perpetrators" and
anyone else who passively stood by. Countless families have been decimated by these sorts of allegations, as Dr. Michael Yapko details in
Suggestions of Abuse:

> There is disturbing evidence that some therapists unintentionally insin-
> uate into the minds of their clients memories of abuse that never hap-
> pened. Therapists often find this hard to believe, because they
> underestimate the potent influence they can wield in the lives of clients
> and they certainly don't often *feel* powerful, pointing out that it is excru-
> ciatingly difficult to get their clients to make even the most meager
> changes. Nonetheless, the capacity to be therapeutic—to encourage, to

soothe, to help shift world view, to change perceptions—is equally the capacity to be anti-therapeutic—to inculcate a mindset and a point of view, to project a vision of reality to the client that may not only be false, but ultimately damaging. Whether therapists like to admit it or not, they can convince people to adopt beliefs that might either help or harm them. [5]

There is great controversy in the mental-health field. Many claim that reports of therapist-induced memories are grossly exaggerated. Perhaps. If nothing else though, the latest uproar in the professional community about the viability of therapist-induced memories has sensitized people to the suggestibility of human beings. And if what really happened is unclear, why not view our memories through rosier lenses?

I remember talking to a professor when I was in graduate school about how involved my mother was in my life when I was growing up. I commented with a hint of disappointment in my voice that my father seemed less interested in my daily goings-on. He always seemed to be extremely involved in his work. My professor quickly pointed out that, with my mother being so invested in her children, perhaps there was little room for my father to do the same. I had never thought about it that way, and once I let the idea percolate a while, I felt better about the role my father played in our family. Had my professor, whom I greatly respected, criticized my father, he would have reinforced my view of him, making it harder for me to love him. Instead, I began to appreciate the unique ways my parents' individual strengths contributed to the overall well-being of our family.

At the time, I had no idea how lucky I had been in choosing my professor as my confidant. Since he was my professor and a well respected psychotherapist his viewpoint carried a lot of weight. Fortunately, his take on my situation was benevolent, leaving me with a good feeling about my family. I was not aware at the time that his view was, nevertheless, just an interpretation, not a fact. Psychotherapists are just people, complete with beliefs, attitudes, and opinions that stem from their own backgrounds as well as their professional training. And since how something is interpreted depends so heavily on the *interpreter*, relying on others to decipher your past is an extremely chancy business.

In addition to the fact that memory is unreliable and highly suggestible, there are other good reasons to bypass the past in a search for solutions. Human beings and their problems are incredibly complex. Naturally, how we were raised has a great deal to do with who we are, but it's absurd to think that you can isolate an event, interaction, or experience in the past that *caused* you to be the way you are. Strict Freudians believe that much of who you will ever be is defined by the age of four or five, but newer theories suggest that people continue to change and grow throughout their lives and that here-and-now experiences can be as formative as childhood ones. In addition, biological, genetic, and environmental forces can be significant contributing factors to any kind of personal or interpersonal problem.

Here's an example. Robert, twenty-five, is depressed. In therapy, he reveals that he felt unwanted as a child and that he has had little contact with his father since his parents divorced, when he was twelve. A below-average student, Robert never really excelled in anything, not even sports. Now he is in a turbulent relationship with a woman who, according to Robert, is verbally abusive. His job as a tool-and-dye maker is dead-end, and Robert can't begin to guess how to help himself to feel better.

It's entirely possible that feeling unwanted and unloved by his parents started Robert on the path to making a career out of depression. He already believes that, to some extent. But how depressed would he feel if his job and his love life were more satisfying? Is he dissatisfied with his life because of what was lacking in his childhood, or because more recent developments have been so unrewarding?

In truth, no one will ever know. A precise cause of an emotional problem can never be pinpointed. Theories about causes are just that— theories. It's no more *correct* to attribute the cause of Robert's depression to his job and relationship than to his shaky beginnings. If a particular theory about the cause of a problem helps someone change, it's worth considering. If not, forget it. But some plausible theories, such as that Robert was emotionally thwarted by his parer ⁀an end up destroying primary relationships. In fact, linking the ca ⁀t problem to the distant past usually results in a blame with parents typically the target.

Parent bashing has become a national pastime, a' are leading the charge. In case you have been asle magazines and newspapers or watched TV for a dɾ

Blaming parents for what they did or didn't do has become a national obsession and big business. . . . [I]ncreasing numbers of people are now referring to themselves as "Adult Children," a curious metaphor. With self-help groups and a spate of books such as the best-selling and pointedly titled *Toxic Parents* to guide them, plus magazines and TV talk shows eager to air their dirty laundry, Adult Children are definitely front and center on the American scene.

The movement began about 10 years ago with survivors of extreme abuse: children of alcoholics and drug abusers or victims of incest and physical or mental violence. . . . But the scope of the movement has grown enormously. It now includes a cadre of parent-bashing Adult Children eager to tell their parents, It's your fault we love too much or not at all and *never* the right person; that we don't trust ourselves or anyone else; that we are "afflicted and addicted," as a *Newsweek* cover story declared; that we are divorced, drunk, desperate, and—pardon the jargon—"dysfunctional." These Adult Children are looking for the Answer—and many think their parents are *it*.[6]

What's wrong with blaming others for our current predicament? Plenty. In addition to jeopardizing rather than enhancing important relationships, blaming has other distinct disadvantages:

Blame leads to impotence. Once we blame others for what we feel, we no longer take responsibility for ourselves. We create rationalizations for our unhappiness: "I can't have a committed relationship because my parents fought all the time." "I drink because that's what I saw growing up." "I can't hold down a job because my parents told me I would be a loser." In day-to-day relationships, blaming others means there is nothing we can do to correct our situation except wait for the person or people causing us pain to change. When we determine that our childhood experiences are to blame for our dissatisfactions in life, not even waiting will help, since the past is irreversible.

Blame keeps us stuck. Over my years as therapist, I have noted that, as long as a person focuses on the injustices of the past, the pain persists. Blaming parents doesn't free people to move forward in their lives, as some suggest. Whether we like it or not, we are the biological by-products of our parents, so condemning them is tantamount to con-
ning ourselves. When we fuel the fires of hate, a piece of ourselves

goes up in smoke. It can be liberating to realize that many other people in the world share our pain and that we are not alone in our struggles, but some Adult Children never move beyond the misery-loves-company stage. The inability to forgive traps people in a time warp and prevents them from growing emotionally.

Blame is blind. When we are so single-mindedly focused on what our parents did wrong, we also tend to forget what they did right. A woman in my practice spent several sessions talking about the hurt and rage she felt because her father had fondled her inappropriately many times as a child. Her pain was wrenching. One day she sheepishly told me that, despite her rage about the abuse, she loved her father very much. She was his favorite. She recalled the times he read stories and poetry to her, consoled her when her friends disappointed her, and encouraged her to do well in school. She asked me whether it was "sick" to have these positive feelings in light of his irresponsible behavior.

I assured her it wasn't and urged her to tell me more about the healthy side of her father. The session flew by. She later told me that our discussion gave her permission to love her father despite his failings as a parent, which in turn made it easier for her to accept herself. There is at least some good in most relationships, and although the bad may outweigh it, the good should not be annihilated.

Blame is often unjustified. Tempting as it may be to blame your parents for causing problems you experience as an adult, study after study has shown the correlation between childhood trauma and adult dysfunction to be surprisingly low. Childhood experiences, good or bad, do not dictate how one adjusts to life's demands as an adult.[7]

The recovery movement tells us that the child of alcoholics is four times more likely to become an alcoholic than someone whose parents were not alcoholics. The risk of becoming an alcoholic is 7 to 8 percent in the general population, so the risk for people who grew up with alcoholic parents increases to approximately 30 percent. But *70* percent of them will *not* become alcoholics.[8] Similarly, approximately 70 percent of those who were abused as children do *not* abuse their own children.[9] Despite enormous hardship, many people not only rise above the adversity, but transform traumatic childhood experiences into extraordinary personal strengths. Clearly, experience alone does not dictate outcome, but, rather, the meaning people ascribe to their experiences and the choices they make about how to integrate these experiences into their lives.

I have worked with many people who are grief-stricken as adults because of some childhood abuse. Their pain is real, their suffering intense. Leaving hurt behind is not an easy task. However, those who eventually heal themselves are the ones who let go of the past, the ones who *decide* to change their lives by putting the past in its place. They make conscious decisions to refocus their energies on making themselves whole. They finally accept that, no matter what they do, they can't change yesterday. But they can change tomorrow.

Blame hurts. Perhaps the most striking disadvantage of immersing ourselves in unhappy childhood memories is that the journey is excruciatingly painful. The grown men and woman John Bradshaw leads in guided fantasy back to the time when their parents betrayed or disappointed them sob uninhibitedly as they hold their teddy bears. They are retracing the most painful junctures in their lives in search of their wounded "inner child," an encounter that is supposed to enable them to heal. This is an interesting theory, but it is unequivocally incorrect.

There is absolutely no research to substantiate the notion that people can't heal their wounds without immersing themselves in pain or experiencing a "catharsis"; indeed, considerable research suggests just the opposite. The more people think, talk, and worry about the painful past, the more difficult it is to leave behind. The more obsessed we become with analyzing what happened and why it happened, the stronger the forces preventing us from moving forward.

I have watched people weep as they relive their childhood memories in seminars like Bradshaw's, and I have felt an incredible yearning to shout at the top of my lungs, "Listen, people, there's an easier, more humane, less painful way to take hold of your life!" I have observed time and time again that, once people direct their energy to creating the future rather than dismantling the past, they feel transformed and the pain disappears. You really can make peace with your past without going to war.

But the most important reason to stop looking to the past for solutions is that *what caused a problem often has nothing to do with what solves it.*

I know this runs counter to conventional wisdom, but consider the following story.

A colleague of mine was working with a woman who was suffering from bruxism—the technical name for grinding your teeth at night, which can cause headaches, a sore jaw, and excessive wear on your teeth. This woman experienced all of these symptoms. My colleague suggested that the woman switch sides of the bed with her husband and watch closely for any differences. Two weeks later, she and her husband returned and reported that, although she had some trouble sleeping the first night, she did not grind her teeth for the entire two-week period.

Now, anyone in his or her right mind is probably asking, "What does where you sleep have to do with grinding your teeth?" The solution seems bizarre if you are accustomed to believing, as most people do, that the nature of a problem dictates a particular solution. Since bruxism is thought to be stress-related, the logical solution would be to identify the causes of the stress and eliminate them. But there are other ways to think about the problem.

For instance, problems often occur in particular contexts or settings. It is possible that there are subtle cues in the settings that trigger the problematic responses. Cigarette smokers will tell you that certain contexts—smoky bars, satisfying meals, or sexual encounters—act as catalysts, prompting them to light up without even thinking. Similarly, the woman's teeth-grinding might have been triggered by her position in the bed, the pajamas she wore, a ritual warm glass of milk before retiring, or any of a multitude of other factors. Therefore, it was possible to break the chain linking the problematic behavior to its context by varying *anything* about the setting. By adopting this philosophy, my colleague was able to help the woman stop grinding her teeth without knowing much about bruxism or the possible stress in her life![10]

Insight about the past doesn't lead to change. Understanding *why* you overeat, feel shy, tend to procrastinate, overreact, fill in the blank, *doesn't solve the problem!* If you enjoy putting pieces of your life puzzle together, then by all means do it. But if you want to get on with your life, put the past in its place. Let bygones be bygones, and begin to look forward. Here's a story about someone who did.

John had a history of long depressive periods, starting at age sixteen, but when he felt suicidal at age forty he sought professional help. The psychiatrist he consulted prescribed medication and weekly therapy sessions to deal with the incest and battering he had experienced as a child. In addition to his depression, John also had a symptom of pulling out his fingernails, which made him feel more depressed. Neither the medication nor the four years of weekly sessions curbed his depression or his self-mutilating behavior. Acupuncture and hypnotherapy proved equally ineffective.

Fifteen thousand dollars later, John went broke, "which was the best thing that could have happened—at least I couldn't afford therapy anymore." He sat down and made a list of what was *currently* making him miserable: his excess weight, and an emotional void due to a lack of relationships with others. Then he devised a specific plan to overcome these problems: find a jogging partner and start jogging, join Weight Watchers, and get a dog for companionship. He told his therapist he was going to quit therapy and did so, over his therapist's vehement objections. Then he set about implementing his own plan to improve his mental health.

Here's what resulted: a complete absence of depression for the first time in his life, a weight loss of thirty-five pounds, new friendships through jogging and his Weight Watchers group, and a beloved German shepherd. When asked about the reasons for the changes, John said: "Part of it is about successful partnerships—something I'm now looking at in my life—but mostly it's about finding my own solutions extra-therapy. I knew what to do instinctively; all I needed to do was stop the therapeutic relationship, which—I now think—had re-created all the horror of my childhood in my adult life."

When I tell people in my seminars that even the most insightful explanation about why you're doing what you're doing doesn't offer solutions, I always see smiles of recognition. Everyone knows what it's like to become an expert on *why* you happen to have a problem while remaining a novice at how to find a solution. At bottom, we all know that understanding the root causes of a problem leads—at best—to understanding the root causes of a problem, but not necessarily to change. Yet millions of dollars are spent every year in therapy offices by people desperately seeking solutions to all kinds of problems. But I ask you: Why not trust your instincts? Why not assume that you are right to question the usefulness of analyzing things to death? Rather than assume there is something wrong with you when understanding your problem doesn't make it go away, why not assume that maybe, just maybe, there's something wrong with placing so much emphasis on the past?

Of course, in the spirit of being solution-oriented, I wouldn't think of criticizing familiar approaches to problem-solving without offering a better alternative. Simply understanding that understanding doesn't work isn't enough. You have to have a plan. You need a brand-new way to think about what to do when you feel stuck. Rest easy, that's what the rest of this book offers—a step-by-step blueprint for change.

ee

The Anatomy of Change

THE CHANGES I'VE witnessed over the years I've been helping people find solutions are truly miraculous, but the *process* of change is no longer mysterious to me. Although each person and each problem I encounter is unique, the mechanics underlying the transition from problem to solution are remarkably similar for everyone. In this chapter, I want to share with you what I have learned about how people change. Since the method you will be learning frequently triggers dramatic and sudden changes in people's lives, it is important for you to read this section; otherwise you might think these changes have occurred by magic.

The Solution Is Within

"Never give advice. The ignorant won't heed it and the wise don't need it."

Believe it or not, the solution for which you are searching is within you. I realize you may not believe this right now. You may feel that you haven't a clue as to what to do. But I guarantee that, on some level, you know a great deal more about how to take control of your life than you think you do. In fact, after years of working with people plagued by all kinds of problems, I can comfortably say that the only experts on people's lives are themselves. They just don't know it.

Take Lisa, a friend of mine, who said in her usual tongue-and-cheek manner, "Michele, if you're so smart, tell me how to lose ten pounds." "I don't need to tell you how to lose weight," I said. "You know what you need to do." Somewhat puzzled, she replied, "I do?" I happened to know that Lisa had read every (maybe every other) diet book on the market, and I was certain not only that she knew what the experts had to say about losing weight but that she knew enough about her own patterns of behavior to design a successful weight-loss program without input from me or anyone else. I told Lisa I felt certain that there were times in her life when she ate sensibly, and she agreed. Then I asked her what was different about the times when she ate more sensibly. After lengthy consideration, she said, "I can always tell at the start of the day how things will go. I'm more likely to eat a small but healthful lunch if I like the way I look, which depends on how I dress in the morning. If I wear one of my favorite outfits and I think I look good, I find that I eat smaller amounts." She went on to tell me that, in addition to dressing well, if she starts her day by exercising she feels good about herself and is more likely to eat well throughout the day.

"Anything else?" I asked. "Yes," she replied. "If I go through long periods without eating, I don't feel great and I get famished and then overeat. If I pack some snacks—a piece of fruit, raisins, or a small salad—I munch on them during the day and never get starving, so I don't overeat when I sit down to meals. I know it sounds crazy that I lose weight when I pack food for myself, but I have learned that I eat more sensibly when I plan my food for the day."

Maybe you are thinking that Lisa's plan would not work for you, and you may be right. The point is that Lisa knew just what *she* needed to do, she just hadn't realized it. She took her own advice and very quickly lost the weight.

I took up golf several summers ago. As most golf fanatics will attest, though the game is truly addictive, it is also incredibly frustrating, because it's hard to be consistent. Although my game had been showin definite signs of improvement, I had one seemingly insurmoun stumbling block—ponds. I knew that I was capable of hitting considerably farther than the length of any pond at my something faltered inside me each time I had to hit the ball over even a tiny body of water. Without a doubt, I was the club's greatest donor of water balls.

One day my husband said to me, "You always tell people that the solutions to their problems are within them. What would have to be different for you to get over your water phobia?" I thought for a moment. I realized that what I agonized about when I teed off over the pond was that I was going to lose my ball, which had gotten to be an expensive habit. I joked, "If I could use someone else's balls, I wouldn't be so concerned about losing them and I could get them over." Then I realized what I'd said: if I were less concerned about losing my balls, I would relax. Two days later, I went to the store and purchased a mega-supply of the cheapest golf balls I could find. And from that day forward, my balls have been sailing over the water.

You may be thinking that losing ten pounds or playing better golf is no major feat compared with the challenges you face. Maybe not. But I can tell you that, no matter how serious your problems seem, no matter how overwhelmed or frustrated you are, the answer for which you are searching is also within you. Let me tell you how I know.

Several years ago, I was observing a therapy session conducted by a colleague of mine. A mother had brought her twelve-year-old son in because his school performance was deteriorating. For approximately forty-five minutes, the woman ranted and raved about his laziness and lack of motivation and her anger about having to go meet with his teachers. Just as the session was about to end, however, she casually mentioned that her son had been trying much harder in school for the last two or three days. Then she started to complain about him some more. The therapist stopped her, turned to the boy, and said, "So you decided to turn over a new leaf. What do you need to do to stick to your resolution?" The boy described a step-by-step plan for staying on track.

I was extreme   ntrigued by the fact that, in between the call to make
the first session, this boy had begun to solve his
help from a therapist. As I noted in chapter one,
n with my colleagues, and many of them reported
'e also noticed that, like the boy's mother, most
significance to such presession changes, so we
incidence of these kinds of improvements was

higher than our clients reported. We decided to test our theory with an informal, brief survey of new clients:

1. Many times people notice in between the time they make the appointment for therapy and the first session that things already seem different. What have you noticed about your situation?
2. (If yes to No. 1): Do these changes relate to the reason you came for therapy?
3. (If yes to No. 1): Are these the kinds of changes you would like to continue to have happen?[1]

Two-thirds of those we surveyed reported concrete changes between the call for therapy and the first appointment. In other words, a great majority of people who thought they needed professional advice had actually begun to find solutions on their own.

One mother, who had been concerned that her ex-husband's over-powering personality was intimidating her daughter during visits to his home, noted that, for several days prior to the first session, her daughter became more assertive and her ex-husband more calm. As a result, mother and daughter were more relaxed at work and in school.

Another family had been concerned for months that their daughter's teacher was not treating her fairly. After they called for a therapy appointment, the parents scheduled a meeting with the principal and the teacher to air their differences. The meeting was extremely productive and the problem was solved.

A middle-aged man, severely depressed after his wife initiated a divorce, considered attempting suicide, which scared him enough to schedule an appointment. Then he decided it was time to take hold of his life. By the first session, he was feeling so much better that he wondered whether he really needed therapy, since he seemed to know precisely what he needed to do. I wondered about that as well.

Recently, I got a letter from a massage therapist who had read about my interest in self-induced changes. "I, too, have noticed that some people begin to improve between the phone call and first visit," she wrote. "Some are strictly physical as in 'I hurt my shoulder last week, but now it's better.' But sometimes it's stated as 'I have chronic neck pain, and it hurt when I called you, but it's OK now.'"

It is clear that the decision to seek help is in itself a decision to change. Once people truly commit themselves to making things different, they apparently know what to do next.

Yet, from the countless stories of presession change that my colleagues and I have collected over the years, it is apparent that most people are surprised to hear themselves talking about the solutions they've discovered. They are so focused on their problems that they overlook the steps they already have taken to make things better.

We are so much more capable and powerful than we know. Spontaneous "cures" are documented in the medical literature as well. Terminally ill people with dire prognoses mysteriously rid themselves of their diseases. Once thought to be hocus-pocus, this phenomenon has been receiving considerable attention in the scientific community.

Bernie Siegel, M.D., a surgeon at Yale University, has devoted much of his life to studying the cases of what he calls "exceptional patients." He feels that the term "spontaneous cure" is a misnomer, because it says nothing about the person's own contribution to getting rid of the disease. He believes that there are important lessons to be learned about people's natural healing processes and that the scientific community has been too quick to dismiss this kind of explanation for cancer remissions.

A 1990 Gallup poll found that 90 percent of over one thousand Americans sampled had successfully overcome a major health, emotional, addiction, or life-style problem, and that all but 3 percent of them did so without professional intervention.[2] Moreover, most were able to maintain their new behaviors over time. It appears that, once change takes hold, the "new and improved" life-style is so rewarding that sustaining it becomes less and less of a challenge.

Why, then, if people are capable of resolving the seemingly unresolvable problems in their lives—and are even able to conquer supposedly irreversible physical illnesses—are we so easily persuaded that without the assistance of "experts" we are helpless?

To begin with, when we are apprehensive, tense, anxious, angry, or sad, we generally don't think clearly. Preoccupied by our dilemmas and the feelings associated with them, we often overlook the simplest solutions. We stumble along on automatic pilot, doing the same old thing even though it has never worked. Then we get frustrated and tell ourselves that there is nothing we can do. Our frustration blinds us to what might work.

There is another reason we have lost confidence in ourselves and our problem-solving abilities. It's hard to feel strong and resourceful when everything you read, hear, or see assists you in diagnosing your flaws! It's the "in" thing to do right now. Just turn on your television sets. Talk-show hosts and their guests will say that everyone (yes, even you) has an "illness." We eat, drink, work, shop, love chocolate or sex, and exercise too much. If you don't fit one of those categories, don't feel left out—chances are you are codependent (according to the experts, 96 percent of us are). Thanks to the recovery movement, we have discovered that we *all* come from dysfunctional families, so no wonder we feel like damaged goods with no inner resources.

If you have not been successfully indoctrinated into believing that you are diagnosable, the experts will tell you that you are in denial. In other words, you are just fooling yourself, and when you become a healthier individual, you will recognize your darker side. Unfortunately, we seem to have a national obsession with pathology, which encourages a lethal introspection. "What's wrong with me?" we ask. "Am I a woman who loves too much?" "Am I codependent?" "Do I have a fear of intimacy?" "Am I a good enough mother?" The problem with this sort of introspection is that it diverts you from a more important endeavor: taking an inventory of your strengths. If you were to spend half as much time thinking about the skills you could bring to problem-solving as you have spent worrying about your shortcomings, you would be well armed to tackle any obstacle before you. In fact, many people with whom I have worked have discovered solutions to long-standing problems simply by identifying and using personal strengths they had overlooked or thought irrelevant. Here is an example.

Beth was at the end of her rope when she started therapy. She told me she loved her husband, Tom, but she had been totally frustrated by his lack of energy. Although he held a full-time job and worked conscientiously, when Tom came home from work, it seemed he had nothing left in him for her. They never went anywhere together and he did little around the house. Beth wanted to stay married to Tom, but when she couldn't think of anything else to do to motivate him, she threatened to leave him. That's when she consulted me.

Early in my discussion with Beth, she informed me that she was a special-education teacher who taught children with learning disabilities (LD). In the beginning of my career, I had spent two years working with LD teachers and their students, and I remembered that most of the teachers I met shared some notable strengths. At the close of the session, I brought this up with Beth.

MWD: Beth, you mentioned you're a special-ed teacher. I know from experience with other special-ed teachers that you probably have a great sense of humor and you're unusually creative and flexible. If a student isn't learning properly, you don't label him as stubborn or resistant and give up on him. Unlike many other people, teachers know that students have different learning styles, and if a student isn't learning with one method, you try a different method. If something you are doing isn't working, you take a back-door approach, right?

BETH: That's right. I know what you mean. Some students learn auditorily, some visually, and some kinesthetically. [Beth was referring to the fact that some people learn better when they can see information (e.g., written examples on a blackboard), some when they hear information (e.g., listening to an audiotape), and others when movement or touch is involved (e.g., doing a lab experiment). A good teacher matches the teaching method with the student's preferred learning style.] And maybe, with my husband, I have been relying too heavily on the *auditory* method, talking too much rather than doing.

MWD: That's right! I would like for you to do an experiment. Tonight, when you go home and you see your husband, I would like for you to pretend that he is a student in your classroom. No matter what he does, pretend that he is a student. [Beth laughs.] Then see if you can't get him mainstreamed. [Mainstreaming is what happens when a student with special needs gains sufficient skills to return to a regular classroom.]

BETH: (Still laughing) You know, I was just written up in a professional journal for being really good at mainstreaming students!

At the start of the session, Beth felt inept, incapable of finding new solutions to her old problem with Tom. She left the session feeling resourceful and empowered. By recalling her strengths and skills in another, seemingly unrelated area, she felt a renewed sense of energy, optimism, and possibility. Beth had much to be proud of in her work with children, yet she had never considered how she might apply what she had learned there to her marriage. Once I reminded her of the way she meets challenges in her classroom, she was able to transpose those methods to her marital stalemate.

The next Saturday, Beth woke up early, as she usually did, but instead of urging Tom to get up and spend time with her, she quietly got dressed, ate breakfast, put the dog on a leash, and went for a walk. She stopped in at a friend's house for coffee and stayed there until noon. When she returned home, Tom was awake and very curious about her whereabouts. Beth told him what she had done and what a good time she'd had, without ever suggesting that he should have joined her. He listened attentively. Later he suggested that they go to the park—the first time in months that he had suggested they spend time together.

Beth was practicing what she knew worked in another context. Recognizing that Tom was not an "auditory learner," she stopped relying on words and became more "kinesthetic" with him, expressing her needs through action. It worked. Eventually, she posted a sign on her refrigerator door to remind her to act rather than talk. It read, "Just do it!"

Another example. A woman in her late thirties came to me for therapy. She owned a successful business that required outstanding people skills: she taught managers to train their own staffs. When I asked her what she wanted to change in her life, she told me she thought time was running out for her to find a suitable mate. "I want you to help me understand why I always get involved with the wrong kind of guy. I need to explore my fear of intimacy. Perhaps you can help me figure out what happened in my past that makes intimate relationships so difficult for me. I just feel so uncomfortable in social situations, I fall apart."

After we discussed her situation for a while, however, it became clear that her interest in an intimate relationship was relatively new. Moreover, in the last eight to twelve months, she had actually been involved in two meaningful relationships. I had a choice to make. I could either explore her "fear of intimacy," as she suggested, or I could look beyond her pessimism to find a way to work with her obvious strengths. I chose the latter.

Rather than talk about her fear of intimacy, I asked her, "If one of your clients came to you with this problem, what would you advise her?" She blushed. "Well, I've actually been thinking of that," she confessed. "I was thinking back to what I did when I was trying to get my business off the ground. I knew I needed lots of contacts: it's a numbers game. So what I did at that time was to join lots of groups, all different kinds of groups, just to meet people. It worked—my business started to sky-rocket. So I thought, 'That's what I need to do, join groups,' and I've already started." She told me she had joined two gourmet groups, a health club, and the Chamber of Commerce, and had begun taking group golf lessons. "In order to be more marketable," she continued, "you need to increase your visibility." Going to bars, she thought, was like "cold-calling"—the process of randomly contacting prospective buyers as opposed to working from leads of potentially interested buyers. Cold-calling was seldom an effective strategy. "So I thought I needed to join groups with people who share similar interests."[3]

At first she was embarrassed to admit that she approached her love life with a "marketing strategy" and wondered if I thought that a man would think it weird if he were to learn he was a "marketing objective." Absolutely, I said. But why did she have to tell him? Did she tell potential clients about her marketing strategies?

In the weeks that followed, she met several men, some of whom she went out with. Some dates went remarkably well, others were disappointments. In the past, disappointments had left her hibernating for months. But now that she considered her search for a committed relationship her "new project," she was determined to approach disappointments in her personal life much as she did in her professional life. When business deals fell through, she didn't allow herself the luxury of sitting around feeling sorry for herself, but quickly picked herself up and started seeking out other opportunities. No more sitting around for weeks waiting for the phone to ring. If someone failed to call, she was out "networking" lickety-split. Within a couple of months, she met the man of her dreams, and one year later, they decided to "close the deal." A year and a half after that, they "expanded their business" with a bouncing baby boy.

Obviously, this woman had all the necessary skills to find a suitable mate, but she had lost confidence in herself. My challenge was to help her recognize her hidden resources and begin taking advantage of them. Frequently, what a person does professionally is fertile ground for identifying problem-solving skills. This is also true of hobbies or avocations. In fact, anything anyone does with confidence is a good place to start hunting for solution-oriented strengths. The following questions will help you begin taking stock of your own abilities:

What is something I enjoy doing and feel I do well?

Remember, this could be an occupation, a hobby, or simply an interest.

What skills are necessary for me to excel?

As you think about your interest, analyze the personal strengths that have made it possible for you to do well in this area.

How might these strengths come in handy as I try to improve my current situation?

Most skills are transferrable. Be creative. Think how you could apply what you do in situations where you feel confident and successful to other situations. Let your imagination be your guide.

Keep this inventory as you continue reading. Regardless of how stuck you feel at the moment, these skills will soon come in handy.

Just Do It

For years I've been talking to people who want to be happier, thinner, smarter, richer, better athletes, or less overworked. I share with them what I know about accomplishing their goals and wait to see what happens next. Most of these people eventually do become happier, thinner, smarter, richer, better athletes, or less overworked, but some don't; they remain stuck. For as long as I have been working with people, I have been fascinated by these different outcomes. Why are some people able to take a little bit of information and turn their lives around, but others, armed with the same tools, change nothing? The answer is simple: action.

What the winners have in common is that they have put their thoughts, dreams, and plans into action instead of passively waiting for things to change. People who live their dreams are those who stop considering all the angles, weighing the pros and cons, and just go do it. They are not always "in the mood" when they begin, but they do it anyway. They've come to realize it's time to stop talking to their friends, families, or therapists, stop listening to tapes on self-actualization, stop reading self-help books, and begin living. Without action there is no change.

Without change there is no excitement. Without excitement life becomes dull and monotonous and we become boring. We must move for there to be movement in our lives.

Unfortunately, many people have the misconception that they have to be in the right frame of mind before they can do what it takes. "I must feel more confident before I call for that job interview," they tell themselves, or "I know it would help me feel less depressed if I got some exercise, but I just don't feel like it." You get the picture. These folks are sitting around waiting for their feelings, attitudes, and perceptions to change *before* they act. But research demonstrates beyond a shadow of a doubt that the most expedient way to change how you think or feel about something is to take action.[4] Once you do something, *anything*, about your situation, you will notice immediately that you feel better. As D. G. Myers observes in his book *The Pursuit of Happiness*:

> Those who seek greater happiness can exploit one of social psychology's arch principles: We are as likely to act ourselves into a way of thinking as to think ourselves into action. In experiments, people who feign high self-esteem begin feeling better about themselves. Even when manipulated into a smiling expression, people feel better; when they scowl, the whole world seems to scowl back. So put on a happy face. Pretend optimism. Simulate outgoingness. Going through the motions can trigger the emotions.[5]

A woman I was working with complained of low self-esteem and marital problems. I asked her about the times in her marriage that seemed to go more smoothly. She told me that she and her husband used to spend lots of time together, going to sporting events, eating dinner out, playing bridge, and just talking. I asked if she had been doing these things lately and she said, "No, I haven't been feeling like it. I like to go out more when I feel better about myself."

Now, you don't have to be a rocket scientist to wonder whether spending lots of time together, going to sporting events, eating dinner out, playing bridge, and talking with her husband gave her pleasure and therefore contributed to her overall sense of well-being. In other words, participating in enjoyable activities with her husband helped her to feel good about herself, and *not* doing those things contributed to bad feelings about herself. She saw that she had a choice. She could do these things and see if they'd make a difference, or she could sit around waiting for self-esteem to happen. Eventually, she chose the former, and felt better immediately.

The longer the agoraphobic stays home, the more fearful and intimidating the outside world becomes. The longer the school-phobic child skips school, the further she slips behind her peers, the more she gets stigmatized, and the less likely it is that she will ever go to school willingly. The more a shy or self-conscious person avoids social situations, the fewer his opportunities to develop social skills, and the more likely he will continue to avoid social situations. The more inactive a depressed person is, the less likely he will get out and do something, and the more depressed he will be about his inertia. *The antidote to these vicious cycles is to step out of them by doing what you know you should even though you may not feel like it.*

Did you feel like getting out of bed this morning when your alarm clock sounded? Probably not, but you did it anyway. If you hadn't, you might have missed an important meeting or your kids' school bus. Do you *feel* like paying taxes on April 15 (or any other time, for that matter)? But you do, because you believe the consequences of *not* paying (a compromised conscience, fines, or jail) are unacceptable. Do you *feel* like forgoing your summer-vacation plans when you're short of funds? Of course not, but the alternative doesn't sound so great either. Do you always *feel* like exercising when you go to the gym or your aerobics class? I doubt it. But since you love how you feel afterward, you push yourself out the door.

The bottom line is, stop catering to your feelings and allowing them to rule your life. Feelings are just feelings. They come and they go. Show negative or self-limiting feelings the door by ignoring them and taking action. "Just do it," ran Nike's massively successful ad campaign, tapping into a truth everyone—young or old, big or small—recognizes.

READY. FIRE. AIM.*

Lack of motivation is not the only reason people procrastinate about taking action. Sometimes they fear that they haven't examined their

---

* Motto of an executive at Cadbury's.

situations carefully enough. This uncertainty about the value or effectiveness of a particular solution becomes an excuse not to try it. I tell people like this that I may not be an expert on what works but I am definitely an expert on what doesn't work. I can guarantee that continuing to do nothing doesn't work. Compared with the risks of attempting something new and unpredictable, the risks of doing nothing are monumental.

In the early eighties, authors Tom Peters and Robert Waterman set out to investigate the management style of the top companies in the United States. After thorough research, they laid out the principles that seemed to give companies a competitive edge in their book, *In Search of Excellence*. The number-one principle was a strong emphasis on taking action, doing *something*, rather than analyzing data and having endless committee meetings. Instead of attempting to ascertain the usefulness of a particular plan, top managers acted first, then observed the marketplace to evaluate their success.

> "Do it. Fix it. Try it," is our favorite axiom. Karl Weick adds that "chaotic action is preferable to orderly inaction." "Don't just stand there, do something" is of the same ilk. Getting on with it, especially in the face of complexity, does simply come down to trying something. Learning and progress accrue only when there is *something* to learn from, and the something, the stuff of learning and progress, is any completed action.[6]

The message in all of this? Don't waste another second clipping articles or gathering support from experts, friends, relatives, or yourself before you launch your next plan of attack. Just do it—then watch the results. There is no such thing as failure, only feedback as to how to modify your next step. One of the most important prerequisites to putting the program in this book to work is to adopt a trial-and-error philosophy about change. It is remarkably freeing to realize that there are only two ways you can really screw up. One is by not trying anything new for fear of failure. Even if your first efforts aren't as successful as you wish, I promise you will feel better just for having done something about your situation. In fact, see failure as a sign that you are taking control of your life by experimenting with new solutions. Top managers agree:

Quality performance doesn't mean absence of failure. In fact, failure is the fuel of growth. It shouldn't just be expected, it should be encouraged. Recently one of our client companies came up with a new way to legitimize failure and to encourage discussion and learning from it. A new column was introduced in the corporate newsletter: "Failure of the Month." It was up to every vice president to contribute one column. Not to have erred was not to have pushed the limits of the business. . . .

In a society that worships winners, we have a low tolerance for the losses that lead to winning. We glorify Edison's achievements and forget his words. When asked about the 2,000 failed experiments that led to the discovery of tungsten as the appropriate filament for light bulbs, he said, "I have eliminated 2,000 possibilities; that narrows the field for success."[7]

The second way to screw up is to ignore the outcome of something you tried: wasting time convincing yourself and others that it *should* have worked when it didn't. Remember, the proof is in the pudding. If it works, don't fix it; if not, do something different.

KEEP YOUR FEET MOVING

A colleague of mine recounts a story from a book entitled *The Third Eye* about a Tibetan ceremony for those who wish to become enlightened. The name of the ceremony is "The Room of a Thousand Demons," and only those who have studied with the Dalai Lama are permitted to participate.

Before the ceremony begins, the Dalai Lama explains the details of the ritual to his robed disciples. He tells them that they are about to enter a small room, and when they do the door will shut behind them. The only exit is another door on the opposite side of the room. Although the distance between the doors is not great, many people never make it out. The few who do become enlightened.

He goes on to explain that the room is filled with a thousand demons who are able to read people's minds. Whatever the person fears most appears to materialize. Those fearful of snakes enter a room that seems to be filled with snakes. Those fearful of insects find themselves swarmed with crawling insects. Those fearful of heights discover themselves teetering on the edge of tall buildings. Although the frightening images are not real, they are so vivid that they feel real. Most people become paralyzed with fear.

To those who decide they are able to meet the challenge, the Dalai Lama offers two suggestions. First, they should remember at all times that the images created by the demons are not real. Many people find this advice difficult to heed, so he offers a second suggestion. No matter what they are seeing, thinking, feeling, or hearing, they must keep their feet moving. As long as they keep their feet moving, they will get to the other side.

For the past ten years, in addition to seeing clients and writing books, I have done an enormous amount of public speaking, usually to standing-room-only crowds. At seminars, people frequently stop me in the hall to ask a question or share a comment. Lately, I've heard two comments with some regularity: "It's great to see that a woman can accomplish what you've accomplished. How did you do it?" and "It's great to see someone with a master's degree teaching doctors, psychologists, and other Ph.D.'s. Does the level of education of your trainees ever intimidate you when you teach?"

At first I had a hard time responding, since I hadn't given these questions much thought. Then, one day, I realized that the fact that I *hadn't* given these issues much thought was precisely the reason I've accomplished what I have. Perhaps I was incredibly lucky in my upbringing (thanks, Mom and Dad) or incredibly ignorant about political issues, but I have always believed that I could do whatever I set out to do.

Now, don't get me wrong. I recognize the tremendous injustices and inequities in our society and know that opportunities commensurate with women's talents are not always available to them. Similarly, I'm familiar with the rigid system that values those with more advanced degrees over others. But I've been too busy setting goals, determining what I needed to do to get there, and then doing it, to pay much attention.

I feel compassion for those who ask me these questions. They tell me they would love nothing more than to have the opportunity to teach, write, or tell their own story. But their self-limiting beliefs stop them from taking action. They're too female, too uneducated, too short, not funny enough, too nervous—the list is endless. It's not that I don't have my own share of insecurities and fears. But I have never allowed them to stop me from going after my goals, because that would be giving in to my worst fear of all.

Several years ago, I was in the midst of doing a major international presentation when, instead of focusing on the information I was discussing, I began to focus on the hundreds of faces staring at me. Normally, I derive energy from having an audience, but this time I saw a wall of faces staring at me. The more I focused on them, the more nervous I became. Fortunately, I have done that particular workshop so many times that I could continue talking and panic at the same time.

Within minutes, my mild discomfort had deepened into abject fear, to the point where I didn't think I could go on. "Now what do I do?" I wondered. We had just had a midmorning break between workshops, but I looked up at the audience and said, "While all of you were on break, I wasn't able to go to the bathroom because so many people were asking me questions. I apologize about this, but when you gotta go, you gotta go." As everyone laughed, I untangled myself from my microphone and hightailed it to the bathroom. After several minutes of deep breathing and pep talks to myself, I returned to the stage. I decided to change the workshop format, forcing me to concentrate on my presentation instead of on fear. It worked. I can't say I felt great, but I can tell you two things: no one had a clue about my devastation, and the participants said it was the best workshop they had ever attended.

I must tell you that I considered it a major accomplishment just to have finished the day without conjuring up some excuse for not continuing. But, in my estimation, the real coup was overcoming the temptation to phase out future speaking engagements from my professional endeavors, an idea I had strongly considered. Although there were no major panic attacks at subsequent workshops, I remained fairly tense, dreading a recurrence. Weeks later, I was still asking myself, "Why am I subjecting myself to this torture?" On a deeper level, however, I recognized this as a rhetorical question, because I knew the reason I persisted. I don't allow fear to run my life. I accepted the fact that I would be "gun-shy" for a while, and I kept my feet moving.

I tell this story not to boast about my accomplishments but to make point. Most people think that those who succeed do so because come easily or naturally to them. Not so. NBC's Willard Scott, the well-known weatherman, has said that he struggles with stage fright every morning of his life before appearing on national television. But every day he is there, rain or shine. Don't fool yourself into believing that your fears or apprehensions make you different from people who reach for the stars. Those who succeed have their fair share of anxieties and setbacks; they just don't stand still long enough to allow themselves to become paralyzed.

Sometimes it's helpful to have others remind us to keep our feet moving. A woman I know who has a fear of heights told me a story about a time she and her husband went backpacking with friends. On their first anniversary, they climbed a ten-thousand-foot peak. About two-thirds of the way up, they stopped for a rest. Looking ahead, she saw that the trail seemed to fall away on both sides, which made her extremely apprehensive. When she shared her fear with her husband, he did not respond. Irritated at his apparent lack of concern, she promptly restated her fears. Again, no response from her husband. Without realizing it, she began to focus more on her annoyance with her husband's insensitivity and less on her abject fear. This distraction tranquilized her until she reached the difficult stretch of trail. Once upon it, she realized it wasn't as treacherous as it had looked, and they completed the hike. Later, her husband told her that he had been completely aware of her anxiety but chose to downplay it by ignoring her comments rather than magnify it by acknowledging it. Smart guy!

You might not be worried about making presentations or scaling mountains. You might be dreading an exam, saying "no" when everyone around you expects you to say "yes," asking for a raise, allowing yourself to be really intimate with a partner, getting yourself out of an unhappy relationship, telling your parents something that might disappoint them, being firm with your child, or taking the next big step in your life. Ask yourself, what would you do differently in your life if you didn't allow a fear or an uncertainty to hold you back? What actions would   to keep your feet moving in spite of your feelings? here things you would *stop* doing if you weren't so might happen if you were to try something different? swer these questions, envision how your life will ke the decision to keep moving forward no matter

Expect Success

What is the greatest predictor of a college student's grades? If you answered high school grade-point average or SAT scores, guess again. The single best predictor of one's performance in college is one's level of hope as a freshman. A recent study showed that what sets students of equal intellectual ability and past academic performance apart is the extent to which they expect to do well.[8] Amazing, isn't it?

Academic performance isn't the only thing influenced by hope. Research shows that those with higher levels of hope do better in most situations requiring personal strength and resilience, from work and athletic performance to recovery from critical illnesses or debilitating accidents. The bottom line? The more hopeful you are, the better you do.

Some people tell me they are convinced that change in themselves or others is impossible. "Besides," they say, "if I expect the worst, I won't be disappointed." Although on the surface this seems like a practical philosophy, in practice it is deadly. As writer Norman Cousins observed, "We fear the worst, we expect the worst, we invite the worst." Negative expectations bring about negative ends.

THE PYGMALION EFFECT

Robert Rosenthal, a prolific psychology researcher in the sixties, was interested in the phenomenon referred to as "experimenter bias"—the influence of an experimenter's expectations on the outcome of an experiment. He devised a twist on an experiment that every graduate psychology student is required to do at some point, teaching rats to run through a maze by rewarding them with a piece of cheese. Rosenthal and an associate told each student that the rat he or she was responsible for teaching was either "maze bright" or "maze dull." In other words, each student was led to believe that he or she had either an intelligent or a dumb rat. Although the rats had in fact been randomly assigned, the rats thought to be "maze bright" performed significantly better than those thought to be "maze dull." Obviously, the students' expectations about the rats' abilities influenced their handling of the rats, which, in turn, influenced the rats' performance.[9]

Rosenthal's best-known experiment involved children and teachers in an elementary-school setting. He gave all of the students a standardized IQ test, then randomly selected 20 percent of them and told the teachers that these students were of superior intelligence and could be expected to outperform the other students. At the end of the school year, he returned to readminister the IQ test. He found that the students whom he had selected showed a significantly greater gain than the other students. Somehow, the teachers' expectations had been communicated to the students. And when the "bright" students then began to achieve more than the others, the teachers' expectations were confirmed and their behavior was reinforced. Naturally, this in turn reinforced the students' level of achievement.

Rosenthal's experiments call to mind the story of Pygmalion in Greek mythology. Pygmalion was a sculptor who created a statue of a perfect woman. His love for this statue was so intense that it came to life. The Pygmalion effect describes how our expectations of others influences our behavior, which in turn influences others. In other words, we unconsciously act to bring about the very results we expect.

The Pygmalion effect is alive and well in all human interaction. If rats were sensitive to the subtle differences in how the students handled them, don't you think the people in your life can detect your expectations by virtue of your behavior? You bet they can! Consider just a few examples:

- A man who has problems with rapid ejaculation brings on the worst by expecting the worst. The more he worries about his performance during sex, the more nervous he gets, and the less likely he is to be able to relax and sustain his erection.
- The quickest way to ensure the onset of a panic attack is to start worrying about having one. The more intense the fear, the more extreme the physiological response—panic.
- Insomniacs generally become apprehensive as night falls, anticipating another uncomfortable evening. The anxiety over lost sleep makes drowsiness less likely and wakefulness more probable.
- A manager who thinks an employee is lazy and irresponsible becomes distrustful, delegating few responsibilities. The employee is not challenged and, as a result, feels less motivated to perform.

Erring on the side of caution may be okay if you're predicting rain on the day of your family picnic, but it's disastrous if you're thinking about the possibilities for change in your life. I guarantee that if you anticipate failure you are broadcasting that message to everyone around you. Even if you are not doing so intentionally, consciously, or verbally, you are undoubtedly sending nonverbal messages. If you are in doubt about this, remember the rats. They had no difficulty knowing whether they were supposed to be dull or bright, and I don't think they spoke English.

If expecting success is the precursor to success, why do people anticipate failure? There are several reasons.

"I feel crummy today, I'll feel crummy tomorrow." Some people come to feel hopeless because of a bad track record. If a relationship has been turbulent for a long time, they assume that it will always be turbulent. If they have struggled with bouts of depression, they assume they will always have to fight depression. Some parents at war with adolescent children believe they have lost their children forever. When normal hormonal changes wreak havoc with women's moods, it sometimes seems to them that they have always felt this way and always will.

When you are unhappy about something, it's easy to feel hopeless. You get so entrenched in thinking about your predicament that you convince yourself you will never, ever feel better. You even begin to question whether you were in denial during the "good times." Research shows that when people are in conflict or despair they lose sight of the future. The pain of the past and the present can be so overwhelming that the fact that there *is* a future is overlooked. It's like looking down at your feet when you walk instead of at the horizon.[10]

"People just don't change." Those who share this pessimistic outlook believe that undesirable behaviors are deeply entrenched personality characteristics that defy modification. It is not unusual to hear these people say things like, "I'm not surprised my business partner reacted like that—he's just an angry person," "I didn't apply for that job because I'm not a risk-taker," "She is such a nag," "He is strictly a C student."

There is a real danger in thinking about people's actions as nothing more than a series of automatic responses programmed by their personalities. The woman who convinces herself that her business partner is "just an angry person" will become vigilant in her search for evidence that she is correct. Each time he becomes angry, she will make a mental note of it. "See, here he goes again," she'll say to herself, or "I knew it." She will also begin to see him as anger incarnate—nothing *but* anger. She will fail to notice the times he is pleasant or reacts calmly to provocative situations. Her blinders will prevent her from seeing that he is not an *angry man* but, rather, a man who occasionally expresses his anger unreasonably. If he is unusually placid, she will tell herself, "He must want me to do something for him, he is on his best behavior," or "He must be so tired that he doesn't have the energy to get mad." Her conclusions about his behavior allow her to continue thinking of him as an angry man, and her view of him never changes.

"What's the problem with that?" you ask. Let's imagine that this man recognizes that he has a problem with anger and consciously attempts to change his behavior. Unable to fit such a possibility into her view of him, she does not give him the positive reinforcement he needs. After a while, having received no encouraging recognition for his efforts, he will probably get angry, providing her with further evidence for her view.

The truth is that some things about people aren't changeable. But, looking back at the years I've been a therapist, what stands out is the amazing extent to which people can change. I've seen them become self-confident, assertive, thinner, sexier, relaxed, happier, wealthier, gentler, less controlling, and so on. Although science tells us that about 50 percent of the human personality is inherited, 50 percent is learned. What is learned can be unlearned. If the glass can be half empty or half full, why opt for half empty? Why not expect change?

I was working with a woman who wanted to lose a considerable amount of weight. She was fairly convinced she would never be able to do it, because, as she put it, "I am a quitter." I asked her what she meant by that and she told me that she quit everything she ever started— craft projects, home-decorating projects, books, and so on. It was fairly obvious that, given her belief about herself, her chances of losing weight were slim. "How, then," I asked, "do you explain your marriage of thirty-five years—which hasn't been all rosy—and the fact that you've remained at the same job for fifteen years? I'm quite confused." After a moment, she replied, "You know, I never thought about it that way."

Seeing herself as a person who is tenacious and able to commit got her off to a better start than seeing herself as a quitter. As Martin Seligman observes in *Learned Optimism*:

> The optimists and the pessimists: I have been studying them for the past twenty-five years. The defining characteristics of pessimists are that they tend to believe bad events will last a long time, will undermine everything they do, and are their own fault. The optimists, who are confronted with the same hard knocks of this world, think about misfortune in the opposite way. They tend to believe defeat is just a temporary setback, that its causes are confined to this one case. The optimists believe defeat is not their fault: Circumstances, bad luck, or other people brought it about. Such people are unfazed by defeat. Confronted by a bad situation, they perceive it as a challenge and try harder.
>
> These two habits of thinking about causes have consequences. Literally hundreds of studies show that pessimists give up more easily and get depressed more often. These experiments also show that optimists do much better in school and college, at work and on the playing field. They regularly exceed the predictions of aptitude tests. When optimists run for office, they are more apt to be elected than pessimists are. Their health is usually good. They age well, much freer than most of us from the usual physical ills of middle age. Evidence suggests that they may even live longer.[11]

So what are you waiting for? Start to imagine yourself living out your dreams. Envision what might happen if you allowed yourself, just for a moment, to feel what it is like to expect change. No more nagging thoughts about the intractability of your problems. No crushing feelings of disappointment or frustration. Picture yourself accomplishing what you have been yearning to do for years. It really *is* possible. I have worked with so many people who changed their lives in incredible ways once they began to entertain the possibility that they could.

Here's a letter from a woman whose belief in herself turned the stuff dreams are made of into reality:

> When I was about 8 years old, I was failing all my subjects and my teachers told my mother that I had a learning disability. She took me to UCLA to meet with a psychologist to determine what the problem was. Meanwhile, I felt very stupid and insecure since I had to be placed in a

remedial class. The teachers treated me as if I were stupid. Since they set low standards of me, I began to set low standards for myself. My mother decided that I had more potential than that, and she encouraged me to try hard in school and work on my attention deficit problem. If even a pencil were to drop on the floor while the teacher was lecturing, my attention went to the pencil and I had difficulty concentrating on what the teacher was saying.

I had to work three times as hard as any of my friends and was teased by them all the time. Although they hurt my feelings, I decided that one day I was going to be smarter than them and then I would shove my new found abilities in their faces by getting A's when they were getting B's. Well, I struggled through high school but I graduated with a low B average and was more determined than ever to continue learning and improving myself by attending college.

My family thought I was crazy for trying and even attempted to discourage me because they thought I would fail. I guess they were trying to protect me from getting hurt. I took it as more of a challenge—I was going to prove my family wrong! I had my doubts at first because San Diego State University denied me admission but I appealed their decision, begging that they give me one semester to prove myself. Thankfully they granted me temporary admission and I did very well. I graduated in four years with a B average then went on to get my Master's degree and graduated with a 3.9 GPA, and in December of 1994, I graduated with my Ph.D. in psychology with a 3.94 GPA.

I feel great about myself. All of my sacrificing of social events, vacations and sleep was worth it! The best feeling is just knowing that I proved to all my teachers, my fellow students and even some of my family that they were wrong about me. I could do anything I set my mind to.

This is not to suggest that positive thinking is all you'll need to reach your goal. You also must have a plan, and I will help you to construct it. But by virtue of the fact that you are motivated enough to be reading, you are already within arm's length. And by believing that this is so, you just got even closer.

Chapter Four

The Whole Is Greater Than the Sum of Its Parts

SEVERAL YEARS AGO, the rabbit population in a certain part of Canada mysteriously dwindled. Scientists who studied the situation concluded that the rabbit population must have been decimated by an illness, but further investigation failed to reveal any signs of disease. A few years later, the rabbit population suddenly increased, then just as suddenly decreased again shortly thereafter. Around the same time, equally dramatic population fluctuations were noticed among the region's foxes. Again, scientists who studied them were baffled. By chance, another scientist read all the reports about the cycles in both the rabbit *and* fox populations. As the fox population increased, he noted, the rabbits diminished, and when the number of foxes diminished, the rabbit population grew. He unraveled the mystery: The growing rabbit population provided an ample food source for the foxes, who then grew in number as well. When the foxes ate too many rabbits, their food source dwindled, and they, too, began to die. With fewer predators, the rabbit population again increased, creating a new food supply for the foxes, who again multiplied. Clearly, the cycle was self-perpetuating.[1]

The rabbit-and-fox story illustrates an important point. If your field of vision is too narrow, the meaning of an event may elude you. Nowhere is this more true than in human relationships. Take the Hanson family, a fairly ordinary family who are having trouble getting along with one another. As you read what they have to say about the possible causes of their family problems, you will see how each person is missing the bigger picture, just like the rabbit and fox scientists. It's no surprise they are stumped about what to do next.

DONNA

I feel utterly hurt, frustrated and angry. Steve and I are going to bed in silence once again. Before I got married, I believed that people shouldn't go to bed angry, but we now do it on a regular basis. I've lost count of the nights I've fallen asleep wishing things were different.

Tonight's fight, like many of our fights, was about Jennifer, our fourteen-year-old. In all fairness, I must say that Jennifer isn't our only problem, but let me start with her.

Jennifer was a good student in elementary school, like her sister, Allison, who's three years younger. When she turned twelve, though, it was as if her hormones kicked in, and since then all she seems to be interested in is her social life. I'm pleased that she seems to be so popular, but I worry about her future if she refuses to take herself seriously now. I was always a good student and very conscientious, and I'm certain that those habits have paid off in my life. My career as personnel director for a large company is quite demanding, and I would not be where I am today if I hadn't kept my nose to the grindstone when I was younger. I want Jennifer to be able to do whatever she wants with her life, and that's why she needs to lay the groundwork now. Steve and I agree on this much, but then our differences begin.

I'm sure Steve cares about Jennifer, but he has a strange way of showing it. He is very critical of her and everything she does. When she was little, he hugged and kissed her, gave her baths and played with her, and beamed with pride at each milestone she passed. But now, instead of enjoying the little time we have left with Jennifer at home, he acts like a drill sergeant at boot camp. He rarely has a pleasant thing to say to her. I can't blame Jennifer for rebelling the way she does and being fresh to her father. How else can she express her feelings? How else can she tell her father that she needs support, not ridicule?

Today I got home from work around 5:00 P.M. While I was making dinner, Jennifer showed me two deficiency notices from school, warning that she was in danger of failing science and math. Jennifer had gotten D's before but never F's. I was livid. But when I imagined how Steve would react, I put my anger on the back burner and began to strategize the best way to break the news to him. I was convinced that, without a plan, all hell would break loose. I decided to talk to him about it after dinner, when we were alone.

You know the expression "Life is what happens when you're busy making plans"? Steve came home from work in a reasonably good mood and we were having a nice quiet dinner when Allison asked whether Steve had seen Jennifer's deficiency notices. Just as I'd imagined, all hell did break loose. Steve demanded to see the notices immediately. Jennifer handed them to him, and I could see the fire in his eyes as he read. He glared up at me and asked, "Did you know about this?" and when I said I did, he flew into a rage, right in front of the girls. "Why didn't you tell me? I thought you and I were supposed to be a team, but instead you and Jennifer are allies. Of course she's failing in school—you don't do a thing to prevent it. She never has consequences for her behavior. I give up. She's all yours. You figure out what to do with her."

Before I could tell Steve that I had fully intended to discuss it with him in the privacy of our bedroom, Jennifer accused Allison of being a tattletale. Steve thanked Allison for telling him and went to our bedroom, slamming the door. I couldn't decide who I was angriest at, Jennifer for her lack of motivation, Steve for his unreasonableness, or Allison for not minding her own business. Only our cat was exempt from my wrath.

The funny thing is, I agree with Steve that Jennifer should have consequences, but his punishments never fit the crime. If she gets a bad grade on a test, he wants to ground her for a month. If she talks back to him, he wants to forbid her to go to school dances. I think her punishments should be more reasonable and more immediate. Maybe I wouldn't feel so bad about his approach with Jennifer if he would balance it out by being more affectionate, too. It's been ages since he has spent any time alone with her. Although school hasn't been one of her fortes lately, she is growing into a lovely young lady, and he is missing that. He doesn't see how sensitive and loving she has become. It is unfortunate, because they are both missing out. She could be a source of incredible pride for him, and she needs her father.

To compound the situation, Steve pays a lot of attention to Allison. Allison is good in school and polite at home; she's Steve's favorite. They look alike and even have the same mannerisms. They like doing similar activities. Even when Allison behaves like Jennifer, she doesn't suffer the same repercussions. Jennifer sees Steve enjoying Allison, and I know it hurts her feelings. She must feel that nothing she does pleases him.

After most fights I try to reason with Steve, but tonight I have no interest in talking to him. I will probably go into Jennifer's room to see if she is okay. I know how upset she gets when he yells. Since Steve is so harsh with her, I feel I need to compensate by trying to understand her point of view. At least she knows she can turn to me if she needs something.

But as I said before, Jennifer is only part of our problem. Steve has changed so much over the eighteen years we've been married, I hardly recognize him. When we first got together, he was so romantic. He flattered me constantly and made me feel like I was number one in his life. He was never the world's most talkative guy, but when we were first married we used to discuss our jobs, world events, the children, and we would gossip about our friends.

But something changed after Jennifer was born. Steve spent increasing amounts of time on his job—he's an executive for a computer-software company. It's true that he brings in the lion's share of our money, but that's no reason to neglect us. We rarely go out anymore, and when we're home he prefers to read or watch television. When I try to initiate conversation, he usually gives me one-word answers. I've tried to get his attention in different ways—inviting him out for dinner, asking him to take a class with me, trying to interest him in going anywhere together—but he tells me that he works hard during the week and wants to relax on weekends.

When we do talk, it's usually me doing the talking. I try telling him about my day at work or sharing some frustration I've had. But he never just lets me talk—he starts lecturing me on how I should have handled the situation differently. He doesn't understand that I don't want his advice as much as I want him to listen and be empathetic. I don't know why I even bother talking to him. It only makes me feel lonely and distant from him. I guess I'm not surprised that I have no desire to make love anymore. He complains that I'm not very sexual, but it's hard to feel sexual when I don't feel connected to him. We have become two strangers living in the same house.

STEVE

Damn it! I am at my wits' end. Donna and I simply cannot agree on Jennifer, and I'm tired of having my opinion discounted. I find it absurd that our eleven-year-old has more sense about what's right or wrong than Donna does. The annoying thing is that Donna and I have discussed many, many times the importance of presenting a united front. I can't understand why she ignores my pleas to make Jennifer more responsible for her actions. I probably shouldn't have left the dinner table as I did, but I am so frustrated that I don't know what to do anymore. I feel like a second-rate citizen around here, so I might as well be somewhere else.

Part of my frustration is due to the fact that problems with Jennifer are nothing new. She started to slip in school several years ago, but she had a bad attitude long before that. For years teachers have have been telling us, "Jennifer is really quite capable but she doesn't apply herself." If I've heard that once, I've heard it a million times. Somehow we never learned to set limits for her, and now we've got no one to blame but ourselves.

Of course, kids are different these days. They have no respect for authority. My father would have cracked me one if I'd ever talked to him the way Jennifer talks to her mother and me. Sometimes I think Donna approves of Jennifer's freshness. If she didn't, she wouldn't put up with it. Thanks to her permissiveness, trying to teach Jennifer right from wrong is like swimming upstream. I can't do it by myself.

Sometimes I wonder, "Where did we go wrong?" I really love Jenny and it hurts to see her not living up to her potential. She should be setting an example for her younger sister, but actually Allison could set an example for Jennifer. It's not that Jennifer is stupid or incapable, it's just that she doesn't try. If it weren't for Allison, I would feel like a failure as a parent.

I really believe that if Donna would stop babying Jennifer I could get her on track, but Donna refuses to follow through with any of the plans we make. Doesn't she realize that we just have a few more years to teach

Jennifer how to take care of herself? I've always wanted my children to get a college education, but at the rate she is going, no college will accept her.

There is so much tension in our house, and not all of it relates to Jennifer. I feel an enormous responsibility to provide for my family financially. Donna's salary helps, but it won't put two children through college or allow us to live as comfortably as we do. I appreciate her contribution and know how hard she works, but I don't believe she recognizes how overwhelmed I feel that our family's future depends primarily on me. I'm not complaining, I would just like a little appreciation once in a while.

Donna seems so wrapped up in her work, and when she isn't working, all she cares about is the kids. I feel like an outcast. When we were younger, we enjoyed doing things together, going places, laughing, and, well, just spending time together. Our sex life was much better then, too. Donna never initiates sex and doesn't seem very excited when I initiate it. I can't help but feel rejected—I miss the closeness. But Donna thinks my desire to have sex is purely a physical need, like having an itch that needs scratching. She's wrong about that, but I don't think I will ever be able to make her understand that making love allows me to feel connected and intimate with her. Many of our closest times have been when we were really in sync sexually. She'll never understand how I feel about that.

I must admit that I've given up trying to put energy into our marriage, because I'm bitter about her making everyone beside me a priority in her life. Our problems with Jennifer serve as a reminder that what I feel is not important. All Donna ever does is nag. Even when I try to help out with the housework or cooking, she criticizes what I do. Complain, complain, complain. So why should I bother?

You know, now that I think about it, Donna has always been that way. When the children were little, she'd complain that I wasn't helping enough. So I'd jump each time one of them needed a bottle or a clean diaper. But, inevitably, I didn't fasten the diaper the right way, or I wasn't holding the baby in the correct position. When I took the children on outings with me, she'd complain that I picked the wrong place or stayed out too late. She acts as if she is the Parenting Expert. It's like living with Dr. Spock. Nothing I ever do is right. Even when we have conversations, she's always telling me I don't say the right things. Does she think I'm a mind reader? When I try to support her by giving suggestions, she tells me I'm lecturing her. I give up. Sometimes I think about divorce, but I don't really want to go through with it. We have both worked too hard for what we have to destroy it. But I wish that, instead of pointing fingers at me all the time, Donna would take a look at herself. I'm not the one who needs to change—she is.

JENNIFER

School sucks! I don't know why my parents make such a big deal about my grades. They are always on my case. If they would just leave me alone, everything would be okay. Every day when I come home from school my mother starts in on me. "Do you have any homework?" "Did you have any tests?" "What happened in school today?" Why do parents always ask what happened in school today? Do they think kids want to tell them every little thing? I hate coming home, because I know that the first thing that will happen is twenty questions. I mean, I don't even have a chance to get a snack before she hassles me.

And then Dad comes home, as if Mom weren't bad enough. He lectures me endlessly about the same things. "Don't you realize how important schoolwork is?" "How will you ever get into college with those grades?" "You are so lazy." Dad grounds me all the time, even when I haven't done anything wrong. Doesn't he know that if it weren't for my friends I'd go nuts? At least when I'm with them, I feel good about myself, I feel happy. Being at home with my family is depressing. I can't wait until I'm old enough to move out.

The weird thing is, even though my parents start out hassling me about school, they end up fighting with each other. The other night, I was on the phone with Jamie, my boyfriend. Well, he's not really my boyfriend, just a boy friend. Anyway, Dad came into my room—without knocking, I might add—and starting screaming about my homework not being done and why was I on the phone when I still had work to do? Can you believe that he would embarrass me like that? I told him I would get right off, but he wouldn't leave until I hung up. In the middle of all this, Mom walked in and told Dad that he was being unfair, which really pissed him off. He stormed out and she went after him. So I called Jamie back, and we got in a good half-hour before Mom noticed that I was on the phone again. This time she told me to get off, that Dad was right and it was time to do my homework. Well, which is it, Mom? Then, when my dad found out I called Jamie back instead of doing my homework, he told me I was phone-grounded for a month, at which point Mom again started in on him about being too strict. And off they went yelling again. I wonder if other kids' parents are as strange as mine.

It seems like people are always fighting around here. Which reminds me of Allison. Boy, is she a brat. Why can't she stay out of my life? She is such a goody-two-shoes. When we get into a fight, it's always *my* fault. "Jennifer, you should know better, you're the older one," or "Jennifer, you should be setting an example for Allison, she looks up to you." Well, let me tell you. Allison isn't perfect. She usually starts the fights, but my parents *never* see that—Dad especially. Sometimes I just hate her.

One time (and I really mean one time), Allison and I had a fight and Dad blamed Allison. I almost died, I was so surprised. I even felt sorry for her, because I know what it feels like to be blamed. She and I ended up going to a movie together, and we didn't argue at all. I guess she isn't totally rotten, just most of the time.

The other thing that is totally unfair is that, when Mom and Dad are mad about something, they take it out on me. If they have a bad day at work, or if they are in a bad mood, they start yelling at me for no reason. Why don't they take it out on someone else and leave me out of it for a change? Mom says that she wants to have a better relationship with me, that she wants me to be more open with her. Yeah, right. Why should I want to have a better relationship with either of them when all they ever do is yell at me? If they would be nicer to me, maybe I would be nicer to them. Maybe I'd even be more cooperative. But they just ground me whether I'm nice or not, so why bother?

Sometimes I worry that Mom and Dad are going to get divorced. Even though I'm mad at them a lot, I don't think I would want that. Lots of my friends' parents have divorced, and it doesn't seem so great. Sometimes I even wonder whether their arguing is my fault. That means that if they got a divorce I would have caused it. I feel bad when I think about that. But when I try harder nobody notices anyway. I'm just going to watch some TV. That will make me feel better.

ALLISON

I wish Jennifer would move out. I try to be nice to her. I loan her things, let her use my hair dryer, watch what she wants on TV, but she acts like she has it all coming to her. She never even says thank you. When her friends are over, she's even meaner. "Get out of my room, Allison. Leave us alone." Just wait until she wants something from me. I'll remind her of how she treats me.

The worst part about Jennifer is that Mom and Dad are always yelling at her. It seems like she's grounded all the time. If she would pay more attention to her schoolwork and less to her friends, like Mom and Dad say, she wouldn't be punished so much. Even though she's mean to me, I feel kind of sorry for her. Just the other night, I tried to talk them out of grounding her. I do that a lot, and it works once in a while. But she never stays ungrounded for long.

I wouldn't want to be in her shoes. That's why I try to do what my parents tell me. I don't want them screaming at me, too. Plus, I feel bad for them. When I go over to my friend Kim's house, her parents are lovey-dovey with each other. They don't fight like we do here. I bet my parents would be happier if it weren't for Jennifer. That's the other reason I try to be considerate of them. They don't need any more grief. Jennifer gives them enough for both of us.

You know, it's funny, but Jennifer gets more attention for her bad grades than I do for my good grades. I brought home a book report the other day that I had gotten an A on. After dinner I showed it to Mom and all she said was, "That's great, honey." Can you believe it? Three measly words. Jennifer gets a trillion. Dad was working late that night, so I didn't even get a chance to show him.

I wish Jennifer would realize that Mom and Dad are just trying to help her. She acts like she hates them. I even think that she goes out of her way to be a problem. Last summer they went on vacation for a week and Grandma stayed with us. As soon as Mom and Dad set foot out the door, Jennifer was incredibly sweet to Grandma, and even nicer to me. I thought to myself, "What's the big idea—now that Mom and Dad are gone, you turn into a nice person?" But I didn't say anything, because I didn't want to get her mad at me. When our parents returned, Grandma told them how well we had gotten along, and I'm sure they thought Jennifer had just fooled her. The truth is, Jennifer is always nicer when they're gone. I think she stirs up trouble when they're home just to get at them. And trust me, she's pretty good at it.

There's one other thing that I don't understand. Mom works late once in a while, and I always get nervous that Jennifer and Dad will kill each other while she is gone. But it's just like when Mom and Dad both leave and Jenny and I get along—when Mom isn't home, Dad isn't on Jennifer's back quite as much. As soon as Mom returns home, it's business as usual. Jennifer does something bad or the two of us fight, Dad yells, and Mom jumps in. Then Mom and Dad fight. That's how it always goes. When I grow up and have my own family, I want things to be different.

A Word to the Why's Is (More Than) Sufficient

As a therapist, I hear stories like the Hansons' all the time. People come to my office, each of them intent on conveying "the real story" and anxiously awaiting my judgment on whose view is "correct." Each is secretly convinced that I will, once and for all, set the record straight and help the others to "see the light." They remind me of a cartoon I recently saw, which pictured a married couple in a therapist's office. The wife was telling the therapist, "I already told him what's wrong with him, but he wants to hear it from a professional."

How can each member of the Hanson family feel so confident that his or her view reflects what has actually happened? Part of the problem is that as observers we confuse the facts of a situation with our interpretations of it. The facts are indisputable—they either did or didn't happen. Jennifer's receiving the deficiency notices, Allison's informing Steve about them, and Steve's leaving the dinner table are all facts—observers would agree that these events took place. Interpretations, on the other hand, are people's personal reactions to their observations, or their hypotheses as to why these events took place.

For example, if you say that Jennifer gets D's, you are reporting a fact. But if you say that Jennifer gets D's because she is lazy or spiteful or to seek attention from her parents, you are making an interpretation. Interpretations are not factual in nature; they are simply opinions. Relationship problems arise when people act as if their preferred interpretations ("We're having these problems because Steve is so controlling," or "Jennifer would be a better kid if Donna weren't such a softy") are *facts.*

Why is this a problem? When each person in the family believes that he or she alone holds the correct interpretation of the nature or cause of a particular problem, an inordinate amount of time is spent debating who is right and who is wrong. Arguing about important matters feels like problem-solving, getting to the root of things, but nothing is further from the truth. The longer they debate, the more stridently they express their respective positions, the more convinced they become that they are correct, and the less likely they are to consider other views. They become prisoners of their own rigid thinking.

Steve and Donna both love Jennifer and want her to do well in school. They even agree on the importance of her being more conscientious. But because Steve believes that she needs discipline and structure, he condemns Donna for taking a nurturing approach. Donna, who believes that children need tender loving care to flourish, criticizes Steve's more stringent approach. Donna is waiting for Steve to change. Steve is waiting for Donna to change. In the meantime, the problem with Jennifer is getting worse. From a broader perspective, one could say that what's causing the problem with Jennifer is not anything Donna or Steve has done to her directly, but their ongoing arguments about the best way to solve the problem. Although it's natural for Donna and Steve—and Jennifer and Allison, for that matter—each to believe that his or her way of seeing things is the only accurate one, that's a very shortsighted and impractical perspective.

Remember those foxes and rabbits? Well, the Hanson family are doing what the scientists did at first: they are looking "inside" each family member for the cause of the problem. Donna thinks the problem resides with Steve's impulse to control. She might also blame Jennifer for her refusal to put more energy into her schoolwork. From Steve's standpoint, Donna and Jennifer are to blame—Donna for her laxness and Jennifer for her laziness. Jennifer, on the other hand, believes the problem is her parents' interference—and Allison's troublemaking. Allison simply blames Jennifer for all the problems at home.

But just as the scientists failed to notice the correspondence between the rising and falling of the fox and rabbit populations, the Hansons fail to notice the interconnections between all of their behavior.

For example, is Steve stricter than Donna because he's simply a rigid person (as Donna would have us believe), or to compensate for Donna's more relaxed style? Let's examine how this might be possible. Each time Jennifer disappoints her parents, Steve takes a strong stand and Donna disagrees with his approach. In order to convince her, Steve escalates his position. He yells louder, criticizes Jennifer more harshly, and punishes her more severely. Donna, unable to let her daughter be so "mistreated," intervenes more vigorously in Jennifer's behalf. Donna's interference makes Steve grow even more determined to parent Jennifer his way, which, needless to say, steps up Donna's efforts to defend her. And so on and so on.

Put another way, is Donna's more relaxed style a result of poor judgment or lack of character (as Steve would like to think), or is she simply responding to Steve's authoritative tactics? Although Steve would say that the argument around the dinner table occurred because Donna didn't tell him about the deficiency notice, Donna would say that, if she could count on Steve to be more even-tempered and reasonable, she would have told him earlier. As seems always to be the case in their home, when Steve responds explosively, Donna feels the need to contradict him in order to minimize the "damaging" impact on Jennifer. The more emphatically Steve asserts himself, the more Donna feels the need to protect her.

The antithesis is also true—Steve dampens in Donna any inclination to take a stronger stand with Jennifer, and Donna squelches any inclination in Steve to be tender. Note that Donna was initially "livid" with Jennifer, but, in anticipation of Steve's reaction, she "put my anger on the back burner." If Steve had been calmer in his response, or if they were divorced, chances are that Donna would have taken a stronger stand that evening. In fact, she might have exploded in much the same way Steve does. But because Donna is responding not only to Jennifer but to Steve, she modified her initial reaction.

Steve recalls being more nurturing when the children were young, but feels that, because Donna criticized him, he stopped. If Donna had praised Steve for his efforts (even if they weren't perfect), or if Steve had been a single parent, he might have expanded his parenting repertoire.

There is yet another mystery. Donna and Steve see their daughters as arch-enemies. So why do they get along better when their parents leave? Why don't they act out in their grandmother's presence? Perhaps it is, again, that the girls are responding not simply to each other, but to their parents and to the interplay between them.

Clearly, people's behavior is better appreciated in the context in which it occurs. But even this vantage point does not yield absolute explanations about who *caused* a problem. Rather, it reveals the circular fashion in which behavior is connected: Jennifer gets a poor grade, which leads to Steve's phone-grounding her, which leads to Donna's attempt to rescue Jennifer, which leads to Donna and Steve's fighting, which leads to Jennifer's getting back on the phone, which leads to Steve's further rage, which leads to Donna's intervening, and so on. Ironically, each of them elicits from his or her partner the very behavior he or she resents.

This broader, systemic perspective is an outgrowth of research spearheaded in the early fifties by Gregory Bateson, a well-known anthropologist. Of the researchers' many findings, one is particularly relevant here. [2]

Schizophrenia had been considered an illness *inside* people causing them to experience disjointed and distorted thinking and to be totally out of touch with reality. But the researchers observed that, immediately following visits from family members, hospitalized schizophrenics frequently relapsed for several days. This confused the researchers, because they had assumed that these patients were incapable of tuning in to their environment. Apparently, they were wrong.

As they continued their research, they also noticed that these schizophrenic patients experienced episodes of acute psychosis whenever their parents argued intensely. It appeared that, when things got tense between the parents, the child got sick, which in turn diverted the parents' attention from the marital discord, forcing them to band together to handle the crisis. As soon as the discord abated, the psychotic episode ceased.

The researchers reasoned that family members operate like a system—that is, they act in highly predictable patterns that maintain an equilibrium, or a balance. The findings of this research group were replicated by other scientists in the years that followed and were considered groundbreaking in that they provided a systemic understanding of family functioning and human behavior.

However, these early efforts to understand psychotic behavior from a broader perspective failed to appreciate the circular connections in such families. While these studies suggested that chronic marital problems were *causing* schizophrenia, it is equally plausible that the marital conflict was a *result* of the stress felt by parents dealing with a psychotic child. Today we know that there is also a genetic or biological component to schizophrenia. Simplistic as it was, however, the researchers' characterization of schizophrenia provided the rudiments of a new and completely different way to understand behavior in general. Problems stem from problematic interactions *between* people. It is inadequate to look solely *within* individuals for causes of problems.

Unfortunately, the Hansons are too busy looking for causes within one another to notice how patterns of interactions between them are perpetuating the problem. If they did, they could conceivably *interrupt* the sequence by doing something different. If Jennifer did her homework instead of using the phone, her father wouldn't ground her. If Steve handled Jennifer more gently, Donna wouldn't intervene. If Donna didn't intervene—or if she supported Steve—they wouldn't argue. If Steve and Donna didn't leave Jennifer's room to argue, Jennifer wouldn't get back on the phone. But instead of figuring out how to alter the flow of events, each person spends an inordinate amount of time looking for the cause of the problem. Which is itself a cause of the problem.

Regrettably for the Hansons, the search for causes has extended to other parts of family life. Donna and Steve are convinced that Jennifer's behavior precipitates their marital problems and feel they would get along better were it not for their arguments about her. Though this is undoubtedly true, the formula can be reversed: do Donna and Steve fight because Jennifer acts out, or does Jennifer act out because Donna and Steve fight? Everyone agrees that there is far too much yelling and dissension in the family, and this tension must affect Jennifer as well. It's entirely possible that her preoccupation with the tension at home makes it difficult for her to concentrate at school. Hence the poor grades.

Steve and Donna feel that they can't put energy into rebuilding their marriage because Jennifer's problems interfere, but, again, there is another way to view the situation. Does the marital relationship take a back seat to Jennifer's behavior, or do Steve and Donna focus on Jennifer in order to avoid their marital problems? In other words, does

Jennifer sense that it is safer for her parents to argue about her grades than to address the underlying problems in their relationship? Is she unconsciously protecting their marriage by providing them with an arena where they can avoid more painful problems?

Perhaps Jennifer is protecting her parents in another way. Maybe she is giving them the opportunity to work through their differences indirectly and therefore less threateningly. For example, Donna expresses regret that the only time Steve talks to Jennifer is to criticize her. Later, Donna mentions that she, too, feels ignored and criticized by Steve. She also says, "I can't blame Jennifer for rebelling the way she does and being fresh to her father. How else can she express her feelings? How else can she tell her father that she needs support, not ridicule?" Is it possible that Donna is really referring to her own needs? Is it also possible that Donna unconsciously perpetuates the problematic cycle because, on some level (as Steve suspects), she approves of Jennifer's rebellion against Steve's way of handling things?

When Donna and Steve do address their marital difficulties, again, each blames the other. Donna believes that if Steve were more attentive and affectionate outside the bedroom she would be more interested in sex. Steve believes that if Donna were more sexual he would be more loving and animated around her.

One can't help wondering how Steve's feeling of rejection plays a role in the interaction of all the family members. Perhaps he is threatened by what he sees as the closeness between Donna and Jennifer. Inadvertently, he may displace these negative feelings onto Jennifer and draw closer to Allison. Conversely, Donna may feel excluded by the closeness between Allison and Steve, which may strengthen her bond with Jennifer.

In addition, other factors may contribute to the Hansons' difficulties. Each member of the family interacts with people outside the family. If these interactions are pleasant, family members return home feeling cheerful. If they are unpleasant, family members reunite feeling grouchy. Inevitably, the moods are contagious.

Undoubtedly, Donna's and Steve's high-pressure jobs take a toll on both of them from time to time. Jennifer observes, "If they have a bad day at work, or if they are in a bad mood, they start yelling at me for no reason." While it is unlikely that Donna and Steve get angry for "no reason" at all, it is very likely that, when they feel overrun by their responsibilities at work or when they have negative interactions with co-workers, their mood is influenced, and thus their ability to cope with family tensions. A classic example of this game of Mood Tag: a father comes home from a rough day at the office and argues with his wife, who yells at the oldest child, who picks on the younger sibling, who kicks the dog, who bites the cat, and so on.

Now that you have looked at the Hansons' problems from many different angles, you may be scratching your head and thinking how much simpler things seem when you acknowledge only your own point of view. But, as you are about to discover, solutions become self-evident when you consider the bigger picture. Were the Hansons to view their situation from a broader perspective, they could prevent much of their arguing and dissension. By keeping the following principles in mind, you will be able to do the same.

There are many ways to view any given situation, and no perspective is more "correct" than any other. As you read the Hansons' accounts, you probably found yourself agreeing more with one than the others. You were undoubtedly rooting for whoever most closely shares your values or resembles you in temperament. But now you know that any single point of view is by definition narrow and incomplete— just one piece of the puzzle. Although your reactions may mostly coincide with those of Donna, Steve, Jennifer, or Allison, it's important to remember that any one point of view is no more valid or correct than any other.

Then why is it so easy to think other people are simply "wrong" when they disagree with you? The blind man touching only the elephant's trunk believes that elephants' bodies are long and tubular, whereas his blind friend touching only the elephant's stomach disagrees; it is obvious to those who can see the whole elephant that both men are right. Although your own viewpoint is the natural starting place; you must keep in mind that it is only one way to look at a situation, and certainly not the only "correct" way.

In fact, that's why, when you go to your next-door neighbor with your troubles, you may get a good shoulder to cry on, but you probably will not get the best advice. What you have shared with your neighbor is strictly your own biased perspective, which prevents him or her from seeing the "whole elephant." From hearing only your side of the story, your neighbor will probably join you in blaming others, leaving you with no alternative but to wait until they change first.

No matter how convinced you are that you and you alone hold the truth as to the "real cause" of your problem, don't believe it. This self-righteous attitude will diminish your ability to find solutions. Regardless of how different other people's points of view might be, they are not groundless. The more you allow yourself to appreciate other people's perspectives, the more abundant the potential solutions.

How we define the problem dictates the solution. Steve thinks Jennifer is lazy and irresponsible. Donna thinks she is longing for attention and TLC. For simplicity's sake, let's say that Steve sees Jennifer as "bad" and Donna sees her as "sad." Since Steve sees Jennifer as "bad," he uses punishments to correct her behavior. If prohibiting her from going to a school dance on Friday night doesn't improve her performance—if she goes from "bad" to "worse"—Steve ups the ante and grounds her for a week. If that doesn't work, the consequences become even more severe. At no time during this process does Steve consider showing Jennifer affection, because it would not fit with his belief that she is "bad." In his mind, showing a "bad" child affection will only reinforce the undesirable behavior.

Donna, however, seeing Jennifer as a "sad" kid, feels that she needs more compassion and attention. If Jennifer brings home a poor grade, Donna tries to talk to her about her feelings about school, family, friends, and so on. She tries to find out what is bothering Jennifer in order to help her feel better. If a heart-to-heart discussion fails to improve Jennifer's schoolwork, Donna assumes she didn't probe deeply enough or find the right words. She may try to pursue the conversation, or she may try to cheer Jennifer up by taking her out for dinner or on a shopping spree. The more stagnant Jennifer's school performance remains, the more Donna searches for ways to help her feel better. At no time would Donna contemplate abandoning her approach to set strict limits for Jennifer, because she believes that a heavy-handed approach will just make Jennifer feel worse about herself, making it more difficult for her to concentrate in school.

Donna and Steve are so fixed on their respective points of view that they are oblivious to a third possible explanation for Jennifer's poor grades: that the cause of the problem is outside Jennifer's control. She might have a learning disability, or what is referred to as an attention-deficit disorder. In this case, neither punishment nor TLC would be an effective solution; rather, specialized instruction or medication would be in order. But unless Donna or Steve can even consider the possibility that Jennifer is behaving involuntarily, it won't occur to them to have her evaluated.

As you can see, once we assume we know the *cause* of a problem, we are disposed to favor a particular solution to it, and to be oblivious or adamantly opposed to any others.

Since our view of a problem dictates the solution, and since all views are viable, choose a perspective that offers a solution. By now you can understand that the way you see a particular problem suggests certain solutions while concomitantly closing down other possibilities. You also know that your view of any situation is an interpretation, not a fact. Steve and Donna would be better off if they keep that in mind in thinking about Jennifer. Why? If they did, they would see many solutions to Jennifer's problems. Since what we do to resolve a problem is dictated by how we see it, the more flexible we can be in how we see things, the more alternatives become available to us. With this kind of solution-oriented thinking, if an approach stemming from one point of view wasn't working, Donna and Steve could easily shift to a new point of view and try another strategy. If they weren't so locked into their respective positions, a spirit of experimentation and cooperation would evolve between them.

For instance, if Donna and Steve appreciated that their respective opinions about Jennifer were not right or wrong and that both were plausible, they could do a number of things. Together they could agree to set firmer limits for Jennifer and observe the results. If this worked, it would make sense to view Jennifer as someone who needed more structure. If it didn't, they could try to nurture her more and see if the situation improved. If nurturing helped, Donna and Steve could conclude that Jennifer needed more TLC. If it didn't, they could try yet another strategy.

The bottom line is that views leading to effective solutions are the ones to adopt, whereas views leading to dead ends are worth dropping. Since none of the Hansons' individual views alone has helped them to find a way out of their rut, a new perspective is in order. That's why the broader, systemic view, which takes into account all of their individual perspectives, adds another dimension. It's not that this more expansive view is any more "correct" than the individual views, but that, because of its comprehensiveness, it gives family members a new vantage point and offers ample opportunities for them to stop going in circles.

I hope this bird's-eye view into the Hanson family has loosened up your thinking about your own situation. If you've reached an impasse, it's probably because you've fallen in love with your explanation for why you are stuck, and this, in turn, has narrowed your range of responses. But maybe now you can see that your love is blind and it's time to consider a different perspective.

Chapter Five

The Butterfly Effect

IN THE EARLY sixties, meteorologist Edward Lorenz established that small, almost imperceptible changes in weather could affect global weather patterns—a phenomenon he called the "butterfly effect" because, as he put it, a butterfly flapping its wings in Brazil might create a tornado in Texas.

The butterfly effect is alive and well in human systems, too, which is great news. It means that a single change, no matter how small, leads to other changes. If you take one small step to change your life, the positive changes start to snowball, taking on a life of their own. It also means that, if you change your behavior, people around you will also change.

The process can begin just about anywhere. Once you see how problematic patterns of interaction between people get them stuck, practical solutions leap out at you. Instead of blaming others and waiting for them to change, anyone can start the ball of change rolling. That's exactly what Donna did. Once she decided to put on her solution glasses, she saw the irony of her fights with Steve, because, with respect to their feelings about Jennifer, they are both right. All children require a healthy dose of both discipline and nurturing to develop into successful adults, she acknowledged, and families that do not provide both these elements are missing something essential. The key is in the balance between the two. Donna knew that if she could construct a plan that incorporated both discipline *and* nurturing, they could solve Jennifer's school problem.

Donna also realized that what she disagreed with was Steve's harshness toward Jennifer, not his belief that she needed to be responsible in school. Realizing how much they agreed made Donna even more eager to design a plan that would prevent conflict at home.

With the help of one of Jennifer's teachers, Donna set up a reporting system whereby Jennifer recorded the assignment for each day and obtained a signature from each teacher to verify that the assignment was correct. Her assignment notebook was checked daily by either parent. At the end of every week, Jennifer was required to get grades from tests or reports from each teacher as well. This way, Steve and Donna were aware of her performance on a regular basis and did not have to wait until the end of the term or for deficiency notices to be sent home. If necessary, they could intervene before the problem got out of hand. Donna had Jennifer sign a contract that spelled out what was required of her in order to receive and maintain privileges, such as doing and handing in her homework in a timely fashion, receiving nothing lower than C's on tests and reports, and attending school regularly. Steve and Donna both signed, too.

Steve was somewhat surprised that Donna had taken this step, but he was also pleased and supportive. The structure seemed to help—Jennifer began to hand in her homework assignments more regularly, and her grades showed some improvement. Because of this, she was allowed more freedom with her friends, something she desperately wanted. Her curfew was extended and she was permitted to go places that had previously been off limits. Each week when Jennifer came home with a good report, she was praised and, on the rare occasions she allowed it, hugged. On weeks when she hadn't done her work, her privileges were withdrawn. Since the rules were set down in black and white, Donna and Steve did not argue with Jennifer; they just pointed to their agreement. Donna liked the new approach because the yelling stopped, and Steve liked it because everyone seemed to understand and respect the family rules.

Donna's new plan had other benefits. Since Steve and Donna had stopped arguing about Jennifer and presented a united front to her, she no longer worried about her parents' marriage. As a result, she was better able to concentrate in school and found it easier to stay with a task. Because of this and her own improved relationship with her parents, Jennifer felt better about herself. She went to school feeling happier. Her teachers noticed the difference rather quickly, and told Jennifer so. This reinforced her desire to achieve in their classes.

Once the tensions between Donna and Steve lessened, Steve found himself wanting to talk to Donna about topics other than their daughter. He was genuinely more interested in how her day went and asked her about it regularly. He even invited Donna out for dinner several times. She enjoyed the opportunity to be with Steve without discussing Jennifer, and without fighting. After their third dinner date, Donna felt romantic and started kissing Steve "the old-fashioned way." When they returned home, she seduced him.

For the first time, Steve realized that building a relationship with Donna was the shortcut to more closeness with her, and not just Donna's excuse for avoiding intimacy. She really did respond positively and lovingly to his attentiveness. Not only was he truly enjoying the time they were spending together; he was also getting the affection and sexual responsiveness he'd wanted in the first place.

As weeks passed, there were times when Donna noticed lulls in their relationship, times when there seemed to be more distance between them. In the past, she would have made a minor effort to get things back on track, but if Steve did not immediately respond to her overtures, a wall would go up and Donna wouldn't want Steve to touch her.

But Donna was feeling so much better about Steve in general that she decided to do something different. One weekend, the girls were visiting friends and they had the house to themselves. Although she hadn't been feeling particularly close to Steve for several days, Donna sat beside him on the couch and put her hand on his leg. Surprised by her touch, Steve put down the magazine he was reading and smiled at her. Instead of complaining about their lack of closeness, she started being physically affectionate. Donna wasn't "in the mood" when she started kissing Steve, but his responsiveness caught her off guard, and before she knew it, she got in the mood and they made love and spent the rest of the afternoon together.

Donna learned two new things about her marriage that afternoon. First, she recognized that feeling close to Steve was not the only prerequisite to her feeling sexual toward him. She learned she could jumpstart her own sexual feelings by giving herself a slight push to reach out to Steve physically. Even if Donna was only partially interested in being sexual with Steve when she touched him, the idea "grew on her" as they connected.

She also saw how attentive Steve was to her *after* they had sex. They spent a pleasant afternoon together having lunch, working in the yard, and going for a walk. Without complaining or feeling bad, Donna got exactly what she wanted from Steve: more togetherness.

Donna discovered that, although she and Steve are different, she can still get her needs met in their marriage. By accepting their differences and not judging Steve negatively, Donna was able to take better care of his needs, which prompted him to be more accommodating of hers. There was another bonus to Donna's taking better care of Steve; she became aware of how much better she feels about *herself* when she gives freely to him. "This is how marriage is supposed to be," she commented.

There was no doubt about it—Donna and Steve were on the right track again. There were fewer arguments, and they were communicating more. Every once in a while, when Donna would talk about negative feelings, as in the past, Steve would jump in and offer suggestions. But instead of taking his comments personally and getting angry, Donna calmly reminded him that she didn't want solutions—she simply wanted him to listen. Since he didn't have to defend himself, he was happy to oblige. Conversely, when Steve was quiet, instead of assuming something was wrong in the relationship or that something was bothering him, Donna appreciated that he just needed some time alone. Donna found it infinitely easier to give him space when they were getting along better. And the more she respected Steve's need to be alone and quiet, the less he seemed to need it.

Something else wonderful happened in the Hanson family. As Donna and Steve became less divided and the tension in their home subsided, they noticed that Allison and Jennifer were getting along better. Maybe they had stopped competing for attention. Maybe they no longer felt they had to divert their parents' attention from more serious problems. Maybe they were mirroring their parents' relationship. Maybe, maybe, maybe. Whatever the reasons, as Donna and Steve became more loving, so did the girls. There were occasional sibling squabbles, of course—after all, they were still human. But in their new spirit of unity, Donna and Steve refrained from jumping in, and somehow, magically, the girls managed to resolve most of their differences. Donna and Steve realized that their intervening in the girls' fights as often as they had in the past had inadvertently undermined their daughters' abilities to solve their own problems.

Thanks to the butterfly effect, improvements in the relationship between Jennifer and her parents spilled over to her parents' marriage and her relationships with her sister and teachers as well. In all likelihood, Donna and Steve brought their "new and improved" attitudes to work and their co-workers benefited, too.

The Avalanche Effect

Not only does one change lead to another, but change tends to happen exponentially. Motivational speaker and author Tony Robbins has this to say about the change process.

> Think of two arrows pointing in the same general direction. If you make a tiny change in the direction of one of them, if you push it three or four degrees in a different direction, the change will probably be imperceptible at first. But if you follow that path forwards and then for miles, the difference will become greater and greater—until there's no relation at all between the first path and the second.[1]

Donna believed that her new plan might help Jennifer and also might curb the dissension between Steve and her, but she had no idea how quickly these changes would occur, nor did she anticipate the actual breadth and magnitude of the changes. She didn't foresee the extent of the changes in Steve, their sexual relationship, and their communication, or the improvements in the girls' relationship. That's because Donna wasn't aware that change happens exponentially. Many people are amazed to see how minor shifts in behavior and attitude make monumental differences in their lives. When life feels overwhelming, it's difficult to imagine how a small change can make any difference at all, let alone a major difference. But it can and it does.

A woman once told me that she felt depressed about so many different aspects of her life that she didn't even know where to begin trying to help herself feel better. She felt that, even if she were to resolve one problem, it wouldn't begin to make a dent in her overall feeling about her life.

Despite her pessimism, she decided to force herself out the door one Friday evening and go shopping for clothes. At a mall, she found a dress she really loved, and this boosted her spirits a bit. Because she was feeling somewhat upbeat, she called a friend when she got home. Her friend was pleased to hear from her, since there had been little contact between them recently, and she invited the woman out to lunch the next day.

As a result of their lunch date, the woman realized how pleasurable it was to spend time with friends and made more of an effort to contact other people. Her social life picked up considerably, and within weeks she met a man with whom she fell in love. Needless to say, her depression became a thing of the past.

But think about it for a moment. What do you think this woman would have thought if, when she told you of her despair, you suggested she go shopping? Undoubtedly, she would have felt insulted and believed that you really didn't appreciate the depths of her anguish. Going to the mall hardly seems like a cure for depression—until you appreciate how one small change can mushroom into mega-change.

IT TAKES ONE TO TANGO

Let's go back to the Hansons for a moment. As you recall, their lives began to change for the better when Donna decided to set up a reporting system for Jennifer rather than to keep coming at the problem in the same old way. She didn't get Steve's approval or commitment to participate. She just did it. But any of the others could have been the one to initiate change, by changing any element in the cycle of events. No single starting place is better than any other starting place. The key is that *someone* decides it is time for a change. It doesn't matter who, or even what.

Envision a mobile. As one segment begins spinning, the other segments are set in motion. So it is with relationships. If a wife changes her behavior toward her husband, the marriage will change—no matter who was "at fault." If a father handles his children differently, the children's behavior will inevitably change. If a man who is unhappy at his job treats his boss differently, she must respond differently. When one person in a family changes, the interactions among other family members also change. The bottom line is, *you can get more of your needs met in any situation by changing your behavior first.*

A standard self-help axiom suggests that "the only person you can change is yourself." Don't believe it for a second. You *can* change other people, but you must *begin* by changing your own actions. Just as Donna had been unintentionally provoking Steve to respond negatively, and vice versa, she was able, consciously and intentionally, to provoke him to respond positively. Certain actions, however, have infinitely more power to elicit change than others do. In other words, not all efforts to get people to be kinder, more thoughtful, less sarcastic, less controlling are created equal. In a given situation, some approaches are simply more effective, and this book will help you to identify them.

The good news about all of this is that you can be the catalyst for change, without explicit help from anyone. You do not require the knowing participation or acquiescence of reluctant spouses, rebellious children, or overbearing employers. You do not have to ask, beg, or bribe them to read this book, or even leave it lying conspicuously around the house hoping they will notice the heavily highlighted parts. Once you figure out how to push their buttons in a positive way, you will begin to see the results for which you have been hoping. Remember, you are the pivot point for change. You can learn how to tip the balance in any relationship.

But why me?

Sometimes people ask, "Why do I have to be the one to change?" That's a good question. I am not suggesting that you and you alone be the one to change. That would never work. I am suggesting that you *initiate* change, for a very specific reason: to get more of your needs met. If it doesn't work out that way, something isn't working, and this book will help you determine what to do next. I am not suggesting that you be a martyr and correct the errors of your ways, I'm suggesting that you take the bull by the horns and make a change to get a change. I can guarantee that, once you identify how to trigger change in other people by changing yourself, you will wonder why you ever wasted time asking, "Why me?" Try it and you'll see how quickly and dramatically it happens.

I'm not saying that this will be easy. I know how doing the same old thing, ineffective though it is, feels as comfortable as your tattered flannel PJ's. But I also know that, if you don't try something different now, it will be even harder for you in the long run. I guarantee, the pain of being in the same place and feeling the same way three months from now would be much more intense than the discomfort of doing something different immediately. I say, go for it. Make a decision right now to start the dance.

Chapter Six

If You Don't Know Where You're Going, You'll Probably End Up Somewhere Else

FRIENDS OF MINE watching the 1994 Winter Olympics noticed that, before the races, German bobsledders stood together, their eyes closed and their bodies swaying back and forth. The commentator explained that the bobsledders were envisioning the run, and their bodies were responding to the twists and the turns they were imagining. They were visualizing themselves excelling through the course, and in so doing rehearsing the maneuvers necessary to perform competitively in the race.

Many top athletes learn to outperform others by creating mental pictures of themselves giving peak performances. Golfers visualize themselves hitting the ball so that it sails through the air and lands on the green. Baseball players see themselves hitting a home run. Runners envision themselves crossing the finish line. Olympic gold medalist Greg Louganis pauses for several seconds before each dive, imagining himself bounding off the board in defiance of gravity and hurtling through the air with grace and precision. Gymnast Mary Lou Retton uses a similar strategy. The night before winning the 1984 gold medal, she "did what I always do before a major competition—mindscripted it completely. I mentally ran through each routine, every move, imagining everything done perfectly."

Visualizing success is not hocus-pocus. Researchers theorize that this kind of mental rehearsal helps create a blueprint for action. Chinese pianist Liu Chi-kung would probably agree. In 1958, he placed second to Van Cliburn in an international competition. A year later, he was arrested for political reasons and sent to prison for a seven-year term, during which time he never touched a piano. Yet, within several months of his release, he was on the road again, receiving accolades from the critics. Many people wondered how it was possible for Kung to maintain his level of expertise without the hours of daily practice that piano virtuosos generally require. Kung assured them that he had practiced daily, mentally rehearsing all of his music note by note.

When I met Mary, the thought of excelling at anything could not have been further from her mind. The only image she had of herself was one of a depressed person. She lived and breathed thoughts of hopelessness and helplessness. "I can't seem to get out of this slump I'm in," she told me. "The harder I try, the worse it gets. Usually when I get down, I give myself a pep talk and then I am up and running again. But this time it's a little deeper. It kind of scares me. My usual methods for breaking out of this cycle just aren't working anymore. Work has lost its meaning, and I find everyone around me annoying, including my husband and kids." Consumed by negativity, Mary had *become* her depression.

Pervasive as her depressed mood seemed to be, I asked Mary to imagine what her life would be like when it lifted. I said to her, "Imagine for a moment that, after you leave here today, you go home, and tonight, in your sleep, a miracle happens. This miracle would make it possible for all your worries to disappear, for everything that you have been feeling down about to vanish into thin air. My question is, how could you tell that the miracle had happened in your sleep? What would you be doing differently tomorrow morning?"

It was a hard question, but Mary gave it a try. "I would feel happy again. I wouldn't feel so overwhelmed by everything. I get into such black moods. That would be gone." I pressed for more details. What would her life be like? If I came over to her house, what would I see "the happy Mary" doing?

As she spoke, Mary began to flesh out a picture of herself as a happier, more fulfilled person. The more she described this person, the clearer the vision became, and the more I could see her mentally stepping into the positive picture of herself.

MARY: Well, I guess I would be putting more energy into my work. I'm in sales, and I haven't been meeting my monthly goals. This depresses me, and I have been avoiding doing what I know I have to do to get back on track. If I were in a better mood, I wouldn't procrastinate anymore. I would just do what I have to do to make more sales. Even if I just worked one hour a night making phone calls and outlining what I need to do tomorrow, that would help.

MWD: So focusing more on work would be part of this miracle picture.

MARY: Yes, absolutely. Also, if this miracle you're talking about happened, I would be more patient with my family. Even my kids are telling me I have been crabby lately, and believe me, "crabby" is a nice way of putting it. Everything they do irritates me. I know kids get on their parents' nerves, but I feel like a time bomb with them. Every little thing sets me off. I don't like myself after I holler, but I feel like I can't help it either.

MWD: So, after the miracle, you'd be more calm with them?

MARY: Yes, just not so much yelling. And we would sit down for meals together. Now, because of my lack of energy, meals are "catch as catch can." There's no sense of togetherness anymore. We've stopped doing things as a family. I used to be the driving force for family outings, but, because I've been depressed, I've given up, and when I don't organize family activities, no one else does either.

MWD: So let me see if I've got it straight. After the miracle, you would feel happier and would be spending an hour or so every night focusing on your work, you'd be calmer with the kids and spend more time together as a family, such as eating meals together. Is that right?

MARY: Yeah, and I would notice that my old energy level is back, not just with the family or work, but in other areas of my life. Right now, I don't feel like doing anything. I haven't seen any of my friends for a long time. And I haven't gone to church, which I used to do fairly regularly. I don't want to burden other people with my problems, so I stay secluded.

MWD: But remember, this miracle happened. What's different now?

MARY: I would feel the zest for living I used to feel. I would call my friends to say hello and ask them how they are doing. I wouldn't be so self-absorbed. And then there's church. Members of my congregation have been asking me why I haven't been there, and instead of coming up with excuses, I would just go. I know, if I would force myself out the door, I would feel better. I usually feel inspired when I'm there. You know, I realize now that, if the miracle happened, I would show more interest in *anything* other than my depression. I've had such a one-track mind lately.

MWD: What else would you be thinking about?

MARY: Anything. I am a planner. When I'm feeling good, I love to think about the future, maybe plan a trip or decorate a room in our house, start a new exercise plan, or whatever. When I'm depressed, I don't do that at all. I will know that I am feeling better when I start planning again.

MWD: In addition to all these things you've been mentioning, what might your husband notice about you after the miracle? If I were to ask him what you would be doing differently after the miracle, what would he say?

MARY: Hm . . . That's interesting. He would probably say that I would be nicer to him and show more interest in his life. I would ask him questions about his day and, oh yes, he'd probably say that I would be more affectionate.

MWD: When he talks about affection, what does he mean?

MARY: Mostly he'd been referring to the fact that I haven't been feeling up for having sex too often, but I think he'd also say that I haven't been paying enough attention to him. We used to go out more, but lately I haven't felt like it. He's complains about that once in a while, so I guess he would notice me going out with him again, out to dinner, the movies, things like that.

Just as my friends could see the German bobsledders swaying to the imagined curves of the course, I could see Mary's affect changing as she imagined herself being happier again—and so could she. As she heard herself talk, she was reminded of the part of her that was *not* depressed: the patient, energetic, loving, hardworking person who was only dormant, not dead. As the picture of a happier Mary began to crystallize, she remembered where she wanted to go. And that made getting there considerably easier.

The Goal of Goal-Setting

"If you aim at nothing, you'll hit it
every time."

—ANONYMOUS

Setting an effective goal is a prerequisite to solving problems. It will help you identify where you want to be, provide clues as to what you need to do to get there, and offer a way of knowing when you've arrived. I frequently ask my clients, "How will you know when we can stop meeting like this?" If we start out with a clear goal in mind and keep this goal in our peripheral vision throughout, our energies remain focused, and the goal is accomplished rapidly.

What sets the program outlined in this book apart from others is its emphasis on solutions over problems, and the single most important prerequisite to finding solutions is establishing goals. The very act of setting goals makes vague aspirations concrete and begins to define the steps necessary to accomplish them. It also stops people from focusing on the past or what's wrong with their lives currently, and projects them into the future, a process that renews hope.

Perhaps you are telling yourself that you can skip this part because you already have a handle on what needs changing in your life. "I want more self-esteem," you say. "I want my wife to be more considerate toward me." "I feel I deserve a promotion." But half-baked goals such as these are deceptive—they give you the illusion that you know where you're headed when you really don't. Even if your goals are already fairly well defined, I encourage you to keep reading, because, the more precise you can make them, the quicker you will get there. In fact, it helps tremendously to write down your goals. The mere act of committing your goals to paper transforms your ideas into action.

"So what are you hoping to change?" That's the first question I ask when I work with people, to get the process of goal-setting started right away. I have been asking that question for seventeen years now, long enough to know how difficult it can be to answer and how easy it is to get sidetracked. To shorten your problem-solving journey, I'd like to offer you a crash course in goal-setting, so that the destinations you set for yourself will help you to discover the most effective ways of getting there.

Identify What You Want, Not What You Don't Want

When I ask people how they want their lives to be different, they typically respond by telling me what they don't like about themselves, others, or circumstances in their lives. We are experts on what makes us unhappy, and amateurs in knowing what might give us more satisfaction. Take Mary in the example above. When I asked her to imagine the miracle happening, she told me, "I wouldn't feel so overwhelmed by everything. I get into such black moods. That would be gone." Although Mary didn't like feeling overwhelmed by her black moods, she didn't at first say what she wished would happen instead. But when I prompted her, she came up with a very specific objective: she would put more energy into her work, spending one hour a night making phone calls and outlining what she needed to do the next day. Now we were on to something.

Here are some other responses I've heard recently to "What do you want to change?": "I can't stand myself when I'm ten pounds overweight." "My daughter wouldn't be so fresh." "My husband would stop being so sarcastic." "I'd stop worrying so much." "I wouldn't feel so tired all the time." Again, these responses don't offer much information about how these people envision their lives *without* their problems. Why is this so important?

Positively stated goals are more informative. Although describing
what you don't want may come more naturally, it is not nearly as helpful
as describing positive goals. The client who answered, "I'd stop worrying so much," hadn't told either of us what she needed to do next to feel
more carefree. But when asked what she would be doing when she
stopped worrying or worried less, she replied:

> I will be more active in my life. I will stop thinking of everyone else and
> start doing more for myself. I will take some classes at the local college
> and get out of the house more often. Also, I will learn how to budget my
> money, because I'm always worried about overspending. I noticed that
> the college offers a course to help people get their finances in order, and
> if I were to take it, that would kill two birds with one stone. I would be
> getting out, plus I would get a better grip on my financial situation.

Once she described her goals positively, the solutions became self-
evident. She now had a road map to guide her.

As you begin to define your own goals, make certain that you are
thinking about what you want to happen, not what you want to stop. If
your first inclination is to respond negatively (for example, "I won't feel
so tired all the time"), ask yourself, "What will happen *instead?*" (in
other words, "What will replace the feeling of fatigue?") Another way to
put this to yourself is, "What will I do that I haven't felt like doing
recently?" What new actions, feelings, or thoughts will replace the old,
objectionable ones?

Negatively stated goals evoke negative mental images. Another
good reason to keep positive goals in mind is that negatively stated goals
summon unpleasant mental pictures. A woman who wishes that "my
husband would stop being so sarcastic" will invariably picture in her
mind's eye a situation where her husband was sarcastic; then she will
tell herself, "Not that." If you don't believe me, try this exercise: whatever you do, do *not* let the image of a pink elephant enter your mind
right now. . . .

What happened? I bet you imagined a pink elephant! I know that
I am picturing one right now. Even though you instructed yourself *not
to* imagine one, you had to. Similarly, if you say to yourself, "I want
to be less depressed," you inevitably conjure up a vivid image of

yourself feeling depressed, not exactly a great starting place for someone who wants to feel better. Picture Greg Louganis on the edge of the
diving board. Can you imagine him saying to himself, "I won't do a
belly flop"?

***When your goal involves others, negatively stated goals sound
like nagging or complaining.*** Goals can be thought of in two categories, personal and interpersonal. A personal goal might be to increase
your income by 30 percent, lose fifteen pounds in three months, or
spend one day every weekend doing a project around the house. Personal goals describe the changes you want to make in yourself. Interpersonal goals, on the other hand, describe how you would like the other
people in your life to change: "I would like my daughter to spend at least
one hour practicing piano every day." "I want my husband to ask me out
once in a while." "My employees need to be more prompt in meeting
deadlines."

In short, having interpersonal goals means that you want someone
else to change. There is an art to influencing others to alter their behavior to suit your needs. If you want someone else in your life to
change, there is a distinct advantage to thinking of positive goals. If you
have a positive image in mind, you are more likely to express your
requests of other people positively, and you are therefore more likely to
get the results you want.

For example, suppose you think your son is a bump on a log. If you
have been in the habit of thinking of this negative image, in all likelihood you also have been talking negatively to your son. Maybe you have
been saying, "You never want to do anything, you are a couch potato.
You are really lazy." If this is what you have been doing, all I can say
is, "Good luck!" It is my experience that personal attacks generally
yield defensiveness and counterattacks, not change.

If, on the other hand, you were to imagine what you *want* rather than
what you don't want, you might tell your son, "I noticed that the YMCA
was offering some fun courses for kids your age. Would you be interested in taking one?" To which comment would *you* be more willing to
respond positively? Similarly, do you think you would have better results informing your spouse, "You aren't involved enough with the children; I feel like a single parent," or "It would really help if you put Seth
to bed every night while I helped Roger with his homework"? Undoubt-

edly, asking for what you *want* rather than saying what you dislike is a far better strategy to win friends and influence people.

Be Specific

Bud and Linda decided that the answer to their relationship problem was that they needed to feel more connected. One week later, they came for a therapy session. I asked how things were going. Simultaneously, Bud said "Great" and Linda said "Lousy." Confused, I asked them to account for the disparity in their responses. Interestingly, they both alluded to what had occurred the previous evening. They had watched television together all night. Bud said he enjoyed it because he could feel Linda's presence beside him and he felt close to her even though they weren't talking. Linda said that she couldn't believe Bud's response because she had been bored to tears and felt that their silence was indicative of the distance between them. The very same incident constituted progress in Bud's mind but regression in Linda's. How is that possible?

Bud and Linda's downfall was that they were not specific enough when they defined their goal. "Feeling more connected" meant one thing to Linda and another to Bud. Apparently, when Linda spoke of feeling connected, she was hoping for more active interaction with Bud. Bud, on the other hand, was satisfied with just having Linda in the room with him. Part of their problem was that their goal focused on *feelings* (i.e., "I want to feel more connected") instead of observable *actions*. Since feelings are subjective, internal, and not quantifiable, Bud and Linda didn't know that they didn't have a consensus about what feeling connected meant. They could avoid this misunderstanding by translating their feeling goal into an action goal. For example, Linda could tell Bud that, for her, feeling more connected means getting a babysitter so they can go out alone, having a conversation over dinner, or playing Monopoly in the evening.

Vague goals of any sort present serious problems for people eager to achieve results. Describing a goal in action terms makes the mission clear. Consider the following examples:

Vague goals	Action goals
Be more prompt.	Arrive at work by 7:00 A.M.
Be more sexual.	I will initiate sex at least once a week.
	I will suggest we try something new.
	Wear more provocative clothes for me.
Get in shape.	Lose ten pounds.
	Exercise at least three times a week.
	Start counting your fat-gram intake.
Communicate better.	Ask me how my day went.
	Make eye contact with me when we talk.
	Tell me you heard me even if you don't agree.

As you begin to identify what you want to change, make certain your goal is described as an observable, quantifiable action. Be as specific as you can. Ask yourself, "What will I be *doing differently* when (fill in your goal)," to bring a global goal down to earth. For example, if your goal is to have more self-esteem, ask yourself, "What will I be doing differently when I have more self-esteem?" "In what ways will my life change when I feel better about myself?" "What will others notice about me when I feel stronger?" If someone followed you around with a video camera after your self-esteem improved, what would they see you doing?

Think Small

Several days ago, I was watching a golf pro on television who was competing for a title in a major tournament. She was under tremendous pressure to sink her last putt with one stroke—a challenging feat, since her ball was at least twenty feet from the hole. With great concentration, she swung the putter and sank the ball. Later, a commentator talked with her about her shot. She told the commentator that her success at sinking long putts does not come from concentrating on the hole, but from picking a spot close to the ball that is in line with the hole and using that as her target. In other words, the way to hit a distant target is to aim at something closer.

Her words echoed through my mind as I recalled a fourteen-year-old boy and his parents who were forever at odds over the boy's lack of effort in school. At the time we met, the boy was getting straight F's. I asked his parents, "What will be the first sign that your son is on the right track?" After a momentary pause, the father responded, "He would be getting A's." Admirable goal, I thought to myself, but hardly the *first* sign of improvement. So I responded, "Maybe he will get there some-time, but my question is, how will you know that he is moving in the right direction? What will be the very first sign that he is making progress toward achieving those grades?" After some discussion, the parents agreed that, if their son were to begin to receive D's on his work, that would be a sign of improvement.

Once his father identified a goal the boy believed was attainable, the boy started putting more effort into his schoolwork, which quickly paid off; he received some D's and a few C's on papers and tests. Because his parents had defined D's as a sign of progress, they were encouraged when he brought home those grades. They complimented him on his effort, reinforcing his efforts, and gradually he pulled up his grades even further.

What accounts for the happy ending to this story? It is highly prob-able that this boy had pulled his grades up from F's to D's from time to time in the past, but, because his parents were on the lookout for A's, his more modest improvement didn't get him any positive feedback. In fact, it probably got him continued reprimands. He probably said to himself, "What's the use? Why bother trying when I can't please them?" and quit trying. But when D's were greeted as sign of change, he was rewarded and further improvement was encouraged.

There's a wise old saying that bears repeating here: "A journey of a thousand miles begins with one step." The only way to accomplish an ambitious goal is to break it down into small, achievable steps. If you don't, the task will seem insurmountable and you will thwart yourself.

I remember the day I received the contract to write my first book. I was so elated, my feet never touched the earth. I felt very fortunate to have the opportunity to put my ideas into writing so that I could share them with colleagues. My husband and I went out for dinner to cele-brate. The next day, I sat down in front of my computer. As I stared at the blank screen, the reality of writing a book began to set in. I started to get depressed. I told myself I must have temporarily lost my mind to have agreed to undertake such an enormous project. I decided that my new motto should be, "Be careful what you wish for—it may come true." I told friends and colleagues how overwhelmed I felt, but received little compassion.

Eventually, I noticed that the book was not writing itself, and I forced myself to buckle down and start writing. After a few pages, I reminded myself of what I tell other people all the time: break the goal down into small, achievable steps. I figured approximately how many pages I needed to write in all, took out my appointment calendar, and counted the number of available writing days before the book was due. I allowed for weekends and holidays off and ruled out the days I would be on the road doing seminars or seeing clients. I divided the total number of pages to be written by the number of available days and discovered I only had to write two pages a day! "Two pages a day, anyone could do that," I thought, and I was off and running. I must admit that there were many days I didn't write my two pages, but there were many other days when I wrote much more. What got me going was remembering that a small but persistent effort will yield big results.

Any successful business person will tell you about the importance of sizing down goals into manageable chunks. In *The Seven Habits of Highly Effective People*, Stephen Covey tells readers to use a weekly planner to schedule their days, hour by hour, with activities that reflect their values and priorities.

Distill your goal down to the smallest component you can think of. Ask yourself, "What will be the very first sign that things are getting on the right track?" Like the golf pro in the example above, look for a target closer than your end goal. Think about whether this goal could be broken down any further by asking yourself, "Is there anything I will notice happening before (whatever you have designated as the first sign of change) occurs?" If so, what is it? Remember, like your ultimate goal, this first sign of change must be concrete, specific, and stated positively.

Breaking goals down into small steps was a tremendous help for the client of a colleague of mine, a fifty-year-old man who thought he was at the end of his rope. The man had a successful retail business, but his marriage was threatened because his wife felt that his long hours at work meant that she was not a priority in his life. Although he loved his wife, he believed there was nothing he could do to remedy the situation, because he felt that the success of his business hinged upon his complete involvement. Over the years, he had taken on so much responsibility for the smooth functioning of his business that an employee once called him at home to inform him that a light bulb had burned out.

When my colleague asked this man why he didn't delegate responsibilities, he expressed a fear that his business would fail if he weren't intimately involved in every aspect. He had lost two jobs in the past, and now that things were going well, he didn't want to rock the boat. Every time he envisioned himself spending less time at work, he pictured disaster. In the meantime, his marriage was going down the tubes.

The man told his therapist that his goal was to "regain my old thinking habits and confidence." When asked to be more specific, he said, "I want to have the freedom to leave when I want, to take a vacation and spend more time with my family. I'd even like to take a day off once in a while." The therapist asked him to identify a first step he would feel comfortable taking, and he said, "I would like to leave work for two hours to take my wife out to dinner."

The next evening, he left work and had dinner with his wife at a fine restaurant. She was absolutely delighted. When he returned to work, it was quite obvious to him that disaster had not struck, and he was very relieved—so relieved that, the following week, he took off an entire day to be with his wife. As time passed, he felt increasingly comfortable spending time away from work, and he selected one of his most loyal and dedicated employees to manage the business in his absence. He and his wife lived happily ever after.

Even before this man consulted the therapist, he knew he needed to spend time with his family. The question is, why didn't he? Up until that point, he believed that the damage to his marital relationship was so extreme, it required an extreme solution: long vacations or extensive time at home. These imagined solutions overwhelmed him, so he avoided making any changes at all. But when he was asked to identify the smallest possible change with which he would feel comfortable, he could see himself taking off two hours for dinner with his wife. Once he took this small step, he recognized how much it meant to his wife, which made him feel good. He also saw that he was more dispensable than he had thought. Over time, he learned that his overzealousness at work had prevented others from achieving. Once he spent more time away from his business, he discovered the strengths in some of his employees.

Be Realistic

I once worked with a woman who was starting a new job and was very apprehensive. When I asked her about her goal she replied, "I just want to skip the period of initial discomfort. I want to go there tomorrow and feel like I've been there forever. I just hate beginnings." Though I could sympathize with her, I could not accept her goal as a legitimate starting place for our work together: her desire for instant comfort was not realistic. I commented that beginnings are often difficult and asked, "What could you do that would help you to feel a bit more comfortable tomorrow?" She replied, "It will help to get a good night's sleep and decide what to wear tonight, so I don't have to be frantic in the morning." Once an anxiety-free beginning was no longer her goal, she could focus on one that was achievable—feeling a *bit* more comfortable on her first day.

The best way to fall short of your goals is to choose unrealistic targets. I hear them frequently: "My kids won't fight with each other anymore." "I'll never crave sweets again." "I just won't *feel* like drinking anymore." "My daughter won't ever talk back to me." Once I asked a mother how things were going with her teenage son. Her goal was to get him to comply with the consequences she imposed when he broke the family rules. She told me that things were just okay. I was curious as to why things weren't going better. She said, "When he came in after curfew, I grounded him and he complained about it." I asked, "Did he follow through with the grounding?" "Oh yes," she said, "but he grumbled the whole time."

Now, I ask you, what teenager doesn't grumble about being punished? It's important to keep in mind that, no matter how well things are going, life will never be perfect. Kids will be kids, temptations will always exist, relationships will have ups and downs, work will be uninspiring from time to time, you will have bad-hair days and times you wish you had gotten up on the other side of your bed or just stayed in bed, for that matter. There will never be nirvana, this I can guarantee.

But this doesn't mean that you should abandon ambitious goals, it simply means that whatever you set as a goal should be doable. Let's go back to the unrealistic goals just mentioned and see if they can be transformed into attainable goals:

"My kids won't fight with each other anymore." Since all kids fight from time to time, it might be more reasonable to say, "My kids will get along more often," or "I will be able to tune out their arguing more often."

"I'll never crave sweets again," or *"I just won't feel like drinking anymore."* If you are a dessert-aholic or an excessive drinker, chances are the urge to indulge will not entirely disappear. "I want to eat sweets only once a week" or "I want to drink no more than five beers a week" might be more realistic. You could also say, "I want to learn ways to overcome my urge to eat sweets (or drink beer)."

"My daughter won't ever talk back to me" could be translated into "My daughter will speak respectfully to me more often," or "I will learn ways to ignore her attempts to provoke me," or "I will learn how to take her snippy responses less personally."

As you begin defining what you want to accomplish, ask yourself whether the smaller steps along the way are accomplishable. One depressed woman told me that her goal was to become a rock star. Although she had once sung at a friend's wedding, she had no other performing experience. Knowing that becoming a rock star is not something one can do overnight, I asked, "What will be a sign that you are moving in that direction?" and she told me that she had been thinking about singing at "amateur night" at a local club but hadn't done it yet. She committed herself to taking a friend to the club the next evening and going up to the mike to try singing in front of an audience. This, she told me, would be an acceptable first sign that she was moving toward her goal.

Are you expecting too much, or, worse yet, the impossible? If so, remember to start with small steps and keep in mind that, even in the best of situations, life is never blemish-free. Reach for the sky but keep your feet on the ground.

Sometimes, even when you are satisfied that you have broken your goal down into achievable steps, other people will tell you that your goal is unachievable. Don't let them dissuade you. No one knows what it feels like to walk in your shoes, nor do others know the parameters of your inner strength. Sometimes other people can be more objective about your situation than you are, and they may be able to see that a particular goal is unattainable. But if that is the truth, eventually you will discover it, too. And if you give up before you are sure, you will always wonder, "What would have happened if . . ."

It's important to point out that sticking with your goal despite advice to the contrary is different from sticking with a particular strategy when it's not working. Ineffective strategies should be abandoned promptly. For example, let's say your goal is to get your sister to visit more often. Perhaps your husband and brother-in-law are saying, "Give up on her, she's an incurable couch potato." You can ignore them and keep your goal, but if what you have been doing hasn't been getting your sister to your house, you need to vary your approach with her.

Fast Forward to the Future

If you're having difficulty identifying a specific goal, don't give up. Remember: if you've been longing for a particular outcome in your life—a more loving relationship with your child, spouse, or parent, more satisfaction at work, greater financial rewards, less tension at home—you must be able to envision what your life will be like when it happens. It might help to ask yourself the question I asked Mary—the "miracle question":

> *If I went to sleep tonight and a miracle happened so that whatever problems or negative feelings I have had totally disappeared in my sleep, what would be different tomorrow morning?*
> *How would my (spouse/ friends/ children/ relatives/ boss) know from watching me that the miracle had happened? Who would be the first to notice? Then who? And so on. What would I be doing that would clue them in that this miracle had happened in my sleep?*[1]

Try closing your eyes to imagine yourself in this miracle picture. Make yourself comfortable and take your time. Pretend you are creating a video depicting how things will be different when you have found the happiness or achieved the goal you are seeking. As sole producer and director, you have complete artistic license to develop the scenes and include any characters you wish. If you are having difficulties with someone in your life—a spouse, child, friend, parent, or colleague, for example—imagine yourself interacting with that person in a way that is satisfying to you. Who is in the picture? In what kinds of activities are you participating? What are you saying to each other? How does everyone look? What are the people in your picture wearing? Are you touching each other, and if so, how? How are you feeling as you observe yourself in this new picture? Try to paint as vivid a miracle portrait as possible.

If you're still drawing a blank, perhaps the following suggestion will help. Picture yourself in bed. It's the dawning of the first day after the miracle happened in your sleep. You open your eyes and have this strange feeling that something unusual has occurred. What is the very next thing you do after waking up? Do you stay in bed for a while? What do you decide to do the moment you rise? Pretend there is a video camera following you around and recording everything you do, minute by minute.

For some people, it helps to put the miracle question this way:

If, magically, whatever has been troubling me vanished all of a sudden, what would I do with all the time and energy I have been spending mulling over the problem, arguing, defending, and feeling bad? What would I do instead?

If you are saying to yourself, "I wouldn't change anything that I am doing, I would just change how I feel," then imagine how others around you would respond differently to you with your new inner strengths. *Something* in your life will change when your feelings change; what is it? Once you have envisioned your miracle picture, ask yourself, "What would be one or two small things I could do immediately to begin making the miracle happen?"

Now that you have determined what needs improvement in your life, you probably want to know what you do next. Great! That's what the rest of the book is about. As you read on, you will notice that, unlike in other self-help books, in *Change Your Life and Everyone In It* you will not find your dilemma neatly labeled so that you can scan the pages looking for it. This was done by design. In the true spirit of this book, the following chapters are organized around *solutions* rather than problems. Wondering why? I'll explain.

If the book were organized around problems and you are experiencing difficulties with your son, you would peruse the pages looking for a heading about parent-child difficulties, under which you might indeed find examples of problem situations very much like your own and descriptions of how they were resolved. The solutions that worked for others might work for you, or they might not. In the meantime, however, you would have missed the solutions other people had applied to different kinds of problems (marital or co-worker problems, say), assuming that they wouldn't apply to your situation. Odd as it sounds, that is incorrect.

You see, solutions to one kind of problem can often be generalized to another. For example, solutions for dealing with stubborn children may also apply to dealing with resistant co-workers. Or one person's solution for losing weight—keeping busy and active—might also be effective for relieving depression. The individual solutions or techniques can be thought of as master keys that are able to unlock many different kinds of locks.[2]

Conversely, a particular problem can have an infinite number of solutions. Suppose you are a manager trying to deal with two unmotivated salespeople. What inspires Person A may be entirely different from what inspires Person B. One person may be motivated by increased challenges, whereas another feels overwhelmed, and would respond better if the challenges were reduced. A good manager considers the individuals involved and their strengths and weaknesses when trying to determine what might motivate them, rather than following a rigid program that makes no allowances for individual differences.

So, regardless of what it is that you want to change in your life, read the chapters to come carefully. You may find the solution for which you have been searching where you least expect it. If one idea or strategy does not appeal to you, try a different one. There are plenty from which to choose.

Chapter Seven

If It Works, Don't Fix It

MEET HOWIE, AGE forty-four, a securities trader. When I met him, he had not earned any money for two years. During this time, his family was living off savings and the modest salary Howie's wife, Janet, earned as a librarian. They had two daughters, both teenagers. Howie was convinced that eventually things would turn around. Janet was equally convinced he was a dreamer, and she was devastated that their life savings were rapidly dwindling. They argued about Howie's decision to continue his career as a trader despite the family's financial situation. Janet frequently reminded Howie that their daughters wanted to go to college, which would be an additional burden. Howie felt certain that he would be able to provide for them without changing careers.

Janet's anger faded as she grew more and more depressed about their situation. She worried about their future, but she also worried that she and Howie were growing apart because he was unwilling to "face reality." She felt that he was being selfish and insensitive to her needs and the needs of their family. Her interest in spending time with Howie diminished as her desperation increased. When she learned that he had borrowed money from relatives to pay some bills, she announced that she could not go on as they had any longer. That was when Howie came to me.

Howie believed, "Under no circumstances should people be quitters. You can't be a good role model for your children if you quit when the going gets tough." When asked about his goal, he said that he had to start earning money immediately. I inquired whether some days were better than others with regard to his earning capacity, and he said, "Absolutely. If I trade, I do well. If I just watch the market and am passive, I lose money. It's as simple as that. I like to watch the market on Mondays to get a feel for things but I should be trading four days out of five." I was beginning to smell a solution. I asked, "How do you decide to trade on any particular day?" Howie's response supplied us with all the information he needed to become more successful starting the very next day.

HOWIE: When I walk into my office, I do a self-check. I ask myself how I feel today. If the answer is "good," I feel confident and I start trading. If the answer is "lousy," I just drink coffee, walk around, and think.

MWD: What do you do differently that increases the chances you will feel good in the morning?

HOWIE: I feel good in the morning when I run the night before. I typically run on Sunday, Tuesday, and Friday nights. But since I said that I need to trade on Tuesdays through Fridays, maybe it would be a better idea to run Monday through Thursday nights instead.

MWD: Sure sounds that way to me.

HOWIE: I also feel better in the morning when I get a good night's sleep, meaning that I go to bed no later than 10:30 P.M.

MWD: What increases the chances that you will be in bed by 10:30 P.M.?

HOWIE: I get energized if I work on projects around the house during the week and have trouble going to sleep. I should save house projects for the weekend instead. Also, when I work on projects during the weekend, my wife appreciates it, which makes me feel good and therefore more confident at work.

At the end of the session Howie agreed to make the small changes in his routine we had discussed, and we scheduled an appointment for four weeks later.

Howie returned thrilled to report that he had won the confidence of several investors and was actively trading again. They were pleased with his performance, and word was getting around that he was a reliable trader. He proudly announced that he had earned several thousand dollars since the last session, his first income in two years. Although his wife was somewhat cautious about this rapid turn of events, she was relieved and, for the first time in two years, began to show interest in his work.

How was Howie able to change his situation so quickly? Was it a stroke of luck? Had he simply waited so long that the market had come around? The truth of the matter is that luck or fate had very little to do with Howie's success. He had reversed the powerful negative momentum in his life by understanding a remarkably simple but generally overlooked principle: *If you want more success in your life, identify what is different about the times when you are successful and do more of that.*

Howie and everyone around him knew plenty about what was not working. They all knew he wasn't earning money, that he was falling short in his responsibilities as father and husband, and that the marriage was on shaky ground. He had endlessly explored the possible reasons why. In the process, he had lost sight of a single piece of information that eventually made all the difference in the world: he was more successful some days than others. When we examined those days, it became evident that there were distinct, quantifiable and repeatable differences in his approach to trading. Once I helped Howie identify what he was doing differently on the days that went well, he had a formula he could use to catapult his career to a higher level. He didn't need to read books on trading or consult with experts, because he already possessed all the information he needed to become a better trader. But why hadn't he recognized this long before his meeting with me?

It is easy to see why. No matter how well things went on any particular day, the end result was always the same—at the end of the week, Howie returned home with no income. Janet and the children were not at work to observe the good days. All they noticed was the tension at home and the pile of unpaid bills. Howie knew that some days were more productive, but they seemed insignificant compared with the days he walked around the office drinking coffee and feeling paralyzed.

Howie was not alone. People are much more likely to pay attention to what troubles them and to ignore problem-free times. I have noticed that, when I go to the dentist, I am either in pain or braced for imminent pain. Never am I pain-free, or so it seems. Painful times carry so much more psychological weight than comfortable times that we often fail to notice comfortable times entirely.

Sometimes we notice problem-free times but minimize them. Especially when we are unhappy or angry, we tend to view good times as brief intermissions from the way things "really are." Life seems like one unhappy or problematic incident after another, and exceptions are dismissed.

Just think about it for a moment. If you have a bad day at work, you go home worrying about it. Mulling over the events of your day again and again, you condemn your actions and wish you had responded differently. If you have a fight with a loved one, you spend the next few days replaying the argument word for word, reliving the emotions you felt in the heat of the fight. Although it is natural to reflect on bad experiences, it is unfortunate that we don't give equal psychological air time to good ones.

Admittedly, being aware of this principle and putting it into practice are two very different things. Believe me, I know this first hand.

As I have mentioned, I play golf. I began several summers ago, when my husband took up the game. Not wanting to become a golf widow, I took him up on his suggestion that I take a lesson. For someone who had never held a golf club before, I was doing remarkably well for the first half-hour of the lesson. I was actually able to hit the ball *and* aim it in the general direction that I had intended. I started wondering why avid golfers always complain about the difficulty of maintaining a consistent game. Certainly they were overstating the challenge.

Several minutes later, beginner's luck shifted and I began missing the ball entirely or hitting it in the wrong direction. At one point I turned to my instructor and asked, "Why did that ball just go off to the left when I intended to hit it to the right?" He simply said, "I don't know." I reasoned that he might not have been watching me. Moments later, after another faulty swing, I asked him, "Why did my ball go off to the right this time?" Again he responded, "I don't know."

"This is just great," I told myself. "I am paying good money and this guy doesn't even know the first thing about golf!" The instructor's voice interrupted me right in the midst of that thought. "You know, Michele," he said, "I find this very interesting. For the past thirty minutes, you have done extremely well, better than most beginners. Now you aren't doing quite so well and you want to have a lengthy discussion about it.

I would much rather have you memorize in your mind and in your muscles what you were doing differently five minutes ago, instead of dissecting what isn't working now. If we discuss what you are doing wrong, the next time you go to take a swing that's what you will be thinking about or imagining. Even if you say to yourself, 'Don't do X,' you'll still be visualizing X. So let's not talk about what you're doing wrong right now, okay? Try to remember what you were doing a few minutes ago." I had to admit that his advice sounded kind of familiar.

Envision how it would be if we were in the habit of focusing on exceptions. At the end of a good day at work, you'd ask yourself, "How did I get that to happen? What did I do differently today to get better results?" After a good talk with someone close to you, you'd ask yourself, "What did I do to create an atmosphere for good communication?" or "What were we doing today that we didn't do last week, when we got into an argument?" Clearly, there is much to be learned from what works. In fact, *the solution to most personal and interpersonal problems lies in unraveling the differences between times when the problem occurs and times when it does not.* By doing more of what works, we allow the positive times to crowd out the negative ones.

I have counseled thousands of people experiencing a vast array of problems, and I have seen how studying what works and doing more of it has brought about dramatic and rapid change in their lives. No matter what their concern—relationship problems, low self-esteem, substance abuse, poor health, parenting difficulties, work conflicts, and so on—people are able to identify times when problems abate, times when their relationships run smoothly, they feel better about themselves, drinking isn't a problem, they feel healthier and more vibrant, the kids are more cooperative, and work seems enjoyable. Even in the most entrenched, unhappy situations, there are momentary, daily, weekly, monthly, or even yearly reprieves, when—for whatever reason—things really do go better.

Gail and Brad were eager to meet with me, but because of my busy schedule I couldn't fit them in for two weeks. The only information I had about them prior to our meeting was that Gail had called an attorney to file for divorce, and the attorney had advised her to call me because she was so emotional. So I knew that their marriage had reached the point where she was ready to walk out.

As they entered my office, Brad mentioned that for the last two weeks things had been considerably better between them. Intrigued by this, I said, "Tell me what has been better about the last two weeks."

Gail began by telling me what had happened the night before the session. "I am trying to change my reactions to things. Our biggest fight is our families: I don't like his and he doesn't like mine. We were arguing about our families, but instead of standing there and arguing like we used to, I left for a while and drove around. It really helped to get my mind off of things. When I got back, it was over. Six months ago, it would have become a big, big blow-out fight, screaming and yelling and being mad for days and days and days." Brad added, "That's right. We would have told each other, 'We keep arguing about the same things. We need to get a divorce.' Last night that didn't happen.' "

It became clear to Brad and Gail that, in order to prevent arguments from escalating, they needed to institutionalize a time-out when their discussions began to deteriorate. One of them could go for a drive or a walk, or they could simply retreat to separate rooms to cool down. Granted, taking a time-out wouldn't necessarily resolve the issue at hand—their conflicts over each other's families—but learning how to control their outbursts was a good step in that direction. And if the argument didn't escalate, they would be able to go to bed on good terms with each other.

I asked them what else they had been doing differently in the past two weeks. Brad told me that, although in the past they spent a great deal of time together with their two daughters, their interactions had been focused on the girls instead of on each other. But during the past two weeks, Brad and Gail had related to each other a great deal during family times. They joked, talked, held hands, and made eye contact. Brad reported that the tension he used to feel during family outings was completely gone. They even talked to each other in the car instead of maintaining their usual silence.

Gail said that during the past two weeks she had tried to remember what was different about their relationship in the early years, when they were very much in love. "One thing I know for sure, we used to go out together and enjoy each other's company. We bowled, we traveled, we just did lots of different things. So, when I remembered that, I went out and signed us up for a couples' bowling league, which we start tomorrow. We also went ballroom-dancing, something we haven't done in years. But the big surprise was that, for my birthday, Brad told me that he got reservations at this resort we love but haven't been to for ten years. In fact, we haven't spent a night away from the girls for about that long, so this will be really special. We used to do things like that very often when we were younger."

When Gail reflected on what had attracted her and Brad to each other, she recalled their mutual interests and realized they had stopped participating in activities together. She figured that it might be possible to generate positive feelings by doing things they once enjoyed. Sure enough, as soon as they began to re-enact the "good old days," they breathed new life into their marriage.

Finally, Brad mentioned that he had been helping more around the house. He explained that in the past when a rough day at work or an argument with Gail put him in a foul mood he would withdraw and be less energetic at home. During the past two weeks, he had found his spirits lifting and had started pitching in and being more of a team player. Needless to say, Gail was appreciative of these changes and found herself feeling very loving toward him.

When I asked them what difference these changes had made in their lives over the past two weeks, Gail jumped in. "It's been great. I don't think Brad realizes it, but, although I have lots of friends, Brad is my best friend. For two years it has been hell. We have been on a roller coaster, doubting our commitment on a daily basis—one day on and the next day off. It's been awful. I haven't been able to sleep or eat, and I've been crying all the time. But for the last two weeks, we have been more hopeful, because now we have a goal. It feels great. The best part of all of this is that I have found my best friend again."

Despite the hostility they had felt toward each other for so long, Brad and Gail took a leap of faith and applied a simple principle that changed their lives: "If it works, don't fix it." They determined what worked for them by identifying what was different about the times in their marriage when they enjoyed each other. This is what Brad and Gail recognized that they must do to make their marriage work:

1. If they find themselves beginning to argue in a destructive manner, take a time-out.
2. Continue communicating with each other rather than through their children.

3. Keep active together. Do mutually enjoyable activities such as bowling, dancing, and being with friends.
4. Brad needs to continue being a team player at home.

If you are in a troubled relationship, you may be thinking that it would improve if you followed in Brad and Gail's footsteps. Or you may be thinking that you and your partner are so different from Brad and Gail that their solution wouldn't work for you. Every relationship *is* unique, and the specific steps people need to take to feel better depend on the needs of the people involved and the nature of the relationship. Particular solutions vary from person to person, and from relationship to relationship, but the method for discovering these solutions remains constant: *focus on the exceptions and do what works.*

Another example. A three-and-a-half-year-old girl was taken to a therapist because she had been stuttering, which had her parents extraordinarily worried: the girl's father was a stutterer. At first the therapist focused on the problem, wanting to know the extent of her stuttering and the occasions when she stuttered most. But this information failed to improve the situation. Eventually, the therapist asked the parents to keep track of the times her speech was fluent.

A week later, the parents reported there were many times their daughter was fluent—when her father took her to the park and pushed her on the swing, when she was playing on the slide, when they were lovingly physical with her at home. They also noted that when she played with her baby sister she was able to speak without stuttering. These observations helped the girl's parents to recognize that their daughter was not a "stutterer" but, rather, a little girl who often spoke fluently. After several weeks of keeping track of their daughter's fluent times, the parents stated that these were so frequent, they no longer wanted to keep track. Focusing on fluent times had provided them with specific guidelines to help, but it had also demonstrated to them that the problem was not, as they had thought, all-pervasive. This eased their minds about their daughter, which undoubtedly affected the way in which they interacted with her.

Although the process of focusing on exceptions to discover solutions is remarkably simple, it isn't easy. Here are some questions to help you start sorting out what you need to do more of to achieve desirable results in your life.

Ask yourself: *What's different about the times when I'm feeling better, I'm more productive, my sex life is good, the kids cooperate, etc.?*

Start with the goal(s) you identified in chapter six. Try to recall a recent example of a time when you felt more on track to the goal. Get as clear a mental picture of this occasion as possible and ask yourself: *What am I doing differently in that situation?*

Try to picture yourself as others see you and describe your *actions* as specifically and concretely as possible. For example, you might have noticed, "When I keep my voice at a regular speaking level instead of yelling, my son is more apt to respond positively," or "When I tell my spouse about my day after dinner, he is a better listener than before dinner," or "If I give my sister advance notice that I would like to visit, she is much more hospitable than if I just show up." List as many examples as you can think of—the more, the better.

Sometimes when people answer this question, they describe how their *feelings* differ during exceptional times. They say, "I feel more relaxed," or "I am happier." That's a good start, but it is not enough. In addition to identifying how you might be feeling different, you must be able to identify the outward signs of those feelings if you are to begin to take action. If you are having difficulty identifying actions as well as feelings, ask yourself:

When I feel more (fill in the blank), what does that enable me to do that I don't feel like doing at other times?

For instance, if you feel more confident during exceptional times, what do you have the courage to do that you hold yourself back from doing at other times? If you feel more loving, what do you do for your partner, children, or friends that you might not do when you feel angry? Focus on what you *do* differently as a result of feeling different.

Sometimes when people ask themselves what's different about the times when they get better results, they can only think of changes in the way other people treat them—for example, "I feel better when you are more thoughtful." But since *you* are the one who has decided to start changing, it is more helpful to focus on what *you* do differently when things go better. If you still find yourself focused on other people, ask yourself:

What do the people around me do differently when I feel good? What does their positive behavior enable me to do in return?

Picture yourself feeling positive and recall what others do that directly or indirectly promotes this sense of well-being. Then ask yourself how feeling good alters your response to them. For example, if your mother offers to babysit more often, in what ways do you feel like reciprocating? Are you more complimentary, or more willing to do favors for her? When your kids are more independent, allowing you more time to study, do you find yourself being more patient with them, or spending a few extra minutes with each of them before bedtime?

Although you probably think that your positive behavior is merely a response to the positive behavior of others, I can guarantee that that is precisely what other people think, too. Your children believe they are more sensitive to your needs because you are nicer to them. If you asked your mother why she babysat for you even though she had previous plans, she would tell you that you put more effort into being considerate to her. In fact, you are both right: your behavior may be a reaction to someone else's positive behavior, but your actions encourage additional positive responses from others as well. Ask yourself:

What are we doing differently as a (couple, family, group of co-workers, or social group)?

If your goal pertains to a change in a relationship with one or more people, ask yourself what sorts of activities you participate in as a group when things are going more smoothly. For example, a woman discovered that she and her husband spent more time together during problem-free periods, and listed the specific activities in which they participated. A father who asked himself what his family did differently during peaceful times recalled nights when the television was turned off and family members spent more time talking. A supervisor asked herself, "What do we do differently as a team when we are more productive?" and remembered her employees' positive response to team-building meetings which were no longer being scheduled.

If it seems impossible to recall any recent examples of times when things went well, look further back. Ask yourself:

What was I doing differently in the past that was more helpful?

For example, two nurses who were extremely combative with each other were not able to identify any recent examples of getting along but were easily able to recall more cooperative times several years ago, when they first met. Asked what was different about those times, they agreed that they talked more, frequently complimented each other, and regularly sent memos back and forth. The nurses also agreed that they could begin doing what used to work for them, and left the brainstorming session arm in arm. If recent times have been rough, don't forget successful times in the past. It doesn't matter how long ago these exceptional times occurred, or how long they lasted. It only matters that they happened and you can learn from them.

Sometimes when people recall successful times in the the past, what they identify as having been better now seems inaccessible or irretrievable. "We used to have more disposable income, so we could travel more." "My relationship with my father was better before his stroke." "Life was better five years ago, when we lived in Arizona." If you attribute your happier or more successful times to events beyond your control, you might as well resign yourself to feeling miserable. I don't think that's a great idea, do you? If your answer to the question "What's different about times past when I felt more satisfied?" relates to things you can't change, you can help yourself out of this dead end by asking yourself an additional question:

What was different about my life then?

For example, the man who recalled that his life was better when he lived in Arizona said that his life was different then because "The weather was warmer, and I had more friends and a job I really enjoyed." Since neither he nor I could do anything about frosty Midwestern winters, I put the weather on the back burner and pursued with him the issues of making friends and achieving job satisfaction. As we talked, he realized that he hadn't put any effort into making friends in the Chicago area, as he had in Arizona. He came up with several ideas he could implement to increase his social network. Also, he recognized that part of his dissatisfaction at work related to his feeling undercompensated. He wanted to ask for a raise but hadn't felt comfortable approaching his supervisor. We talked about how he might broach the subject, and he left prepared to do so. In other words, although he initially identified living in Arizona as the key to his happiness, by focusing on what was doable and changeable rather than what wasn't, he was able to take back control of his life.

"I know this will work, but I don't think I should have to do it."
Some people are good at identifying what they need to do to get the results they want but believe that they shouldn't have to do it. For example, parents who were concerned about their twelve-year-old son's

declining school performance commented that, when they reminded him about homework every night, he did a good job and received good grades. But they didn't feel they should have to remind him at his age. When they stopped reminding him, his grades dropped from B's to C's. Granted, it would be beneficial for a boy this age to develop independent study habits, but the fact of the matter is that for some reason, he required additional structure. The arguments that ensued as a result of forgotten assignments and lower grades were hurtful to everyone. It would have been considerably more expedient simply to remind their son of his daily homework, even if they shouldn't "have to."

Similarly, a traveling salesman told me that his wife often got angry about his frequent absences. I asked about exceptions and he told me that if he calls home every night when he is on the road she is much more understanding. "Well," I said, "I guess you know what you need to do, then, right?" He replied, "But she shouldn't need that kind of reassuring. I shouldn't have to call so often."

The fact is, we spend entirely too much time romanticizing about how things should be, and as a result we lose sight of how things *are*. In the situations above, whether their significant others liked it or not, the boy needed structure and the woman needed reassurance. Period.

If you have some thoughts about what might work in your situation but have been holding back because you wish you didn't have to take the action, don't sit back waiting for other people to change. If you have the formula for success and aren't acting on it, you are only hurting yourself. Stop wasting time debating whether it is fair or reasonable, just do it. The results will be well worth it.

"She is only doing it because I want her to, not because she wants to." The corollary of "You don't have to like it, just do it" is, "They don't have to like it either, as long as they do it." I wish I had a dollar for each time a parent complained, "My daughter cleaned her room, but she only did it because I have been on her case, not because she wants a clean room. I want her to *want* things to be orderly," or "When I told him he couldn't go, he obeyed, but he complained all weekend."

Remember that changes in behavior are what we're after; they won't always be done willingly or happily. We should be appreciative when, despite hesitations or resentment, the people in our lives follow the rules or comply with our wishes. Often, a change in attitude follows a change in action. But don't hold your breath. Remember, the *doing* is what counts.

I know a woman who, after years as a full-time homemaker, took a job working outside her home several hours each evening. Her husband had agreed to this plan, but he complained continually how stressful it was for him to work full-time and manage the kids in her absence. This rankled her, since she felt he should take care of the children without complaining, as she had done for so many years. Each time he commented how hard he was working, she became defensive and responded with some less-than-pleasant retort. Needless to say, this never produced very good results.

One day, instead of getting angry at her husband, she wondered whether when he told her of his struggles he was not so much complaining as he was asking for some recognition for his effort. After all, he had supported her decision and carried out his responsibilities. She decided to try a new tack and expressed her gratitude for all he did at home while she was gone. His complaining stopped almost immediately.

She confessed to me that, truth be told, she felt she shouldn't have to thank him for something she did all the time without much appreciation, but when she did express gratitude they got along much better, and she felt more at ease when she left for work. She concluded that complimenting her husband, "even if he didn't deserve it," was worth it in the end.

So far, I have stressed the importance of identifying which of your actions are different when you get what you want in your life. But actions aren't the only things that change during problem-free times; our thought patterns change as well. We all have a little voice inside that offers a running commentary on our lives. Sometimes the voice cheers us on— "Boy, you really look good today" or "Go knock 'em dead." But sometimes the voice is not so supportive. "I just know you're going to blow it," it says, or "There is no way you can do that—you're a woman." It is useful to identify what we spontaneously tell ourselves immediately preceding, during, and after our positive achievements, so that we repeat it intentionally more often. You can increase the impact of your "friendly" internal voice by becoming more familiar with it. Ask yourself:

What do I tell myself when the going gets tough that helps me get the results that I want?

For example, a woman who complained of panic attacks noticed that she experienced an intense panic reaction when she told herself to fight back her fear, but was able to ward off intense attacks when she told herself, "Relax, don't fight it. You will come out the other side. Take a deep breath." Once she became aware of her coping strategy, she was able to implement it consistently, and her panic attacks eventually disappeared.

Similarly, a woman who felt depressed mentioned that one way she maintained her depression was by telling herself, "I have always felt this way, I will always feel this way. Nothing ever changes." Each time she repeated this doom-and-gloom mantra, she felt increasingly depressed. As we talked, however, she also recognized that there were times when she felt better. I asked her what the little voice inside her head said then. After some thought, she replied, "I have several comforting thoughts: 'This too shall pass,' or 'Maybe I'm overreacting.' If that doesn't work and I continue feeling depressed, after a few weeks I eventually hear myself say, 'I'm tired of feeling sorry for myself. This is downright boring,' and I start doing something, anything, different. That usually helps."

Perhaps you are still at a loss as you try to identify problem-free times—you simply can't think of any. If there are no exceptions, another useful question to ask yourself is:

Under what circumstances is the problem less intense, less frequent, or shorter in duration?

A mother told me that her three-year-old son had temper tantrums every day. I asked her what was different about the times when the temper tantrums were less intense or shorter in duration. She agreed that some tantrums weren't quite as bad as others; for some reason, they would occasionally cease without prompting from her. She thought about it for a moment and said, "Now that you mention it, when I leave the room, he stops quicker than if I stay and try to control him. I hadn't thought about it before." Although leaving her son unattended in public places was not a possibility, this woman recognized that, when she avoided a power struggle with him, he was able to control his own behavior more effectively, so she did what worked and eventually his tantrums ceased.

Another woman was devastated to discover that her husband had had several affairs. Because they had been married for twenty-two years and had three children together, she wanted to see if there was some way to overcome her hurt and anger in order to keep the marriage together. The news of the affairs was so fresh that she could think of no time when she felt pain-free. But when I asked her what was different about the times when her pain was less intense, she replied, "I feel better when I keep myself busy. When I sit around thinking about the affairs I feel awful, but when I am active it keeps my mind off them. Also, when I am doing something I enjoy I remember that life goes on."

In addition to exploring problem-free times or times when the problem is less intense, there are several other questions you can ask yourself that will help you discover potential solutions.

What is different about the times when the problem situation occurs but something constructive comes from it?

A woman was determined to lose thirty pounds. After losing fifteen, she found it difficult to stay on her diet. She found that there were an increasing number of days when she gave in to the temptation to overeat. I asked her, "What is different about the times you overeat but something constructive comes from it?" Initially, she thought my question was ludicrous, because her overeating usually led to self-recrimination and more overeating. But sometimes when she overate, she did not use it as an excuse to continue bingeing; she got back on track with her diet and exercise regimen. After some thought, she realized that, when she allowed herself truly to enjoy what she was eating and forgave herself immediately, rather than feeling guilty about it, she was able to get back on track more easily. She also became aware of how these temporary departures from her diet offered her opportunities to demonstrate the inner strength necessary to renew her resolve. This made subsequent dietary blunders easier to contain, and she eventually reached her goal.

A couple with whom I worked told me that they fought all the time. In addition to asking them what was different about the times when they got along, I asked, "What is different about the times when you argue but something constructive comes from it?" They acknowledged that some arguments were more constructive than others and said that in "good fights," as they put it, "we take turns talking and try not to interrupt. We let each other know that, although we may not agree with each other, we understand the other person's position, and, no matter what, we don't go to bed angry. In 'bad fights,' we call each other names, we hit below the belt, and we bring up the past continually. After 'good fights,' we feel that there is some resolution and often feel closer to one another. Sometimes we make love. After 'bad fights,' there is a cold war which can go on for several days."

The couple began to see that not all fights are created equal, and once they were aware of the difference between "good" and "bad" fights, they could begin to pay attention to how their discussions unfolded and decide early in their interaction which conversations to continue and which to end in order to avoid unpleasant feelings.

What is different about the times when the problem situation occurs but it doesn't bother me?

Has anyone ever said to you, "I never know what to expect, because sometimes this bothers you and sometimes it doesn't"? We don't always respond the same way to situations. On certain days the smallest irritant can set us off, but on other days we seem impervious to bad feelings. What's the difference?

A mother told me that her children's bickering drove her crazy. She realized that siblings will fight, but felt that her children did so more than others. She dreaded vacation days because of the fighting. I asked her what was different about the times when the kids fought but it didn't bother her. She told me that, if she took better care of her own needs, she got less emotional when her children bickered. She explained that she sometimes felt housebound, and when that happened, her nerves were on edge and she became particularly sensitive to the fighting. But if she went out with her friends or to her exercise class on a regular basis, she felt calmer and was less annoyed when the children picked on each other. Her solution was clear—take better care of herself.

Mort and Judy, an unmarried couple in their early twenties, each felt that the other spent an inappropriate amount of time talking to members of the opposite sex at parties. Because of this, they both felt very threatened. I asked what was different about the times they went to parties and talked to members of the opposite sex but it wasn't a problem. After considerable thought, Judy said, "For me, the difference is my feeling connected to Mort. If he comes over to me several times during the party and says hello or pats me on the butt or says, 'I love you,' I'm fine for the rest of the evening. I don't care who he talks to then." Mort agreed that he needed similar reassurance to feel relaxed about Judy's conversations with other men.

Think about the particular situation with which you are displeased. Perhaps as you think about it, you can recall certain circumstances when it hasn't bothered you quite so much. Identify what is different about such times and do that.

One last question that many people find helpful when they are in search of solutions is:

How have I gotten the conflict to end?

If you listen to people discussing their disagreements, you will notice that they pay a great deal of attention to how the conflict started. And we all know how conflicts start: "*You* started it!" However, if you continue to listen you will probably also hear, "Yes, but I only did that because of something you said earlier in the day," followed by, "But I only said that because my feelings were hurt by your actions yesterday." And so on and so on and so on. This classic chicken-and-egg debate is truly a go-nowhere proposition. Instead of trying to figure out what started the conflict, it is much more useful to determine what *ended* it. Experts in canine behavior reveal that dogs in the wild have distinct ways of signaling to each other that a fight has gone far enough. A dog might roll on its back and bare its neck, indicating to its opponent that the competition is over. Although people also send highly patterned and predictable peacemaking signs, we are not often conscious of them. These peacemaking signs, which I call "truce triggers," help to diffuse arguments and assuage peaked emotions. Most people fail to see the connection between their actions in a conflict and what stopped it, so they miss an opportunity to discover a solution. Shifting your attention to the events at the *end* of unpleasant times can provide you with information that will enable you to short-circuit future problems.

Perhaps an example from my own life will help. My husband and I have been together for approximately twenty-two years, which has given me ample opportunity to observe our truce triggers. However, like other people, I have always been much more interested in how our fights start. Of course, Jim's always to blame. In one of my more objective moments, however, I thought it might be a good idea to practice what I preach and reflect on what happens when we argue and how we let each other know that it's time to stop.

What I realized is that I am willing to let an argument drop when there has been some closure. I will keep pursuing an issue until one of two things happens: either we reach some resolution, or I get some reassurance from Jim that everything is okay, preferably in the form of a hug. Jim, on the other hand, doesn't necessarily need closure, and the last thing he wants is a hug. Basically, all Jim wants is for me to leave the room. He de-escalates by being alone. I want closeness and he wants solitude. Perhaps you have noticed that these are diametrically opposed needs. In the past, the more I pushed for closeness, the more he wanted separateness. The more he wanted separateness, the more I wanted closeness. Many of our arguments escalated out of proportion to our original disagreement because each of us ignored the other's truce trigger.

The day I figured this out, I went into our bedroom and told him of our dilemma. He joked and said, "The next time we have a fight, we can flip a coin and see who wins, heads-you-leave, tails-I-hug." We laughed and ended the conversation. And, no, we have never flipped a coin, but since that conversation our patterns have changed. Now when we argue, even though I don't really feel like it, I will sometimes muster all my strength and leave him alone. I walk downstairs and busy myself with anything to take my mind off of our argument. I will even do dishes. Shortly thereafter, he will inevitably come downstairs and say something silly like, "Do you want to be friends?" or "Do you want to make up?" and I feel satisfied. Other times, in the heat of our debate, Jim will say, "Come here," and with his arms stretched out as stiff as a board, he will give me a hug, albeit an unconvincing one. As he embraces me, I know he doesn't really mean it, but I am so delighted that he is doing it in spite of his feelings that I good-naturedly get up and leave the room, giving him the space he needs. He is always happy to see me go. We have finally learned that, if I want him to be loving toward me, I have to give him time and space, and that if he wants me to leave him alone, he has to act loving toward me. It's a simple equation.

A father told me that his son never took no for an answer and that their arguments went on forever. Although it was true that he debated with his son longer than he should, their arguments did not actually go on forever. I asked the father to recall a recent incident when his son stubbornly nagged but eventually did what the father requested. Then I asked him to reflect on what he had done to get that to happen. The father said, "Well, I guess that somehow Joe eventually realizes that I mean business." "Yes, but how?" I asked. He replied, "I guess that's when I look him straight in the eye and get closer to him physically and simply but emphatically say 'no' with no further explanations." He had unraveled the mystery to his success.

No matter what type of relationship you are trying to improve, paying attention to how conflicts end is a useful method for discovering solutions. You can do this by envisioning an imaginary videotape of the scene when you and your partner (whether it's your child, mate, colleague, or friend) stopped sparring. Then rewind slowly to the scene just before the fighting ended. What did you do that precipitated a conciliatory response from your partner? You may have done it unintentionally, but since it worked, next time you can do it intentionally.

What's Next?

Once you identify the exceptions, the next step is to start doing them. Although many people apply what they learn about themselves and their exceptional times immediately, I have noted with interest that some people do not. Intrigued by this, I sometimes ask people what is keeping them from doing what they know works. The most common response is that they think that, before they take action, they must be in the right frame of mind. Estranged spouses believe they have to feel more loving before they spend more time together. Depressed people believe that feeling motivated is a prerequisite to getting out and doing something. Anxious people think they must feel more self-confident before they take a risk. But as we have discussed in chapter three, this sort of thinking is upside down.

People who take assertiveness-training classes quickly learn that feeling assertive *follows* rather than precedes an increase in assertive behavior. Similarly, research shows that one of the best antidotes to depression is exercise, even if the depressed person doesn't *feel* like exercising at first.[1] By taking action, even reluctantly, people can change how they feel about themselves. Putting on a pair of running shoes and booting oneself out the door is considerably more expedient than sitting around waiting for self-esteem to happen.

The point is, once you identify what works or what has worked in the past, start doing it, even if your heart isn't in it yet. You will be surprised how taking action leads to changes in how you think and feel about yourself and others, and how they respond to you. Try it, you'll like it.

Chapter Eight

Do Something Different

"Insanity: doing the same old thing and expecting a different result."

—ANONYMOUS

IT's WEDNESDAY, 5:15 P.M., at the Baker household. Rita arrives home from work. Her husband is working late at the office. Their kids, ages ten, thirteen, and sixteen, are doing homework, watching television, and making popcorn. Exhausted, Rita hangs up her coat, rifles through the mail, and hopes no one will tug at her sleeve for fifteen seconds. But, as it does every night, her entrance sets in motion a whirlwind of activity. Before she has a chance to read any mail, her youngest is whining, "What's for dinner, I'm hungry," the thirteen-year-old pulls out two forms that need to be signed and returned to school the next day, and the sixteen-year-old asks if he can borrow the family car on Saturday night. Then the phone rings, the dog barks, and the popcorn burns. Welcome home, Rita.

Although some of the specifics will vary a little tomorrow, the chaos will repeat itself. What will occur, as predictably as Old Faithful's daily spouting, is Rita's reaction: yelling. Every night, for as far back as she can remember, she has dreaded the witching hour—the time when she switches back from a working woman to mom. Without fail, the children demand her attention immediately, and, without fail, she gets over whelmed and lashes out at them. It happens *every night* in exactly the same way. The evening tension has become as predictable a part of family routine as brushing teeth in the morning or going to sleep at night.

Scene two takes place in Stan and Merrill's dining room. For the past fifteen years, Stan has been an accountant for a shoe company. He also augments the family income by hiring out as a free-lance accountant during tax season, when he uses the dining room as a workspace. Merrill abhors having his papers "spread all over the dining room," but Stan contends that "the dining room isn't any messier than the rest of the house." Every January marks the beginning of Stan's free-lance work *and* the shouting matches between Merrill and him. The arguments are so predictable by now that Stan knows exactly what Merrill will say, and vice versa. Not once does either of them say, "Honey, tax time is coming up again. Why don't we try something different to avoid the arguing?" Most people say there are two things you can count on: death and taxes. I say there are three: death, taxes, and Stan and Merrill's fighting.

Scene three: the classroom at Oakwood Junior High School. About midway through the class period, two boys start giggling, Oakwood's version of Beavis and Butt-head. The teacher gets annoyed and repri mands them. They giggle more and the laughter becomes contagious. Soon, half the class is laughing. Outraged, the teacher yells at the boys and sends them to the principal's office. The principal also reprimands the boys, and returns them to the classroom with only minutes remaining in the period. Next day, the boys behave exactly the same way. And so on and so on.

Although the teacher knows with certainty what to expect from these boys when she walks through the classroom door, and she also knows that the principal's reprimands aren't any more successful than hers, her strategy for dealing with the boys' irritating behavior never varies. Like clockwork, the boys interrupt the class, the teacher gets angry, the boys visit the principal, and he sends them back to class. And, the next day, it starts all over.

Rita, Merrill, and the teacher have several things in common:

1. What they are doing to solve their problem isn't working.
2. They know their approach isn't working.

ecurrence of the problem situation is imminent.
ey know, they keep repeating the same strategy
oblem occurs.

But ⸍ news is that Rita, Merrill, and the teacher are not
alone. *Everyone* ˎ en you and I) has those situations and issues that
seem to defy resolution—situations that transform us into robots who
respond in exactly the same manner over and over, even though what we
are doing fails miserably each time. Any of these sound familiar? "Every
time your mother comes into town, we fight about the kids." "Whenever
my business partner and I talk about goals for the company, we end up
disagreeing and cutting the meeting short." "Every Christmas, my sister
and I argue about where the family should get together. It ruins the
holidays." "Whenever we talk about our sexual relationship, it always
turns out the same way—he accuses me of being uninterested, I accuse
him of being insensitive, and nothing ever changes." These troublesome
repetitions—"more of the same"—happen when we keep applying the
same solution even though it doesn't work.

What's the problem with more of the same? There are a few. First and
most obvious, it doesn't change or improve anything. Second, a persistent problem takes its toll emotionally, physically, and spiritually. It's
very discouraging when nothing you do seems to make a difference. But
the fact is, things aren't just not getting better when you do more of the
same; they are actually deteriorating.

The Solution Is the Problem

Have you ever tried to loosen a nut by turning the wrench clockwise,
unaware that you should be turning in the opposite direction? When
your initial efforts failed to loosen it, what did you do? You determined
that you simply hadn't been twisting the wrench hard enough, so you
applied more pressure. When that didn't work, you pushed with all your
might. Unfortunately, not only didn't you loosen the screw; by dint of
your full strength, you tightened it beyond belief. Solving problems by
doing more of the same is very similar.

For example, Barb wanted more intimacy from her husband. One night she told him that she wanted to feel closer, spend more time together, talk more, and have more affection in their relationship. The next morning, at the breakfast table, he picked up the newspaper and started reading. She requested politely that he put the paper down so they could talk. Feeling that they had already had a meaningful conversation the evening before, he resented her request and told her that he was in the middle of an article.

She waited several minutes, but when he continued to read she thought to herself, "He must not have heard me." So she repeated her request more loudly, with a bit of annoyance in her tone. "Please read some other time; I told you last night that we should spend more time together." Irritated, he shouted, "Why do you always have to talk?" to which she responded, "Because we never do." Convinced she was being unreasonable, he stormed out of the room, just the opposite of the result she had hoped for.

The more Barb pursued, the more her husband distanced himself. The more he distanced himself, the more she pursued. More of the same leads to more of the same.

Consider the parents who discover that their teenage son is lying and sneaking. What do they do? They become proficient at spying on him: eavesdropping on his phone conversations, searching his room when he's not there, and so on. But imagine for a moment that this kid finds out that his parents have been spying on him. What does he do in response? He becomes better at being sneaky. He fine-tunes his lying skills until he can look his parents in the face and tell them a whopping falsehood. When his parents catch on that he has gotten more proficient at lying, what do they do? Get the picture? I have worked with families in which this sort of escalation has led to parent's tapping phone lines, bolting doors, locking kids in their rooms, and nailing their windows shut for fear they will escape. Some have even hired private detectives! Imagine how skilled at evasion a teenager would have become by the time he or she had to dodge a private eye.

Take another example. Sue is depressed. Her husband, her relatives, and everyone else around her feels concerned. Naturally, everyone tries to cheer her up. "Things aren't as bad as they seem." "Why don't you take an aerobics class?" "I've been through what you're experiencing, you'll snap out of it." "Tomorrow is another day." But, despite these reassurances, tomorrow isn't another day for Sue. All of her days have taken on a gray sheen, making each feel just like the one before it. Sue continues to feel depressed.

When other people's efforts to cheer Sue up fail, she feels even more depressed, because, in addition to being upset about whatever originally bothered her, she now wonders why it seems impossible for her to "snap out of it." "After all, everyone says I should be feeling better, but I'm not," she thinks. "There must be something wrong with me." Or she feels worse because her well-meaning, cliché-slinging friends and relatives don't seem to understand the depth of her sadness and hopelessness, deepening her sense of alienation.

Why Do We Persist?

If what we do fails to get us what we want or, for that matter, makes getting what we want even less likely, why in the world do we persist in doing more of the same? Why don't we try a brand-new approach as soon as we determine that we're running in place? There are several reasons.

"It should work." Even if a person's problem-solving approach isn't effective, it usually appears to be the most logical and reasonable thing to do. Cheering up someone who's depressed, heavily monitoring a deceitful person, pursuing a distancer are all extremely reasonable and rational things to do. These approaches *should* work, but it just so happens that, in these cases, they don't. But, unwilling to abandon our logic, we keep saying to ourselves, "This should be working; maybe I'm not trying hard enough," as we pursue harder, spy more thoroughly, and console more vigorously.

The classic example of this was a mother with whom I had been working. Her son was not doing well in school, and she believed that the problem was his low self-esteem. I asked her what she had been doing recently to try to help him with his schoolwork. She said, "I talk to him a lot. I ask him, 'What's wrong? Is there anything I can do to help you feel better about yourself? What don't you like about school?' " She had tried no other approach; and his schoolwork had not improved at all, although he did seem to enjoy the attention she was giving him. I asked her how often they had such heart-to-heart talks, and she replied, "It's become nightly." "Are you convinced yet that these talks aren't really working?" I asked. "No," she responded, "I know they will work. I just haven't found the right thing to say yet."

Is it possible that this mother might find something to say to her son that would make a difference? Who knows? I wouldn't bet on it, though. I'd place my money on her trying a new tack instead. And eventually she proved me right. One day, when she had had a bad time at work and her patience was running thin, her son complained about what she was making for dinner. Uncharacteristically, she snapped at him, telling him she didn't care whether he liked the menu or not, he was going to eat it anyway. The boy was so jolted by her unusual response that he not only stopped criticizing dinner, but was very pleasant and solicitous of her feelings for the rest of the evening. In fact, he even started his homework without encouragement from her.

She took note of his reaction and decided that perhaps she had been pampering him too much in general. She stopped asking him what was wrong all the time and started demanding that he stop complaining about what he didn't like and start doing it anyway. Her stern approach was so different from what she had been doing up to that point that he responded immediately. Had it not been for her fortuitous brush with impatience, this mother might still be having nightly talks with her son and getting nowhere. As absurd as that might seem, it was consistent with her judgment that her son was insecure and needed to have his morale boosted. But, no matter how sound you think an approach is, if it doesn't work, it's time to jump ship.

"I've always done it that way." Another reason that we keep doing the same old thing is that people are, by and large, creatures of habit. Most people's routines are so highly patterned that they don't have to think about what they are doing much of the time. For example, you probably get up about the same time each day and do the same things in the same order when you rise. Which comes first, a shower, a shave, or making coffee and eating breakfast? What happens next? Do you feel edgy when someone jumps in the shower during "your time" or your schedule is varied for some reason? Which is "your seat" at the dining-room table? Recall your reaction when an unsuspecting visitor sits in it? What about holidays and family traditions? If something interferes with your usual way of celebrating, does it just not feel right?

Our interactions with others are highly ritualistic. Just think how many times per day you say, "Hi, how are you?" and hear in return, "Fine, and you?" We have our scripts and we act them out religiously. That many of our interactions with others are done on automatic pilot is not a problem. The comfort we feel with friends we know well versus new encounters is due in part to the fact that their actions have become familiar: we know what to expect from them and how we should respond. Routines offer a sense of certainty and stability that we need in order to function. Habitual responses are only problematic when we react automatically to a problem without evaluating the results of our actions. Then we are headed for disaster.

"The devil you know. . ." If following routines and living our lives in patterns comforts us, then the converse is also true: there's uncertainty and vulnerability in newness. People often avoid the novel because they can't predict the outcome. As the saying goes, "The devil you know is better than the devil you don't."

But their fears are misplaced. What is really worrisome is what will happen if they *don't* try something different. The longer people persist in doing what doesn't work, the more intractable the problem appears, and the more hopeless the situation becomes. Conversely, fears about trying a new approach to an old problem become quickly assuaged when small improvements become obvious.

"Who, me?" A final reason why we blindly continue doing what we do even when it isn't working is because we aren't aware of *our* role in maintaining the problem, although we know all too well how others are causing us pain. We fail to see how our behavior is inextricably connected to the very responses we dislike.

Several years ago, I witnessed the following exchange between my husband, Jim, and our son, Zach, then four years old. Although I wrote about it in my last book, it bears repeating here.

ZACH: Do we have any soup?
JIM: I don't see any.

ZACH: But do we have any soup?
JIM: (In a louder tone) I don't see any.
ZACH: (Matching Dad's volume) But do we have any?
JIM: (Now screaming) I don't see any!

At which point Jim turned to me and shouted, "I can't believe he keeps asking the same question over and over!" to which I responded, "I can't believe you keep giving him the same answer over and over!"

The problem in their interaction was obvious to me, since I wasn't caught up in the tornado. From Zach's perspective, the fact the my husband couldn't *see* any soup didn't mean that we didn't have any. Zach thought that if my husband looked a bit more thoroughly he might find some. Therefore, he was determined to repeat his question until he got it answered. Unfortunately for both of them, Jim thought Zach was just being obstinate. Zach would undoubtedly have said the same of Jim if he'd had the vocabulary.

I have my own bouts with this sort of blindness. Over the past few months, my thirteen-and-a-half-year-old daughter, Danielle, has been doing her job as a teenager and testing her limits. Sometimes she is rude and challenges me in ways that I find inappropriate. When she does, I respond with a harsh reminder that her behavior is unacceptable, and occasionally withdraw a privilege. But I became aware that my resentment of her defiant behavior often lingered beyond the incident that had provoked me, causing me to grow short with her in general. Had you been at my house during one of our recent go-rounds, you would have heard this conversation:

ME: You are phone-grounded!
DANIELLE: You have been so mean to me lately.
ME: And why do you think I've been so mean to you?
DANIELLE: I have no idea.
ME: I've been mean because you've been fresh.
DANIELLE: Well, I've been fresh because you've been mean.

At times I've wished I were ignorant about how people get stuck in these relationship knots, because it would be easier to continue to blame Danielle entirely for the problem between us. I could just say to myself, "If she would just shape up, I would feel like being nicer to her."

Unfortunately, I know that is only part of the story. Danielle's version is that I initiate our problem. She thinks that, if I were nicer to her, she'd be more cooperative and respectful. I have to face the fact that I trigger in Danielle the very behavior I wish to eradicate (and, Danielle, if you're reading this, vice versa).

Although it is often humbling to acknowledge your own accountability for problems, it is also empowering. If it is possible that you have inadvertently made things worse, it is also possible for you intentionally to make things better. Our failure to critique our own behavior only delays our finding real solutions to our problems, while we monitor other people in the vain hope that they will change. Which reminds me of a joke.

A policeman making his nightly rounds came upon a man crouched beneath a street lamp, furiously scanning the ground. The policeman asked the man what he was looking for. The man told him that he had lost his keys and had been looking for them for hours. In an effort to help, the policeman asked the man whether he was sure he had dropped the keys near where they were standing. "No, I dropped them over there," said the man, pointing to a dark area twenty feet away. "But I am looking for them here because I can see better under the lamp."

Beyond More of the Same

What are your typical "more of the same" actions? The following questions may help spark your memory:

What problem situation keeps coming up over and over in my life? Answering this one probably won't require too much thought on your part. Most people are acutely aware of those stubborn problems that never seem to get resolved. Perhaps you argue or get upset about particular *issues* (such as money, sex, parenting, substance abuse, irresponsibility, low self-esteem) or *occasions* (such as holidays, weekends, visitation, Monday mornings) or *people* (such as certain friends, in-laws, parents, supervisors, co-workers, ex-lovers) or in certain *places* (such as the bedroom, your parent's house, when you go out to eat). Where do you always seem to get stuck?

What is my usual way of handling this situation? When you answer this, make sure you are explicit. Don't just say, "I get angry." What do you do when you get angry? Do you pout? Do you yell? Do you withdraw? If you get upset, do you overeat, yell, get extremely quiet, leave, cry or "let 'em have it"? Be specific.

How would the people around me say I usually deal with the situation?

This is an extremely important question to answer, because the other people in your life will react to you based on *their* interpretation of your behavior. Chances are, they see you and your actions in a different light from the way you see yourself. Let's say you are a person who wants more intimacy from your spouse. You have tried many different approaches to achieve closeness. From your perspective, you are "working on the relationship." But if I were to ask your spouse, "What has she been doing to try to resolve the problems between you lately?" he might say, "She's been nagging me a lot." Granted, you do not see what you have been doing as "nagging," but since your spouse does, you would have to do something that would not be perceived as nagging in order to get a different response.

Try to put yourself in other people's shoes. See yourself the way they do. Remember, it doesn't matter whether you agree or disagree with their view of you. It just matters that you figure out what that view is. If you are having difficulty, ask yourself, "What do other people tell me about my behavior? When they complain to me, what do they say?" If you continue to draw a blank, go straight to the source for more information. Pick a time when you are not in the midst of an argument, when things are peaceful, and ask the other person a question that approximates: "From your perspective, what have I been doing lately that makes you feel uncomfortable?" When you get your answer, don't argue with it or even comment on it. Just make a mental note.

Do Something Different

Now that you have a clearer picture of your "more of the same" moments, you know what you need to change. You need to quit doing that and do something else instead. But what? The answer is what I love most about this approach: *Anything other than what you have been doing that hasn't been working has a better chance of getting good results. Anything.*

In contrast to other self help-books that offer highly specific advice for solving particular problems without regard to who you are as an individual and what your circumstances, preferences, and goals are, I'm suggesting that you simply vary your usual way of handling things and watch the results. This advice flies in the face of conventional wisdom, which tends to suggest generic solutions. If you have a substance-abuse problem, for example, you're told to join a twelve-step group. If you have had an affair, you're supposed to confess to your spouse. If you have a hyperactive child, you should medicate him with Ritalin. If you are depressed, take an antidepressant. I am oversimplifying here, but not much. Most self-help methods do not take individual differences into account. Some people struggling with excessive drinking *should* go to recovery groups, but a group setting is not the solution for everyone. Some—but not all—depressed people do respond to medication.

The key to immediate change is not to adopt a generic solution. The key is to introduce novelty into your usual problem-solving approach. The last chapter taught you to find out what is working, even minimally, and to do more of it. The message of this chapter is, "If what you are doing isn't working, do something different. *Anything* different might do." If you have difficulty accepting that there isn't a universally correct way to improve your situation, the following story may help.

Renowned anthropologist Gregory Bateson was once asked by concerned zookeepers to observe a group of otters. Since otters are by nature playful animals, the zookeepers had grown worried when they noticed that their otters appeared listless. Bateson observed the otters for several days and took copious notes. It became clear to him rather quickly that the zookeepers were right: the otters were uncharacteristically sluggish.

After several days of observing the otters, Bateson took a sheet of paper, attached a long piece of string to it, and dangled it into the area where the otters were resting. Soon an otter spotted the paper and made his way over to it as if he was curious. He began to paw the paper, which set it in motion. Then another otter came over, as if to see what all the commotion was about. He intercepted the swinging paper with his paw, and the first otter playfully attacked him. Within minutes, the rest of the otters got in on the act, tackling one another. Bateson waited several minutes, and withdrew the paper. The otters continued playing. In fact, the listless behavior was never observed again.

Who in the world would have predicted that a dangling piece of paper would restore the otters' playfulness? The results of Bateson's experiment seem like magic. But his conclusion was simple: If nothing new was introduced into the environment, nothing new would happen. If something unusual was introduced into the otters' environment, the odds of change were greatly improved. Any number of other novel approaches might have produced similar results.

If you've been trying to perfect the generic solutions you read about in a book or learned in a class, stop to ask yourself whether what you are doing is working. If it isn't, don't waste any more time questioning yourself or your skills. Try something different.

When my daughter was four years old, she used to put off going to the bathroom as long as she possibly could, so that she wouldn't miss out on anything. I would observe her crossing her legs and wiggling around like a Mexican jumping bean. Noticing this, I would say, "Danielle, do you have to go to the bathroom?" to which she would respond, "No, I don't." Like clockwork, I would retort, "Danielle, you *do* have to go to the bathroom," and she would reply once again, "No, I don't." Raising my voice, I would insist, "Danielle, you have to go to the bathroom! Go now!" She would start crying and I would complete our little ritual by firmly taking her hand and leading her into the bathroom. By then we were always both upset. And this happened not just every day but several times a day, whenever nature called. When I wasn't busy acting like a robot, my husband filled in for me and did precisely the same thing. Poor us, poor Danielle.

One day I noticed the familiar bathroom dance out of the corner of my eye. As usual, I began my part of the dialogue: "Danielle, do you have to go to the bathroom?" But at the same time, a little voice inside my head said, "Michele, you teach others to be creative; do something different." Nothing occurred to me at first, but just as Danielle said, "Mom, I don't have to go," I suddenly turned to her and blurted out, "Ishkabibble!" in a loud voice. With a startled look on her face, she immediately began marching herself to the bathroom, with no further prompting from me. I don't know who was more surprised—Danielle because of my unusual reaction, or me because it worked! The next time I saw Danielle wiggling and began to remind her to go to the bathroom, she replied, "Okay, but please don't say 'Ishkabibble.' "

As I recall the story, I can't help smiling, since I can't imagine coming across this particular solution in a parenting book. Out of pure desperation, I decided to practice what I preach and, without planning, did the unexpected. I dangled my piece of paper in front of my otter. I can't say that "ishkabibble" worked forever, but I can tell you that the fact that it worked at all served as an important reminder for me to vary my actions when things aren't going well.

Here is another example of a parent who decided to do something different. Arnold is a dear friend and colleague of mine who grew tired of his then seven-year-old son Nathan's complaining, "You never buy anything for me," every time Arnold refused to purchase something Nathan wanted. No matter how generous Arnold was, inevitably there would come a tee shirt, a comic book, or a videotape that he refused to buy, whereupon Nathan would chant, "You never buy me anything." Most of the time, Arnold responded with a long-winded defense of his undying generosity, but Nathan's next complaint was always right around the corner.

One day, when they were driving home from school, Nathan spotted an ice cream store and pleaded for a cone. When Arnold told him, "No, not before dinner," Nathan grumbled, "You never buy me anything." This time, though, Arnold decided to try something new. He turned to Nathan and said in a serious tone, "I wasn't going to tell you this until you got older, but I guess that you are really old enough to handle it right now. When you were born, the doctors handed out numbers at the hospital. Every set of parents receiving a certain number had to agree to participate in an experiment. We picked the lucky number and automatically became part of the experiment. The doctors explained what we needed to do with you. We were told that your mom and I had to promise to give you all the love and hugs and kisses you needed. We also had to vow to give all the food and clothing you required. Naturally, we had to give you a nice home. But we were *never, never* supposed to buy you anything you wanted."

Nathan was silent for a moment, then blurted out, "You buy me things sometimes." Although Arnold was pleased with this answer, he didn't let on. He said, "Don't tell anyone or I will get into trouble. I promised never to buy you anything you really want." Nathan appeared to be quite perplexed. He couldn't tell whether his father was teasing him or not. He was noticeably quiet for the remainder of the evening.

In the morning, he sat down at the breakfast table next to Arnold and said, "You know, Dad, that wasn't a very funny joke." Arnold replied, "Which part, the one about you being part of an experiment, or the one about me never buying you anything?" Nathan got the message and smiled. Arnold added, "Let's make a deal. I'll never say that you were part of an experiment, and you never tell me that I don't buy you things, okay?" They shook on the deal.

Sara and her husband, Paul, have been friends with another couple for many years. Sara and Paul find Alice and Ron absolutely charming and wonderful except for one completely intolerable shortcoming: they are always late. (Alice was an hour late for her own baby shower!) Sara and Paul have to assume that Alice and Ron will show up about one hour after the scheduled time, which they find infuriating. Over the years Sara has had countless conversations with Alice, pleading with her to be more prompt. She even told Alice how resentful she feels when she waits for her. Alice has promised to put a little more effort into being punctual, but she hasn't followed through.

One Sunday, Sara and Paul invited their friends over for brunch. They prepared a gourmet spread and set the table meticulously; Martha Stewart would have been proud. One o'clock, the agreed-upon time, came rolling around, but no guests. One-thirty, no guests. At 2:00 P.M., Alice called to say they were running late (no kidding) and that they would be there in an hour.

Sara hung up the phone and discussed the situation with Paul. They agreed that, if they were to wait one moment longer for their friends, their resentment would be so great that it would spoil the rest of the day. They decided to do something different.

They placed the food on the table, served themselves, and enjoyed lunch together. After eating, they cleared the table completely and replaced the books that had been there. They crammed the leftovers into Tupperware containers and put them in the refrigerator.

At approximately 4:00 P.M., the doorbell rang and in walked Alice and Ron. As they began to take off their coats, Sara said, "Leave your coats on, we feel like going for a walk." "Can't we eat first?" said Alice. "We're starving." Sara acted surprised that they had not already eaten, since they were three hours late, and said, "Oh, sorry, we already ate." Bewildered, Alice asked if there were any leftovers. Sara replied, "Oh, there are plenty, just help yourselves."

In advance of Alice and Ron's arrival, Sara and Paul had decided that, instead of being their usual gracious selves, they would resist the temptation to wait on their friends. But they had also agreed to be in good spirits and keep them company while they ate. At one point during the meal, Alice went into the kitchen and shouted back to Sara, "Do you have any mustard?" and Sara replied, "I'm sure it's in there somewhere, just keep looking." Sara couldn't help noticing Paul chuckling softly, and when their eyes met, he winked at her.

After lunch, Paul and Sara waited while Alice and Ron cleared the table and put the leftovers back in the refrigerator. Then they all went for a walk and had a very pleasant afternoon (at least what remained of it). As Alice and Ron left, they suggested having lunch at a certain restaurant the following weekend. Guess what? For the first time in the history of the friendship they actually arrived on time!

Instead of feeling powerless to change the situation with their friends or having to "learn to live with it," Sara and Paul decided to change how *they* responded when their friends were late. They agreed that, even if their strategy hadn't succeeded as well as it did, it would have made them feel more in charge of their own lives.

It should also be said that, when Sara and Paul devised their plan and considered the possible outcomes, they recognized that their friends might get angry or even wish to terminate the friendship. They decided to proceed anyway, not because they didn't care about the friendship, but because they knew that if they didn't their resentment would eventually impair the relationship anyway.

Let's go back to you now. After you've identified your "more of the same" behavior, tell yourself, "The next time I am about to do the same old thing, I am going to do something different, no matter how weird or crazy it might seem. I'm going to do something I've never done before."[1] Maybe you've had a zany idea about how to approach your situation but never had the nerve to try it out. Well, here's permission. As long as you don't hurt anybody, cast your inhibitions to the wind. Be creative—and don't forget to use your sense of humor.

CHANGE ANY STEP IN THE SEQUENCE

It may help you to map out a step-by-step, blow-by-blow description of the sequence surrounding the problem. Once you do this, you can begin to see how you can, by changing any step in the sequence, change the entire outcome. Start by asking yourself, "What's the first thing that happens? Then what do I do? Then what?" and so on. Picture how each step is linked to the one before it and the one after it. The following example will help you to visualize this mapping process.

Betty and her fourteen-year-old daughter, Gina, sought therapy because Betty was concerned about Gina's relationship with her father, Betty's ex-husband. Recently, each time Gina visited her dad, she returned home upset because of how her father treated her. Since Betty had come to anticipate Gina's being upset when she returned home, Betty waited up to talk with her about the visit. She would question Gina closely about her feelings, and whenever Gina expressed a feeling of hurt, Betty would get extremely upset. Seeing her mother upset made Gina even more upset, and she often had trouble sleeping after their talks. Inevitably, the next morning, Betty would pick up the phone and reprimand her ex-husband, who would then get furious at Betty for not minding her own business and resent Gina for complaining to Betty. Gina would return to her dad's house anticipating his resentment, and she would often be right.

As I heard this story, I began to draw a picture in my mind about the patterns that had developed in their family. This is what I envisioned:

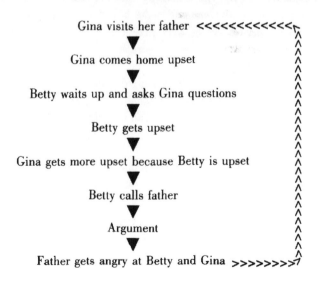

Gina visits her father <<<<<<<<<<<<
▼
Gina comes home upset
▼
Betty waits up and asks Gina questions
▼
Betty gets upset
▼
Gina gets more upset because Betty is upset
▼
Betty calls father
▼
Argument
▼
Father gets angry at Betty and Gina >>>>>>>>>

As I thought about this cycle of behavior, I began to envision how it could be broken. I started by asking if Gina planned on continuing her visits with her dad. She said, "Yes. Although we fight, I still love him." Since Gina's visits with her father were to continue, I talked with her about how she might deal with him differently when he got angry. If Gina were able to interact with her father successfully, she would not come home upset, and the rest of the sequence would be interrupted.

Next, I explored with Betty the importance of Gina's learning how to handle her relationship with her father by herself. I suggested that she not wait up for Gina. Betty agreed that Gina would feel good about being able to resolve things with her father independently. I believed that, if Betty was able to resist the temptation to wait up to talk with Gina, she would not get upset and call her ex-husband. As a result, Gina would feel better that her mother wasn't overwrought, and Gina's father would not get angry at Betty for interfering, nor would he take it out on Gina at a later date.

If, however, Betty felt that she *had* to wait up for Gina, I recommended that she just talk to Gina about what went well on the visit. That would keep Betty from getting upset and exacerbating Gina's worry. If Betty didn't get upset, she would not feel compelled to call her ex-husband. Finally, Gina's knowing that her mother and father were not fighting on the phone would make it easier for her to go to her dad's without worrying that he was angry at her. I anticipated that her more relaxed demeanor might elicit more solicitous behavior from her father when she saw him.

As you can see, there were many possible ways to solve the problem Gina and her mother were experiencing. In fact, it would also have been possible to contact Gina's father and include him in the problem-solving process if none of the interventions I attempted with Gina and her mother worked.

Now let's go back to your situation. If you like to sketch things out, draw a diagram like the one above. Remember to be specific. Then look at each step in the sequence and envision what you could do differently at that point to get a new result. Focus on your steps in the process, because that is what you can change immediately. But remember, once you change your steps, the whole dance will automatically change.

Even if the difficulty you are experiencing is personal rather than interpersonal—you feel depressed, have trouble sleeping, get nervous when you have to take tests—you still behave in highly patterned and predictable ways.

Take Joan, for example, a single woman in her early thirties who feels depressed. She tells me that she can detect as soon as she wakes up whether she will be depressed or not. On depressed days, she has a sad feeling inside as soon as she opens her eyes, and that feeling sends her into her "depressed mode."

In her depressed mode, she procrastinates about getting out of bed until 10:30 or 11:00 A.M. (She can do this because she is self-employed and sets her own schedule.) Even when she gets out of bed, she remains in her pajamas. She sits on the couch and watches television, flipping channels because she finds it hard to concentrate.

At around 2:00 P.M., Joan reminds herself that she hasn't eaten and gets a bowl of cereal and a glass of orange juice. She thinks about getting some work done but feels too depressed to begin. If the phone rings during the day, she lets her answering machine pick it up, because she doesn't feel like talking to anyone. She doesn't want to burden people with her problems. At about 5:00 P.M., she walks down her driveway to get her mail. If the weather is cold, she wears an overcoat to conceal the fact that she is still in her pajamas. In the summer, rather than get dressed, she forgoes getting her mail. Later, she feeds her cat, makes herself dinner, cleans the dinner dishes, climbs into bed, turns on the television, and channel-surfs with the remote control until she falls asleep, which usually happens around 10:30 P.M. She often wakes up at 2:30 A.M. and tosses and turns for two hours before falling back to sleep.

Now compare this pattern with how Joan acts and thinks on days when she is feeling better. On good days, Joan is up and out of bed by 7:30 A.M. She showers, makes herself a cup of coffee, and goes into her home office. She reviews what she must accomplish for the day and works until 10:30 A.M., when she takes a break and calls one or two friends. She chats with them for a while, which she always enjoys, has a cup of tea, and then goes back to work until noon, when she usually meets a friend or business associate. After lunch, she picks up her mail and works in her office until 5:30, when she feeds her cat. She goes to her health club to work out, then has dinner with friends. Back at home, she watches the news, but when the news is over, she turns off the television and listens to music. She usually falls asleep around 10:30 or 11:00 P.M. and sleeps through the night.

Unlike problems that involve other people, personal problems are triggered not by others but by our own thoughts, feelings, and actions. Joan's sadness when she awakes prompts a little voice in her head to tell her, "Uh-oh. You're going to have a bad day. Might as well stay in bed." Once she allows her daily work routine to be delayed by staying in bed, she feels unable to break free of the "bad day" pattern. Arising late leads to staying in her PJ's, watching television, avoiding phone calls and contact with friends, eating little, staying home instead of working out, and so on.

But it's important to point out that Joan is not aware of the choices she makes to remain in a depressed mode once she awakes feeling sad. Subconscious triggers are powerful. Just ask a smoker. He will tell you that he often finds himself smoking without even realizing why he lit up, or even that he did. Certain situations—smoky places, satisfying meals, gratifying sexual encounters, and tense interactions—unconsciously trigger the impulse to light up. Similarly, each of Joan's actions sets off the next, yet she does not realize how deeply entrenched these patterns have become. When I ask her how she turns a bad day into a good day in midstream, she insists that, once she determines she feels sad in the morning, there is no turning back.

But here's the good news: Once Joan understands that she is behaving by rote, she can interrupt her depressed-mode sequence (make herself feel better) with some of what she usually does on days when she feels better. To begin with, she can make a commitment to set her alarm for 7:30 A.M., get up and take a shower, and *then* assess how she feels. Or, no matter how she feels in the morning, she can call a friend and make plans for lunch or for meeting in the evening. Since socializing is something she only does on good days, making a "date" early on a bad day would significantly alter the bad-day pattern. Something as simple as forcing herself to get dressed after she wakes or going to work out would also disturb her depressed-day routine. Joan is correct when she says that feeling sad sparks a chain reaction, but she is incorrect in assuming that once she feels sad there is no turning back. By replacing any step Joan takes when she feels depressed with what she does when she feels more content, she can easily reverse the momentum of her bad days.

What has stopped Joan from doing so is the inaccurate belief that feelings *cause* her to act in certain ways. She thinks her bad feelings *cause* her to stay in bed until 10:30 A.M. and her good feelings *cause* her to rise early and shower, but that is simply not true. Feelings are just feelings, nothing more, nothing less. We override our feelings thousands of times each day. We go to work even when we don't feel like it, wake up in the middle of the night for our children, see the movie a friend really wants to see even though it isn't our first choice, call a relative who never calls us, go to a school play even if we're exhausted, complete a work project even though it is boring. Get the point?

After we talk, Joan decides that she will get up early each morning and make lunch plans regardless of her feelings. Quickly she discovers that breaking the depression habit is considerably easier than she had anticipated. Once she gets up and showers, she simply feels compelled to get dressed rather than get back in PJ's. Furthermore, the calls she makes to set up her lunch dates are made from the phone in her office, which puts her in a convenient location to start her work, which she does. This is not to say that Joan never has another bad day. But when she does, she is able to catch herself sooner and carve another path for her day.

VARY THE WHAT, WHEN, WHERE, OR WHO

"It is circumstance and proper timing that give an action its character and make it either good or bad."

—AGESILAUS

By now, you probably have a new problem-solving idea you want to test out. If so, that's great. Do it! If you are still at a loss, it may help to break down the possibilities by recognizing that you can alter one of several variables: *what* is done to solve the problem, *when* you tackle the problem, *where* the problem is addressed, or *who* handles it. So far I've discussed how to determine *what* you can change. But let's take a closer look at how you might change the other variables of your problem-solving pattern.

Try varying the time of day or week you deal with bothersome issues. A woman told me that, because she and her husband both had demanding careers, they had little time during the week to discuss issues that concerned them. Consequently, they waited until they both got off of work on Friday evenings to confront these issues and each other. And, like clockwork, every Friday evening they fought, which ruined the weekend. They returned to work on Mondays feeling drained and distant from each other. This pattern persisted for months.

One day, the woman decided to see what would happen if they postponed their discussion until Sunday. When her husband got home Friday evening, he initiated their usual conversation, but she resisted the temptation to respond. That got him to stop as well, and they ended up going out for dinner and thoroughly enjoying each other's company for the first time in a long while. Saturday also went well, as did Sunday. On Sunday evening, the woman brought up the usual issue. With three good days under their belts, they felt closer and more cooperative, and they were able to get closure on what had been a chronic problem.

If you can identify a pattern to the timing of your problems, see if you can alter it. Decide in advance on a new time to address whatever has been bothering you, and stick to it. Then see if it makes a difference.

Keep peak performance times in mind. If I have something important to talk to my husband about, I have learned that there are better times to approach him than others. If I want to ensure failure in our communication, I will broach the subject right when he walks through the door, when the children are around, when he is in a bad mood, or when he is busy doing something. Conversely, if I want to increase the odds of securing his undivided attention and an empathetic ear, I will invite him out for dinner, make sure the children are occupied, ask him if he is willing to discuss something at that particular moment, or do something nice for him prior to the discussion.

My husband is no different from anyone else, in the sense that we all have times when we're more receptive, energetic, cooperative, and conciliatory. Clients tell me, "If she'd just approach me sexually after dinner instead of at eleven o'clock at night, we would still have a sex life," or "I'm pretty reasonable on most days, but stay clear of me when I'm premenstrual, because I'm a real grouch." Recognizing the windows of opportunity with those around you will greatly enhance your ability to influence people and solve problems.

You should not overlook the fact that *you* have peak performance times, too. Sometimes you are more levelheaded, ambitious, empathetic, or focused. You need to recognize these times in yourself and take advantage of them. For instance, when Amy discovered that her son, Tim, had recently received three failing grades, her initial impulse was to let him have it as soon as he got off the school bus. But, recognizing that her anger might prompt her to say or do things she would regret, she decided to wait until it had subsided, so that she could look at the situation a bit more objectively. When she was ready, she confronted Tim calmly, and together they were able to work out a structured plan to get him back on track. Amy was smart to wait for a "peak time" to address the problem.

Ask yourself: "When am I most likely to get the kind of results I want?" Even if there never seems to be a perfect time, some times are clearly worse than others. If you carry out your plan during them, it will surely fail. A mediocre plan executed with good timing is a better bet than a great plan ill-timed.

Schedule predetermined times to deal with the problem. Have you ever been in the midst of a glorious day when suddenly someone says or does something that upsets you? Words are exchanged, and the day goes downhill rapidly for you and everyone around you. If arguments with your significant other, children, friends, or co-workers occur unpredictably throughout your week, you might consider scheduling regular meetings to discuss problems. Otherwise, people may feel the need to air anger or resentment instantly, for fear that their feelings will be overlooked or forgotten. When they know that they will have an opportunity to air differences, they may be able to contain themselves until the designated time(s). It also helps to set a definite end to these conflict-resolution meetings, so that they don't drag on interminably.

Vary the where. The Russian physiologist Pavlov became famous for his experiments on something referred to as the "conditioned reflex." The classic experiment involved sounding a tuning fork just as powdered meat was placed on a dog's tongue. The meat made the dog salivate. This procedure was repeated many times, and the dog began to pair hearing the tuning fork with receiving the powdered meat. Eventually, even when no meat was presented, the sound of the tuning fork could produce salivation.

People are also subject to conditioned reflexes. If a stimulus such as a particular location (e.g., the living room) is consistently paired with a particular response (e.g., feeling depressed), it is possible that, over time, just sitting in the living room will trigger a depressed feeling.

Remember Joan? Did you notice that when she was depressed she spent most of her time on her couch, in her PJ's? We often engage in our problematic habits in the same location. One way she might break the pattern of her depression is to get up and go into another room, or take a walk outside.

Fights typically happen in one spot or location—the kitchen, at the dining room table, in the cafeteria, or in the car. Try taking a walk around the block, discussing a problem over dinner in a restaurant, or working it out in the bathroom. Go for a ride in the country. It doesn't matter where you go, just change the environment and watch what happens.

Vary the who. Finally, certain problems seem to defy resolution until someone else takes responsibility for working things out. I can't count the number of times a parent has said to me, "The kids are out of control when I deal with them, but the minute my spouse enters the room, they toe the line." What's happening in homes across America? Do children have multiple-personality disorders? Why do they do what's expected of them in the presence of one parent but not the other? Clearly, they are responding to the fact that their parents have different expectations and ways of treating them.

Many years ago, a colleague of mine was working with a mother who was unable to get her eleven-year-old daughter to go to school. The mother had been receiving help from school personnel on this issue, but she hadn't informed her husband, a traveling salesman, because she didn't want to trouble him.

One day, the woman had to leave town suddenly because of a death in her family. The next morning, the alarm went off and the father went into his daughter's room to get her up for school. As usual, she balked about getting dressed, but because her father was unaware of her "school phobia," he just assumed she was tired and crabby and prodded her until she got out of bed and began to dress for school. He fed her breakfast, ignored her requests to stay home, and drove her promptly to school. When the woman returned, she couldn't believe what her husband had accomplished, and she told him about her past struggles with their daughter. Shocked, the father decided to take responsibility for getting the girl to school for the next few weeks, until regular attendance was more of a habit.

The lesson I learned from this case was that one way to introduce the unexpected into problem-solving is to vary *who* handles the problem. This does not mean that the father was a better parent. But, for some reason, his actions overcame his daughter's resistance to going to school. No matter *why* it worked—it worked, and they should keep doing it.

Many relationship problems can be eliminated by changing who takes responsibility for handling certain tasks. One couple used to fight endlessly about the wife's frivolous expenditures until they decided that she would take over paying their bills. That way, she would be able to see whether there was enough money to purchase what she had bought. This simple solution ended a decade-long fighting marathon.

Another couple had awful fights each time they entertained for dinner. She felt he didn't do enough, and he felt she didn't notice or value what he did do to help out. Rather than assuming that they would work side by side in the future, they developed a list of tasks and divided them up. If you are in a relationship and you find yourself arguing incessantly with your partner about how a certain task is performed, change roles for a while and see what happens. A change in "who's in charge" may make a big enough difference to eliminate unpleasant fights.

This also often works with parents. Now, I know that what I am about to tell you is blasphemy, but since it works, I will tell you anyway. As you probably know, it is not uncommon for parents to disagree on child-rearing issues. When this happens, instead of constructing a plan to help the child, parents end up fighting about whose approach to the problem is better. The longer they argue about the virtues of discipline versus the importance of TLC (or other favorite parenting disagreements), the longer the problem persists. The parents are too busy arguing to take action, or if they do, each undermines the other in a battle for control.

Although most professional and nonprofessional books on parenting suggest that parents *must* come to an agreement about how to deal with their children and present a united front if they wish to be effective, I will tell you, from personal and professional experience, that parents can't always see eye to eye when it comes to some of the deeply charged issues child-rearing involves. What many parents find more useful is to agree to disagree, and then decide who takes charge.

Some parents find it helpful to make a list of issues that require parental intervention and then choose for which issues each will assume primary concern. Mom decides where their teenage daughter may go on weekends, but Dad decides curfew. Mom sets the children's bedtimes, but Dad calls the shots on table manners. Delegation of these responsibilities can be arbitrary, and they can always be renegotiated if who's doing what isn't working.

Often, flipping a coin is as good a method as any of interrupting unproductive debates about whose solution is better. It helps to agree to the approach in advance, and it is essential that the loser not interfere with the winner's method. (This is usually not a problem, because the loser has the consolation of knowing that chance, not superiority, favored the other person's plan.) If you don't like flipping coins, you can decide in advance that on odd days of the month Person A makes the decisions, and on even days Person B. A couple with whom I had been working disagreed on the value of time spent apart from each other. He wanted to feel free to spend time pursuing solitary interests, but she felt they didn't spend enough time together. She also believed that the time they did spend together was not "quality time." They argued for months as to whether "alone time" would be acceptable in their relationship. He blamed her for being too dependent, and she blamed him for being insensitive to her feelings.

They agreed to try the odd-day, even-day technique. On odd days, they would do separate activities. On even days, they would be together doing an activity of her choice. He felt enriched by his guilt-free time alone, and she enjoyed the closeness that resulted from their quality time together. It was a win-win situation.

Even if your struggles are internal, the odd-day, even-day technique can be useful to you. A woman who was trying to decide whether to remain in her marriage or get a divorce noted that her feelings vacillated "a million times a day." I suggested that on odd days she imagine that she was going to get a divorce and immerse herself in the feelings associated with living her life without her husband. She was also to think about the steps she would need to take to free herself from the marriage. On even days, I suggested, she should fantasize about what her life would be like if she were to stay in the marriage, and imagine how she would feel about herself and her husband.

After two weeks she returned, with considerably more clarity on her feelings. She recognized that on odd days—days when she envisioned herself without her husband—she felt a deep sadness. She also noticed that she began to look forward to even days and to imagining herself with her husband indefinitely. As a result of this exercise, she decided to devote her energy to improving her marriage rather than to getting out.

Now that you've finished this chapter, I want you to promise yourself one thing: that you will stop doing what hasn't been working. Tell yourself that, although there may have been good reasons for you to have chosen that approach, there are even better reasons to do something different now. Once you commit yourself to trying something new, you will feel better. Dedicating yourself to being more creative in problem-solving will itself inject more optimism into your life. Don't waste time trying to identify the perfect fail-safe strategy. Just remember Bateson and the otters, and when you get stuck, do the otter thing.

Chapter Nine

Act As If

YOU ARE ABOUT to meet Frances, mother of a challenging three-year-old; Sam, an editor who negotiates book deals; a woman who has trouble sleeping; and another, who wishes her husband would be nicer to her. What they have in common is a belief that they can foresee the future with uncanny accuracy. But as you are about to find out, they are wrong.

Frances, mother of three-year-old Mindy, said she could always tell when Mindy was going to have a bad day. Intrigued by her clairvoyant ability, I asked how she knew. She said she was able to predict Mindy's mood by the tone in her voice when she yelled, "Mommy, I'm up." If she sounded happy, Frances knew Mindy would have a good day; but if she sounded grouchy, all hell was going to break loose.

I asked Frances to tell me about the sequence of events on the mornings she thought Mindy was in a good mood. She told me she immediately went into Mindy's bedroom and sang a song with her. Frances would sing, "How's Mommy's little girl?" and Mindy would echo back, "Mommy's girl is fine." Frances would respond with, "Who loves Mindy?" and Mindy would sing, "You do." Frances would then help her get dressed, and together they would head downstairs for breakfast. I asked Frances to contrast this with what happened if it seemed to her that Mindy was in a bad mood. Frances said that she hesitated to go into Mindy's room on those mornings, because she anticipated a crabby little girl. When she did enter the room, Frances simply got Mindy dressed, without any singing or displays of affection.

As soon as she described the differences between their "good day" and "bad day" routines, Frances recognized how she might be offering

Mindy subtle clues about her expectations for the day. In other words, Frances' predictions about Mindy's mood influenced her own behavior toward her daughter, which might be triggering Mindy's response.

To test this, I suggested that Frances try an experiment. I instructed her to enter Mindy's room each morning acting as if she believed that Mindy was in a good mood. She was to start singing their morning song regardless of the tone in Mindy's voice when she woke. Frances agreed. A week later, she returned saying they had had the best week ever. Mindy had been cooperative, gotten along better with her baby sister, and seemed happier in general. In fact, Mindy had completely toilet trained herself that week! By acting as if she believed Mindy were in a good mood and doing all the things she would normally do on "good-mood days," Frances set a tone of positive mother-daughter interaction for the rest of the day. Impressed with the results, she started to think about other ways she could get better results with her children by changing her own behavior first.

We are so conscious of the impact other people have on us that we lose sight of the effect we have on others. Simply anticipating a situation causes us to transmit subtle messages about our expectations and often brings about the very results we anticipate. For instance, imagine that you and I just met. If I assumed that you were an extremely friendly and likable person, I would be friendly and outgoing toward you. Undoubtedly, you would notice my friendly overtures and respond in kind. Your friendliness would then be taken as evidence that my initial expectations about you were correct. Little would I realize that, had I assumed you to be cold and distant, I would have been more cautious in your presence, which you might have interpreted as "aloofness." In turn, you would probably have kept your distance from me, causing me to assume that my original hunch about you (that you were cold) was correct. Although I would not have been aware of it, my own behavior would have influenced you to evolve into the person I imagined you to be. As you probably know, this is what is referred to as a self-fulfilling prophecy.

Understanding how the self-fulfilling prophecy works can offer solutions to interpersonal difficulties. If you know that your expectations can influence you to act in ways that bring about the very results you expect, you'd better examine what you're expecting. If you are expecting an unhappy ending, it's time to do some quick re-evaluating. Take it from Sam, a friend of mine who works for a small publishing company.

Sam had to call an agent he really disliked about an author he greatly admired. I asked him what it was about the agent that bothered him. In Sam's opinion, the agent was obnoxious and difficult to deal with. "Also," he said, "I like to get straight to the point. I don't like to beat around the bush." In contrast to this, he described the agent as someone who first likes to "schmooze," to make small talk before getting down to business. Sam found this very irritating. Furthermore, Sam said, the agent liked to go on and on about a single point. "I usually cut him off once I understand what he is trying to say. I know he finds this offensive, but I can't stand how long it takes for him to make a point." Sam went on to say that, though he is aware how his negative feelings about the agent must get in the way of their negotiations, he felt that he couldn't help himself. But now that he had important business to conduct with the agent, he was motivated to find a better way of relating to him.

I asked Sam, "What would you do differently if you liked this man?" He said, "I would take more time in the beginning of our conversation to listen to him go on about the weather, the good restaurants he'd been to recently, or whatever. Also, I would probably give him the time he needs to explain himself without interrupting him. I guess I'd be more patient. He can probably tell that I dread our conversations, so I suppose if I were to sound livelier on the phone, as if I were truly interested, he would notice the difference." I left Sam with a simple piece of advice: "Act as if you like him." When he groaned, I reminded him, "I didn't say you had to like him, I just said *act as if* . . ."

Later that day, Sam called to tell me that his conversation with the agent went swimmingly! Sam had been warmer and more patient, and in turn the agent was friendlier and less obnoxious than usual. In fact, Sam said, "I even found myself liking him a little." Within a few days, Sam and the agent had reached an agreement, and the author was about to sign a contract.

It is important to point out here that Sam felt he could not act as if because he couldn't imagine "liking" the agent. The beauty of this technique is that it is not necessary for your feelings to coincide with your actions initially. As long as the outcome is important to you, you can teach yourself how to act as if they do. And once people around you start changing, this tends to change how you feel about them. So, even if your heart isn't entirely in it at first, try it. I think you'll be surprised.

ing as if can also be helpful in situations that involve only one person—namely, you. If you are trying to change something about yourself but don't expect to succeed, you will undoubtedly sabotage your plan. If you act as if you expect the outcome to be a good one, it usually is. Here's an example:

A woman told me that she was becoming an insomniac but didn't have difficulty sleeping *every* night. She said she could usually predict which nights would be particularly troublesome. I asked her what she was doing differently on the nights she expected to have difficulty sleeping. She said that on those nights she set up her bed on the couch, because she didn't want to wake her husband with her tossing and turning. She also checked the TV guide early in the day to make sure there would be a good movie available when she woke up. If no movie appealed to her, she went to the video store and rented a tape to prepare for her night of sleeplessness. On the other hand, when she was expecting a restful night, she went to bed with her husband and paid no attention to the late-night television schedule. She was more active during the day, because she knew she would have a good night's sleep. She also told me that when she expected to sleep she did sleep, and when she expected not to sleep she didn't. Instead of recognizing the possibility that she had constructed a self-fulfilling prophecy, she figured she had become a prediction expert.

I suggested that when she woke up in the morning, no matter what she thought, she was to act as if she were expecting a great night's sleep that night. She was to do all things she normally did on days when she was expecting things to go well: avoid checking the TV guide, plan on sleeping in her own bed instead of the couch, keep active during the day, and so on. She agreed.

The next time I saw her, she reported that she no longer had to predict how her night was going to go. She had found herself thinking less about the whole situation, and had been sleeping just fine.

If you ever say to yourself, "I can just tell by the look on his face what kind of a day he's had, and I know how the evening will go," or "I know how my boss is going to react to my proposal," you are a good candidate for acting as if. The better you think you are at predicting the future, the more you need to experiment with this method. Begin by asking yourself:

When I expect things to turn out badly, what do I do? If you believe you'll have trouble sleeping tonight, or you'll be turned down for

motion, or your spouse will come home in a lousy mood, how do you prepare for the disappointment? Do you avoid your spouse? Are you short
with your boss? Do you become defensive instantly? Note specific actions
you take when you envision the day going sour. Then ask yourself:

If I were to expect things to turn out well, what would I do differently?
I was working with a woman who said she wanted her husband to be
nicer to her. Lately, he had been working long hours and not participating in the care of their son, and when he was home he was critical
and argumentative. She said he used to spend more time with her,
compliment her more, and enjoy spending time as a family. I asked her,
"What's different about you when he is being nicer to you?" She immediately responded, "I've become such a nag lately. I haven't been
very nice to him. When he is nicer to me, I'm much nicer to him." I
asked her what sorts of things she used to do differently when she was
being nicer to him. She said, "I used to make his lunch and put thoughtful notes in his lunchbox. I used to be more affectionate. We're not
physical very often anymore. I also used to get a babysitter and arrange
for us to do fun things together. I've given up on that entirely."

I told her I had a suggestion: "Go home and act as if he is being nicer
to you. Do the things you used to do when you weren't being a nag.
Watch what happens."

Her husband's response was immediate. He became more affectionate, spent more time with her, and called her more often from work.
Their relationship improved dramatically.

Perhaps the idea of "acting as if" sounds interesting but you are still
not convinced that you have anything to do with the way other people
behave toward you. I have a confession. Whenever my husband and I
argue, I'm certain that the argument has everything to do with him and
nothing to do with me. Even though I know I'm wrong about this, it
certainly feels as if I'm right. Isn't it intriguing that we seem to have
radar for detecting how others antagonize or trigger emotional responses
in us but we fail to appreciate how we do the same to others?

So put away your crystal ball and stop predicting dire outcomes. If
you feel you must predict the future, make sure you imagine a positive
one. Then, no matter what, start acting as if. And if you're not sure how
well this technique will work, act as if you are.

Chapter Ten

Do a 180°

MILTON ERICKSON, THE psychiatrist whose pioneering of solution-oriented therapy I described in chapter two, demonstrated his problem-solving abilities even as a young child. Growing up on a farm, he spent many hours each day watching his father do chores. One day, his father and another man were desperately trying to get a cow into the barn. They had pointed the cow in the direction of the barn, and they were pushing with all their might, but the cow had other plans. And the more they pushed, the more firmly she planted her hooves in the ground.

After watching this struggle for a while, Erickson asked his father if he could try. Reluctantly, his father agreed. Erickson promptly got behind the cow and, with all of his strength, jerked on the cow's tail. Startled, the cow darted forward—away from the source of the pain and into the barn.

Solving problems in our lives is often like getting the cow into the barn: the harder we push, the stronger the resistance. The solution? If pushing doesn't work, try pulling. Earlier you learned the importance of changing *anything* in the way you respond to difficult situations—the point being that *any* novel reaction on your part might be enough to get better results. Sometimes, however, a minor change in your behavior is not sufficient. Only a major U-turn will work.

Although on the surface, doing a 180° may seem like a bizarre strategy, the technique has been around for a millennium. Every parent, whether consciously or not, has used this method at some time or other: "Don't you dare eat those peas." "I bet you can't pick up all your toys." "No matter what you say, you can't go to sleep right now. You have to stay up longer." Kids love asserting themselves and defying authority, and most parents have figured out how to exploit that.

I was once asked to consult with a teacher who had a student in her class who refused to speak. Many people, including the teacher, the parents, the school psychologist, and the student's friends and classmates, had tried various methods to get this little girl to open up, but none were successful. I suggested to the teacher that she do a 180°. I told her to tell the little girl, "I've been trying to get you to talk, but then I realized that you probably have a good reason for not talking. I understand now that, if you have anything important to say, you will say it. So, until that time, it's a good idea to stay quiet."

By the end of the day, the little girl was asking questions in class. She talked more and more as the days passed. In fact, the teacher called and asked me whether I had any suggestions for getting her to *stop* talking so much. We laughed and turned our conversation to other subjects.

Another teacher was irritated by a student who consistently raised his hand each time she finished explaining what the class was required to do next. "I don't understand," he would say, "could you explain it again?" The teacher thought he did understand and was just trying to get his peers' attention. She told him that he really didn't need extra help, she reprimanded him, she spoke calmly to him after class, but none of these methods worked. That's when she decided to do a 180°.

The next time she was about to explain an assignment to the class, she preceded her instructions with a special announcement: "Joey, I know that this assignment will be too difficult for you to understand, and that you will have questions as soon as I am done explaining it. Since I'm sure that the rest of the class won't have any problem with it, I will make sure to give you the special help you need." He immediately objected to her evaluation of him. "What do you mean, I won't understand? I will too." Mysteriously, he had no questions when she was done giving instructions. She continued her plan for several days, until she felt sure that Joe's habit of interrupting had been broken.

Perhaps you are saying to yourself, "I'm not a teacher, and my children are no longer young enough to be challenged by my saying, 'Don't you dare eat your peas.' " Well, guess what? The desire to be self-determining knows no age limits. Adolescents also reel in the opposite direction if they are told what to do. Most people of all ages like to feel in control of the decisions governing their lives. Don't you?

Dave and Paula were very angry and frustrated with their son Lance, age twenty, who was still living at home. For many months, Lance, who was unemployed, had been staying out late with his friends, sleeping late in the morning, and not helping around the house. Finally, Dave and Paula threw him out of their home and told him he could not live there until he found a job. Sure enough, Lance returned in less than a week with a full-time job. They allowed him to live at home providing he kept his job and maintained a curfew. For several weeks after his return, Dave and Paula were amazed at how cooperative Lance had become. But they sensed that this pleasant period was about to come to a screeching halt: they knew Lance had plans to violate his curfew on the upcoming weekend, and they weren't sure what to do.

Our first task was to determine what "more of the same" behavior had been in regard to previous curfew violations. "If Lance thought you knew about his plan, what would he expect you two to do about it?" I asked. Paula immediately replied, "He would expect us to get angry, reason with him, ask him why he is planning on ruining our good times together, plead with him not to go, or make him promise he'll be home on time." At first, Dave suggested that, since they knew about his plan, *not* commenting on it would be a 180° for them. After discussing this for a while, however, they saw that Lance might interpret their not commenting on his plan as not knowing about it: Dave and Paula's silence would not have been different enough for Lance to have noticed. They realized that a real 180° would be for them to encourage him to break curfew. But how in heaven's name could they do that without appearing to have temporarily gone insane?

They decided to invite Lance out to dinner, explaining that they had something very important they wanted to tell him. They whetted his curiosity by refusing to give him any more information about their rendezvous, but informed him to dress nicely because they were taking him to his favorite restaurant. As planned, Dave waited until all three of them were done with their meal, then began to speak in a very serious tone: "Lance, your mother and I want to tell you something very important. We want to tell you how much we love you and how we have enjoyed having you live with us as a family."

He went on to describe his pride over Lance's many accomplishments. He did so very thoroughly, in a rather lengthy soliloquy. At the end of his speech he said: "The reason we are telling you this now is that we want to say goodbye to you while we still have good feelings about each other. We know that you are going to stay out past curfew this weekend and that we will be required to ask you to leave again. When this happens, both your mother and I will be very angry, and we will probably say awful things to you. We won't be in the mood to tell you how nice it has been to have you as our son. So we just wanted to say our farewells while the time is right. Furthermore, although we've enjoyed your company in the last few months, maybe breaking curfew is your way of telling us it is time for you to leave home. In a way, it would be easier for us to part ways being angry than if we had good feelings. It would hurt more that way. So, in the long run, your plan to break our rules makes good sense."

Needless to say, Lance was shocked by what he heard and began to dispute their prediction. Dave and Paula responded by telling him they understood that he had good intentions but were certain that the temptation to break curfew would eventually get the best of him. The more Lance argued with them, the more Paula and Dave knew their approach was working. At the next session, they reported that Lance had decided it was more important to prove them wrong than to stay out late on Saturday night. Mission accomplished!

Even full-grown adults respond dramatically when confronted with the unexpected. Liz and Lonnie are partners in a small consulting firm. From time to time, Lonnie feels overwhelmed by the demands their clients place on her. When this happens, she gets extremely frustrated and irritable. In an effort to calm her, Liz reassures Lonnie that she will be able to get the required task done as long as she continues working at her current pace. She reminds Lonnie that she always fulfills her obligations, even when things get harried. Instead of appreciating Liz's efforts, however, Lonnie usually lashes out at her, accusing her of lacking empathy. Naturally, this rankles Liz, who, after all, is just trying to help.

One day, Liz walked into the office and Lonnie was mumbling under her breath as she typed furiously at her word processor. Lonnie complained that one of their clients had shortened the deadline on a project, and she felt it was nearly impossible to meet it. Just then, Liz decided to do a 180°. She exclaimed, "I can't imagine what he was thinking! He must be nuts! It's clients like him we can do without." Lonnie was quiet for a moment; then she looked up at Liz and said, "I guess, if I just keep at it, I'll get it done. I learned some shortcuts at the seminar I went to last week. It will be fine." Liz was stunned. Not nearly as stunned, I bet, as Lonnie was when Liz did a 180°.

Molly complained that her husband, George, often lingered late at work or went out with friends afterward. This upset her, because she felt that they didn't spend enough time together. George worked long hours, and Molly felt that the least he could do was come home directly when his work was completed. Every afternoon, she called him to see what time he would be home. Rarely did he return when he said he would. Most afternoons, she reminded him of this, and their conversations ended on a less-than-positive note.

Molly decided to try something new. She stopped calling him at work to remind him to come home. After several weeks, however, there was no noticeable difference: George continued to return home late each evening. Molly became extremely angry and frustrated and set up an appointment with me.

After we talked for a while, it became evident that, although Molly had tried to do something different to solve her marital problem—she'd stopped calling George at work—it was not different enough to make a difference. George didn't hear from Molly on a daily basis, but he assumed that she still wanted him to return home promptly after work. He may have thought that she was just too busy to call, or he may not have noticed. It was time for Molly to do a 180°.

I asked Molly, "What would George least expect you to do about his staying out late in the evenings?" She said, "I suppose, if I were to insist that he stayed out, that would really shock him." "Perfect," I thought, "now we're on to something." I suggested that Molly call her husband at work the next day and say, "You know, I've really been missing something. I haven't realized how much pressure you've been under lately and how your going out with friends helps you unwind. I'm sorry I've been so insensitive to your needs. Honey, don't rush home tonight. Go ahead and make plans for yourself." I suggested that she call him again later in the week and advise him to stay out since she had made plans to go out with her own friends. I told her, "If he asks what you are doing, tell him you aren't sure yet."

The next week, she returned and reported what had happened. When she called George and told him to enjoy himself out on the town and not to rush home, there was dead silence on the other end of the phone.

Instead of returning home at 10:00 P.M., as he usually did, George got home at 8:00 P.M. In place of her usual twenty-one questions, Molly simply asked him whether he'd had a good time; when he said that he had, she replied, "Great," and asked no further questions.

During the second phone call, Molly told George not to come home early because she had made other plans. Curious, he asked about the specifics, but she had none to offer. She returned at 10:00 P.M. to discover that George was already home waiting for her and happy to see her. Together they enjoyed what remained of the evening. In the weeks that followed, Molly reported a noticeable decline in the frequency of her husband's after-work escapades. In fact, she found him to be more attentive in general. A side benefit of her 180° was that she discovered how much she enjoyed going out with her friends, and she continued to do so now and then even though George was home more.

Here's what you need to do to do a 180°:

Describe to yourself what you see as the problem. In Molly's case, it was George's frequent late nights out with his friends. Identify the behavior you have been trying to change.

Assess how you have been trying to solve this problem. This is the step when you attempt to determine your "more of the same" behavior, or what you've been doing that hasn't been working. In addition to reviewing chapter eight, it may help to answer the following questions:

What single approach do I most commonly use to change undesirable behavior? Although your approach to a particular problem may vary, which is most typical?

How would the person whose behavior I'm trying to change describe what I have been doing lately to get him/her to change? Try to answer this in as few words as possible. Have you been nagging? Pursuing? Moping? Offering advice? And so on.

What words do I most often use to try to convince myself or others to change? If I were to ask those around you what you have been saying to persuade them to change, what would they say? Has it been, "You're really selfish," or "You are too strict," or "All you ever want to do is talk"? The point here is to try to imagine what others would say you have been saying.

Do a U-turn. Because you have become accustomed to doing the same old thing, this is usually the hardest step. Once you identify what you have been saying or doing to solve the problem, do the exact opposite. You must do it in a credible and sincere manner or it will not work. If your new behavior does not seem genuine, nothing will change.

Stick with it. Although it might be tempting to go back to your old ways as soon as you see positive results, don't. Keep in mind that the only reason you got better results is that you tried something completely different. If you go right back to doing the same old thing, you will once again be disappointed. Once the new changes have really taken hold, it will be possible to relax a bit.

Some people wonder whether doing a 180° is "manipulative," but it is no more so than persistently doing the same thing even though you know it won't work. Doing "more of the same," however "sincerely," is still an attempt to influence someone to change, usually to meet more of your needs—it's just an unsuccessful attempt, which is usually hurtful. When you do a 180°, you are also attempting to exert influence, but going about it in a more systematic way intended to abbreviate unhappy situations for everyone involved.

Years ago, before I completely understood how the "Do a 180°" method works, I found myself hesitant to suggest that a person do the opposite of what seems like the most reasonable response to a given situation. However, since the theory guiding me suggested that a dramatic turnabout in behavior would work, I started experimenting. The results were immediate and dramatic, and I was sold. In fact, in the testimonials I've received from readers of my last book, *Divorce Busting*, "Do a 180°" was frequently cited as the most helpful technique in the book.

It's helpful in thinking about this approach to keep in mind that relationships are like seesaws. The more one person does something, the less the other person does of it. When one person is very emotional, this allows the other to be very rational. When one person is a cleaning fanatic, the other person is often a slob. One person is a penny-pincher, the other a shopaholic. Optimists bring out the pessimism in others, whereas pessimists provoke optimism. We interact with and react to those around us and unwittingly behave in ways that create stability in these relationships. Doing a 180° upsets the usual balance and forces others to adjust their behavior to regain equilibrium. Take Molly and George in the example above.

For months, Molly eagerly waited for George to come home and spend time with her. She felt insecure about his frequent absences from home, but the more she pushed him to spend time with her, the more time he spent with his friends. When she suddenly began to behave more independently and encouraged him to stay away, the seesaw tipped the other way. No longer able to take Molly for granted, George became a bit less secure about her feelings. He began to experience some of what Molly had been feeling, which made him more sensitive to her needs. Doing a 180° creates the necessary space for the other person to see what you see, feel what you feel.

This technique is also useful for changing something about yourself that you don't like. Sometimes the very thing we do to help ourselves only makes things worse. For instance, most people who experience panic attacks or depression can attest that, the more they try to avoid feeling panic or depression, the more intense the feelings become. (On a more mundane level, have you ever noticed how much hungrier you feel the moment you decide to start a new diet?) These same people usually say, "Once I gave myself permission to feel depressed, I felt better," or "When I feel panicky, I am able to comfort myself by *not* fighting the panic. I tell myself, 'It's okay, I'll get through it,' and I take a deep breath." Sometimes, the harder we try, the more elusive our goal becomes.

Janice, a writer in her early thirties, complained of difficulty sleeping. She explained that she was able to fall asleep at 10:00 P.M. without any problem but, like clockwork, she would awaken at 2:00 A.M. and lie there tossing and turning for hours. Occasionally she would fall asleep again as it grew light, but there were many nights when she was not able to go back to sleep at all. This had been going on for several weeks. Not surprisingly, she reported being irritated and having a hard time concentrating at work.

When I asked her how she was trying to solve her sleep problem, she responded:

When I wake up I look at the clock, even though I know it is 2:00 A.M. Then I tell myself, "If I don't get back to sleep, I won't be able to edit that article tomorrow." I remind myself of the deadline and begin to feel more desperate and frustrated. I start to worry about my job performance and the adrenaline starts pumping. Once I get this far, I realize I've only made matters worse, so I try harder to quiet my mind, usually to no avail. Then, thinking if I were more physically comfortable I would be able to relax, I try shifting my position in the bed, but that doesn't work either. At this point, although I know it's destructive, I start to wonder what's wrong with me and feel so envious of people who get an uninterrupted night's sleep. The odd thing is that it seems, the harder I try to sleep, the less sleep I get.

Janice was absolutely right: trying harder to sleep was her "more of the same" behavior, which was precisely what she needed to change. I told her how to do a 180°.

If, after you go to sleep, you should awaken in the middle of the night, look at the clock and note the time. Many people awaken for short periods during the night, and this, in and of itself, is not a problem. If you are able to fall asleep within fifteen minutes, that's fine. If, however, after fifteen minutes you are still up, you are to get up out of bed and begin doing something productive. After fifteen minutes, you are no longer permitted to attempt sleep. You must get up and do something about which you've been procrastinating.

After some discussion, Janice proposed that she would either write or edit an article or do housework if she was not able to sleep.

Ten days later, she returned, reporting that, on the first night, when she found herself still awake after fifteen minutes, she arose and began to edit an article. Once it was completed, she felt greatly relieved, lay down, and quickly fell asleep. The second night she awoke as usual and reminded herself of her commitment to write or do housework if she was not able to fall asleep shortly. Almost magically, extreme fatigue overcame her and she dropped into a deep sleep. In the ten-day period, she had difficulty going back to sleep only one night, a marked improvement. What did she do? She got out of her warm bed to begin an article on insomnia.

In the weeks that followed, she only had an occasional restless night and felt tremendously relieved that she was sleeping once again. At our last session, she agreed that, if she ever found herself tossing and turning again at 2:00 A.M., she would write or get out the vacuum cleaner right away. A one year follow-up phone call discovered a well-rested Janice living in a less than perfectly clean home.

One final example. Richard sat down in my office and told me that he had been having tension headaches and stomachaches for years. Being a meticulous person, he had typed me a list of all the methods he had used over the years to rid himself of the tension, including relaxation tapes, exercise, warm baths, and so on. His most recent count of failed methods was seventy-nine. After careful review, it became clear to me that, although the methods he used varied to some degree, they all fell under the same general category—strategies for eliminating tension.

At first I tried to help him figure out whether any of his attempts had worked at all, but when he said, "No, they only made things worse," I knew it was time to do a 180°. I said:

> Richard, you have told me that, the more you try to relax, the more tense you feel. This might sound strange, but I think that stress is your body's way of trying to tell you something. However, since you keep fighting off the stress, the message your body is sending never gets fully transmitted. Therefore, you need to try something different.
>
> After you get home from work and have dinner, you should find a quiet room where you can get comfortable in a chair. Dim the lights, close your eyes, and give yourself permission to feel the tension. As you feel the uncomfortable feelings in your stomach or in your head, notice what you are thinking. See if you can decipher what it is that your body has been trying to teach you. Don't censor thoughts and feelings, just allow the tension to come. In the coming weeks, do this twice each week, for periods of one half-hour each.

Somewhat confused by my suggestion, Richard agreed and left the session.

He returned two weeks later and reported that he had had a hard time following through with my suggestion. The first time he sat down, he noticed himself getting tense, but "the more I tried to keep the tension, the less tension I felt." He said that he sat there for the full half-hour but his mind wandered and he noticed that he was not able to sustain the uncomfortable feelings. The second time he sat down, he reported even greater difficulty experiencing the feelings of tension, and he decided to stop before the half-hour was over. In the time that remained between sessions, he felt no need to set aside another half-hour to contemplate his body's message.

Upon hearing his good news, I told him that whatever he was doing was working, but if he found himself feeling tense again, he should set aside time in the evening to explore the feelings in greater depth. After two follow-up sessions, he reported feeling better than ever and stopped coming for therapy.

Many people worry that doing a 180° will make matters worse. A man worries that he will lose his estranged wife altogether if he stops pursuing her, because she will think he is no longer interested. A parent who has been nagging a child to eat fears the child will become undernourished if she suggests he refrain from eating. A sales manager fears she will only encourage an unhappy customer to make outrageous claims if she acknowledges his initial complaints as legitimate. It's normal to distrust a method that defies logic and habit, but such caution is misplaced. If what you have been doing isn't working, your hopelessness and the persistence of the problem are undoubtedly making matters worse. Doing a 180° requires a leap of faith, but when you think about it, so does doing more of the same.

Chapter Eleven

Easier Done Than Said

How MANY TIMES have you heard yourself say, "I talk until I'm blue in the face," or "If I've told you once, I've told you a thousand times"? Think about it for a minute. Doesn't it seem ridiculous that anyone would do that much talking with no positive results? Yet we all fall victim to the talking trap. We just assume that, if we verbalize our thoughts, feelings, and desires, other people will feel empathy and comply with our wishes. Sometimes things work out that way, but when they don't and we keep yakking, we start to sound like a broken record. I don't know about you; when I hear a broken record, I like to tune it out or turn it off. If you find yourself saying the same thing over and over and over, chances are the other person is no longer listening. When this happens, it's time to stop talking and start taking action.

My daughter, Danielle, had the annoying habit of leaving her boom box playing in her room twenty-four hours a day, whether she was there to hear it or not. My electric bills solved the age-old riddle, "If a tree falls in a forest but no one is there to hear it, is there a sound?" There is. Ask Con Ed. I asked her please to be more thoughtful and turn off her radio when she left her room. "Yes, Mom. I will." Famous last words. Gentle reminders were followed by a series of threats and lectures about waste. But apparently she tuned me out, and the radio played on.

One night when Danielle was staying over at a friend's house, I went into her room to shut her windows. Discovering the radio on, I promptly unplugged it and took it to my room. When Danielle returned, she asked, "Is there any reason my boom box is not in my room?" I replied,

"Yes, I was worried about the wear and tear on your radio since you leave it on all the time. I wanted to help you keep it in working condition by giving it a rest." Even though she promised to remember to turn it off if she could have it back, I told her I would give it a rest for another day or two. Mysteriously, after that, her memory vastly improved. And once again I marveled at how heavily I had relied on words to change her behavior, when actions are so much more effective.

The Talk Tactic

"Be not the slave of words."

—THOMAS CARLYLE

Why is it that we persist in believing that our most significant communications are verbal? Scientists estimate that fifty to a hundred pieces of information are exchanged each second when people are interacting. In fact, only a fraction of these exchanges happen verbally.[1] The rest are evidence that actions do indeed speak louder than words. For example:

- If you ask your mate, "How was work today?" and he says, "Fine," but has a gloomy expression on his face, what are you likely to do? If you are like most people, you would probably place more weight on his facial expression and continue to ask questions: "Did something go wrong today at work?" or "You don't look too happy, what happened?" His grimace speaks louder than his verbal response.
- If your friend fails to let you know she will be coming to your party late, your silence upon her arrival transmits a message of disapproval that she will read loud and clear.
- Although your supervisor frequently tells you that he values your contribution, during committee meetings he asks for input from and makes eye contact with everyone but you. His behavior makes you question the sincerity of his statements.
- You ask your neighbor whether she would be willing to watch your child for a couple of hours, and although she agrees, she takes a

couple of extra seconds to respond. You wonder if you are imposing on her, not because of what she said but because of what she didn't say.

- You see someone at a dance to whom you are attracted. She approaches you and starts talking about the music the band is playing. Although you talk about the band for some time, you are acutely aware that much more is being communicated than a mutual interest in music. The real message is, "I'd like to get to know you."
- A close relative fails to call you on your birthday, although she knows you are sentimental about birthdays. You are convinced that she has made a definitive statement about your relationship though no words have been exchanged.

As you think about it, you can see that we often make stronger impressions on others through our nonverbal behavior than with words. In no area is this more painfully obvious than in parenting. Children watch and mimic our behavior much more readily than they listen to our words. In fact, research substantiates the wisdom of the adage "Practice what you preach" when dealing with kids.

In an experiment, children were given gift certificates for playing a miniature bowling game. They then observed adults in one of four conditions: those who donated their certificates to poor children and discussed the importance of generosity; those who didn't donate but discussed the importance of generosity; those who donated and discussed the importance of taking care of oneself; or those who didn't donate and discussed the importance of taking care of oneself. When the children were offered an opportunity to donate their certificates, it was clear that the children were more likely to heed the adults' actions than their words. That is, if the adult preached generosity but did not donate, the children imitated the behavior and also did not donate. If the adult preached selfishness but donated, the children were more likely to donate.[2]

Brenda learned firsthand how acute children's hearing is when it comes to actions. She was at wits' end with her son Jason, who was argumentative at home and failing school. Brenda believed that she had tried everything. She had reasoned with him ad nauseam about the virtues of hard work in school and the importance of respect at home, without producing any change in his behavior. So she decided to try something new.

Brenda pondered what she needed to do to get through to Jason. "It would really bother him," she concluded, "if I went to school to find out more about the problem. It would make him feel uncomfortable." We talked about her idea, and by the end of our discussion, she had a plan. She would tell Jason that she just couldn't understand why he was having so much trouble in school, and that she had decided that the only way for her to get a handle on the situation was to join him there.

When she told Jason her plan, he clearly didn't take her seriously. A week later, when he got in trouble with a teacher, Brenda called the principal to get permission to visit. She told him that she intended to spend the whole day with Jason, accompanying him to all of his activities. The principal thought it was a great idea.

I asked Brenda how it went. She said:

Last Thursday was Open House at the junior high. Instead of meeting with Jason's teachers, I met with his sister's teachers. Jason assumed I didn't attend his parent-teacher conferences because I already knew he was doing badly. He seemed quite relieved, but his relief was short-lived.

The next day, I beat the school bus to school and was sitting in Jason's classroom when he arrived. Jason entered the room, headed straight for me and in a hushed tone asked, "What are you doing here?" I told him, "Today is Open House." He told me, "You made a mistake, Mom. You should have been here yesterday." But, much to his horror, I responded, "Since I spent the whole day yesterday with your sister, I thought I'd give you your own private Open House day."

Brenda reported that Jason turned green and returned to his desk. All of his friends came over to her to say hello and ask why she had come to school. Jason was mortified. However, after the initial shock, Jason did all of his work and volunteered in classroom discussions. Brenda assumed he was on his best behavior in the hopes that she would go home, but she didn't allow his shining performance to dissuade her from following him around all day. She accompanied him in the halls, to recess, and even to a football coaching session in the boys' locker room. What perseverance! That evening, Jason's older brother loudly announced, "The entire junior high knows about Mom coming to school." When Jason winced, Brenda felt certain she had finally discovered something that would make a difference to him.

Three weeks later, Brenda updated me about the results of her day in school. She said that Jason was getting A's and B's in his classes, and that she had received a letter from his math teacher, complimenting him on his cooperativeness and hard work. Brenda felt confident that, if Jason started to slip again, all she had to do was mention the possibility of her returning to school and the problem would be solved. Because the results of her taking action had been so immediate and dramatic, Brenda promised herself she would never rely on "talking sense" to Jason again.

Parents aren't the only ones who falter when they emphasize the impact of words as compared with actions. Women also tend to overestimate the effectiveness of words with their mates. Much has been written in recent years about gender differences in communication styles, but an in-depth exploration of these differences is beyond the scope of this book. I will, however, mention one major difference between most men and women that wreaks havoc in their lives.

Women tend to derive a sense of closeness from verbal contact. They love talking about personal feelings and revealing intimate thoughts, and they feel strongly connected to others who do the same. Women also enjoy analyzing relationships, focusing on the nuances of how people interact. "Working on the relationship" via verbal communication is a favorite pastime. The problem is that men generally don't derive the same feelings of satisfaction from talking that women do, and when they do talk, they prefer to steer clear of emotionally charged topics. Business, politics, sports, cars, and so on are preferred conversation subjects. The differences between men and women are never more apparent than after stormy conversations about relationship issues: women feel relieved to have aired feelings, men feel discombobulated.

Most men do not comprehend what a woman feels about verbal interaction. But, conversely, most women do not fully appreciate the ways in which men go about achieving closeness with other people. Think about it for a moment. If a women wants to feel close to another woman, she might call her up and invite her to lunch so they can talk. When men desire closeness with other men, they're more likely to do a "male-bonding thing"—engage in team sports, play golf together, go hunting or fishing, or meet after work for a drink during which talk remains superficial. By and large, men are more action-oriented. If they feel stressed, instead of seeking out a confidant, they are more likely to go to the health club to work out. If they need reassurance from their mate,

they're more likely to want to make love than to have a tête-à-tête about their insecurities. Women talk, men act. These differences in communication styles become a problem when women rely strictly on verbal interaction to inform men of their needs.

I knew a woman who was extremely devoted to improving her relationship with her husband. Their problem? "We just don't communicate. We don't spend enough time together. He always wants to be off doing something else." She tried telling him of her disappointment many times: "You never want to spend time with me," or "Why can't you be more like Sue's husband, who enjoys being with his family?" But whenever she mentioned the subject, they ended up arguing.

She decided to attend a course in building communication skills. She learned the importance of using nonblaming "I-messages" (saying, for example, "I feel hurt when you choose your friends over me" rather than "You are selfish and inconsiderate when you run off with your friends") and reflecting back what her husband said to assure him that she had heard. She practiced these and other techniques with a partner in the class until she felt confident that she had mastered them. Now, she was sure, she held the key to solving their communication problems.

She soon had a chance to give her new strategies a whirl. But she was greatly puzzled by the fact that, despite her use of "I-messages" and reflective listening, her discussions with her husband always ended unpleasantly. Her new communication techniques weren't working. Finally, out of total frustration, she confronted her husband and asked whether he had noticed a change in her. He said that he hadn't and added, "All you ever want to do is to talk about problems. I'm sick of talking about problems." Apparently, changing *how* she phrased things was not enough of a difference. Since he was tired of talking about their relationship, there was not much she could *say* that would make him feel she had changed.

Perhaps she could take a lesson from a seventy-year-old woman. She had been married to the same man for forty-seven years, and for forty-seven years he had annoyed her with his habit of sitting down to meals with his shirt off. She consistently explained that she found his behavior distasteful and wished he would take her feelings into consideration. But, in forty-seven years of reasoning, he never complied.

One day, she made her usual elaborate Sunday breakfast and invited him to sit down. As soon as he did (half naked, of course), she excused herself from the table, went into the bathroom, and returned to the table without her blouse and bra. Her husband turned white, left the table, put his shirt on, and never bellied up to the table half clothed again.

This spirited woman succeeded with action where decades of verbal requests had fallen upon deaf ears. In fact, pretending that your partner is deaf and trying to imagine how you might signal your message through actions rather than words is a worthwhile exercise.

Bonnie and Bill argued incessantly about the stairs leading to the back door of their house, which were in desperate need of repair. Bonnie begged, pleaded, ranted, and raved to Bill about fixing them, but he never seemed to have the time to do anything about it. When she considered hiring a carpenter, Bill insisted that it would be a waste of money. So the stairs remained a constant source of contention.

Bonnie decided to try a different strategy, since reasoning with him clearly wasn't working. On a warm summer day, she got out all the tools necessary to work on the stairs and began to tackle the job herself, although she didn't really know what she was doing. To make sure Bill heard her, she hammered as loudly as she could. Curious to discover the cause of the commotion, Bill came out on the back porch, where he saw that Bonnie had taken matters into her own hands. Bonnie had banked on Bill's disapproving of her carpentry and design decisions, and she was right. After thirty seconds of watching her, Bill said, "Here, give me that hammer," and took over the project. Delighted that her strategy had worked, she smiled to herself and went into the house to make some lemonade.

There's no doubt that a simple, straightforward discussion is the best way to resolve differences between people, and you should always try that first. But if talking hasn't worked, don't assume that you can't get people to change. They will probably hear your behavior better than your words. Here's how some other people succeeded by translating their requests for change into action.

Hal took a different back-door approach. His three boys had a terrible habit of leaving the back door unlocked. There had been several recent break-ins in an adjacent neighborhood, and Hal had asked his sons repeatedly to remember to lock the door, but to no avail. One night he even called a meeting to stress the urgency of his request, but when he came home from work the next night, he found the door wide open. "Time for a new strategy," he thought to himself.

Several days later, his youngest son wanted to play softball but couldn't find his mitt. After looking for it for what seemed like hours, the boy asked, "Where's my mitt? I can't find it," and Hal said, "Hm, I noticed the back door unlocked today. I wonder if the robber stole it." He offered no further explanation or argument, nor did he help look for the mitt. The next day, the oldest son was missing his favorite jeans. Frantic, he asked Hal if he knew where they were. Hal said, "The more I think about it, the more I believe we really did have a robber the other day. I know I saw the door open." Again, he offered no argument or further discussion. The boys noticed that for some strange reason the "robber" had been quite selective, choosing only those items the boys really valued. Miraculously, after several days, Hal began to find the door locked when he came home from work. In fact, the boys' memory improved markedly for quite some time. When they began to slip several months later, their possessions mysteriously disappeared again, which quickly stimulated their memories.

Sandy grew weary of having her teenage son leaving his shoes around the house. Although she constantly reminded him not to, he never heeded her request. Eventually, she stopped reminding him and started threatening to withdraw privileges, but that didn't work either. One day when he was out, she found a third pair of shoes on the landing. On impulse, she picked them up and threw them down the laundry chute. She decided that, from then on, instead of getting upset, she would just throw his shoes down the chute.

When her son came home, he couldn't find his shoes, so he asked his mother if she knew where they were. She informed him of her decision. He grunted and headed into the basement to retrieve them. She stuck to her decision, and after several trips to the basement, his memory seemed to improve. Several weeks later, though, she found a pair of his shoes in the living room, and down the chute they went. When he returned from school, she noticed him looking for his shoes where he had left them. Then, as if a light bulb had gone off in his head, he started toward the basement door, muttering, "I know, they're in the basement." Stray shoes were no longer a problem, and she didn't have to nag.

A woman in the small town where I live won an award for her devotion to children. Over the years, she had taken in more than a thousand foster children. She even appeared on the television show *Real People*. Since she often had several teenagers living in her home at one time, she had to be quite creative in managing them. A story appeared in the local newspaper describing one of her more unorthodox approaches to dealing with them.

Like Sandy, she had tried rational and irrational ways of convincing several teenage girls in her care to put their dirty underwear in the laundry basket rather than leaving it lying around. After weeks without their compliance, she took matters into her own hands. One day when they were in school, she gathered up all of their bras and underpants, waited for a gust of wind, and threw them out a second-story window. The lingerie landed in a nearby tree.

When the girls returned from school to find their underwear decorating the tree, they were mortified. They ran to get a ladder from the garage to recoup their belongings. From that day on, for some strange reason, they became markedly more conscientious about getting their underwear into the laundry basket.

Sometimes people tell me they have a hard time thinking "action," but experience has taught me that most people have an inkling as to what they might do in place of talking—they just haven't tried it yet. Let that seventy-year-old woman be your inspiration. A colleague of mine used to prod parents into thinking "action" rather than talking by insisting that they participate in a "game" called After Twice, There's a Price. The rules of the game were simple: After telling children to do something one time, parents are permitted to give their children one more verbal reminder. However, they must say, "This is the second reminder." After that, *anything* but a verbal reminder is fair play. If a parent forgets and reminds the child verbally again, he or she must pay the child a dollar for each additional reminder.

No matter what you decide to do to stop talking and start taking action, do it. Remember, stop trying to figure out how you might vary what you say, since variations in *how* you say something may not be different enough to be perceived as being different. From another person's perspective, "If it looks like a duck, walks like a duck, quacks like a duck, it is a duck."

Chapter Twelve

Smart Talk

BY NOW, IT should be perfectly clear that one of the most effective strategies for influencing other people is to do less talking and take action. Some forms of verbal communication are more persuasive than others, however. I am not referring to the kinds of principles people learn when they take communication-skills courses, such as using "I-messages." Although practicing the improved verbal skills gleaned from these courses can really make a difference for some people, the techniques you are about to learn are generally not covered in the curriculum. They would be much more familiar to people in the business world who have used similar tools for years.

Power Packaging

When Person A wants Person B to change is some way, Person A makes a request. If it isn't honored, the request usually turns into a demand. As you undoubtedly already know, demands typically yield resistance, because nobody likes to be told what to do. What generally follows are dead-end arguments about the validity of the request/demand. Each person then decides that the other person's position is unreasonable, and nothing changes. Some of the world's best ideas are disregarded or rebuffed in this way—not because they are irrelevant, invalid, unfair, or foolish, but because they aren't framed or packaged properly. Here's an example.

Susan and Cal's marriage of twenty years is a good example of how opposites attract. Susan is an extremely sociable, outgoing person. Give her a couple of close friends and a good conversation, and she's set for the evening. Cal, on the other hand, is more of a loner. He does enjoy an occasional party or dinner engagement, but, except for the time he spends with Susan, he has no strong need to socialize with other people and would rather clean the house than make small talk at a large gathering. Give Cal a good novel, a juicy video, or a solo hike in the woods and he is delighted. Amazing they've lasted so long, huh?

When I met Susan, she explained that over the years she had wished Cal would learn to share her desire to socialize. She understood that they were very different people, but she felt that Cal could put himself out a little more to broaden their circle of friends. Although she had tried in many different ways to convince him that a more active social life would be beneficial, so far she had failed to discover the key to changing his mind. One of her tactics was to tell him, "You would enjoy yourself if you'd give it a try," but Cal remained unconvinced. She also tried to persuade him that being with other people would benefit his emotional and psychological development, but Cal wasn't buying that either. When all else failed, Susan relied on the old guilt trip: "I can't see why, even if you don't feel like it, you couldn't do it to please me." But Cal's desire to shield himself from unrewarding social experiences was stronger than his need to make Susan happy, so her appeal was denied. Eventually, Cal settled into deterring Susan from "pressuring" him by saying, "Look, I'm not stopping you from doing what you want. If you want to be with other people, then go do it. Just do me a favor and leave me out of it." This was not the ending for which Susan had been hoping.

But let's take another look at the arguments Susan offered Cal:

"You would enjoy yourself if you'd give it a try." Here Susan is trying to convince Cal that being with other people would be fun for him, that once he immersed himself in a social situation he would discover that he liked it. Susan doesn't realize that, because Cal does not have a strong need to be with others, he is not motivated to overcome his initial discomfort. Therefore, this lure isn't appealing to him.

"It would be good for you." The problem with this approach is that Susan doesn't take into account that Cal doesn't feel he is operating at a deficit. He believes he is a fully functioning human being who just happens to have needs different from Susan's. Odd as it may seem to her, he does not aspire to be more like her. He is quite content with himself the way he is.

"Do it to please me." Although Cal likes to please Susan, he does so in ways that are more comfortable to him. In Cal's mind, it isn't necessary that he *love* everything he does for Susan, but it's important to him that he not dread it either. Although Cal is considerate of Susan's feelings, he is not willing to please her at his expense.

As we discussed the situation, it became clear to Susan why her approach to Cal hadn't been very effective. She saw that her arguments were based on her way of seeing the world, not his. Because she hadn't taken into account what motivates or repels Cal, none of her rationales for his changing were particularly powerful. She was frustrated that she hadn't found a way to overcome his reticence to socialize because she had recently met a couple whom she really liked, and she was confident that, if he just gave it a chance, Cal would like them, too. They had a great deal in common—the women were both teachers, and the men were both in the medical profession.

I suggested that she needed a "hook," a way of enticing Cal. "What motivates him?" I asked. "What interests him? How does he prioritize his time?" She was quick to tell me that one of the most important aspects of Cal's life was his work. Medicine fascinated him, and he spent much of his time off reading professional journals. "Perfect," I thought and sent her home with an assignment: "Find out more about the other man's interests and accomplishments in the field of medicine. When you have more specific information, mention in an offhand way that you met some really interesting people. Tell him about this man's endeavors and then drop the conversation. Wait a few days and give him a few more pieces of information about this man. Mention that he expressed some interest in getting together, but say nothing more. Once again, wait a few days and ask Cal if he has any interest in hearing more about this man's research. See what happens."

Susan followed my suggestions and reported that she was successful in piquing Cal's interest. Spontaneously, he asked Susan to set up a dinner date. Susan stopped herself from showing too much interest or even commenting that it might be fun. She acted as if she were doing him a favor to set up the date. The evening for their rendezvous arrived, and a great time was had by all. Cal and his new friend did talk shop for a while, but most of the conversation was not work-related. Susan was right—it was a foursome meant to be. After a long goodbye, *Cal* suggested that they get together again sometime soon. On the car ride home, Susan resisted the temptation to say, "I told you so."

Susan finally won Cal over by doing something every experienced salesperson does: appealing to the buyer not simply on the merits of the product, but by tuning the sales pitch to the personality, interests, needs, and motivations of the buyer. Imagine a realtor lauding the local school system to a couple, only to discover that they are childless and plan to remain that way. As in sales, in order to persuade someone in a particular direction, you need to frame your request so that it strikes him as a deal he can't refuse. Etymologically, the word "persuade" comes from a Latin word meaning "to sweeten." We persuade someone by highlighting the positive outcomes—by sweetening the deal.

> *How* we put something may be persuasive to one person but not to another. For example, both the bon vivant and the economy-minded person may buy a Rolls Royce, but for obviously different reasons—the bon vivant because of the distinctiveness and status of the car; the other because the engineering and durability of the car can save him money in the long run. Because of these differences in appeal, the salesman needs to make his sales talk different for each customer. How he frames his sales talk can make the difference between customer acceptance or rejection.
>
> . . . When the Rolls Royce salesman confronted by the economy-minded customer emphasizes the engineering and durability of the car, he is enlisting the values ("position") of the customer toward buying it. If, instead, he extolled its virtue as a status symbol, he would fail to tap the customer's own momentum and would actively drive him away; he would not be talking the customer's "language."[1]

Nancy and Phil were sitting on the edge of their chairs in my office, filled with anxiety over their nine-year-old daughter, Jill. "We're here,"

they said, "because we are concerned about Jill. Her teacher suggested
we come for counseling because she is the most insecure little girl she
has ever seen." I asked her what they thought the teacher meant by this,
and they repeated what she had told them:

> Jill is a perfectionist. She has to get perfect grades on everything. If she
> doesn't get a perfect score, she gets incredibly upset and pouts. She must
> have such feelings of low self-esteem to react this way. Also, when I give
> instructions to the whole class about doing a task, to avoid doing anything
> incorrectly, she continually raises her hand, interrupting to ask questions
> about the instructions. But I dare not discipline her in front of the class
> for fear that I will hurt her self-concept even more. Instead, I patiently
> respond to her questions. When the class gets a test, I always hand hers
> back before I grade it so that she can check for mistakes. I know how
> upset she is when she gets something wrong.

Phil and Nancy had observed other signs of Jill's shaky emotional
state. She had persistent stomachaches, for which her family doctor
could find no physiological cause; the consensus of several specialists
was that her symptoms were "psychological" in nature. The doctor also
suggested that Jill's intensifying allergies were stress-related.

When asked what they were hoping to achieve from the counseling
sessions, Nancy and Phil said, "We want Jill to feel better about herself." Nancy told me that she thought Jill's teacher might be right: that
many of Jill's problems were due to her lack of self-confidence. To
combat this at home, Nancy and Phil bent over backward to make sure
they never reprimanded Jill, even when she misbehaved. Jill's sister, on
the other hand, was expected to follow all of the family rules and behave
maturely. Jill was soft-spoken, and her parents said that everyone became silent whenever she talked at the dinner table, to encourage her to
join in the conversation. Even when she was interrupting, no one commented, for fear of intimidating her.

Now that you know more about Jill's problems and how she was
treated by her teacher and her parents, what's your impression? I know
precisely what I was thinking as I listened to this story: "Boy, this little
girl sounds spoiled. She always gets her way. There are no real expectations of her at home or at school. Unlike the other children in her class
or her older sister at home, she gets treated with kid gloves." I was

convinced that Jill's problems could be resolved if those around her started setting some limits for her. I felt certain that she would benefit from some firm consequences when she interrupted her teacher or behaved inappropriately when things didn't go her way. The bottom line was, I believed that Jill was suffering from overindulgence on the part of her parents and her teacher.

But I was careful not to tell Nancy and Phil exactly what I was thinking. They were so certain that Jill's ego was damaged in some way that, from their point of view, coddling her was the only logical response. Remember: how people explain the cause of the problem to themselves dictates the actions they will or will not be willing to take in order to solve it.

As long as her parents believed that Jill was an insecure child who must be protected, telling them that she needed firmness would have been worse than ineffective. They would have felt that I did not appreciate the seriousness of Jill's condition and, by implication, that I was criticizing them as parents. My challenge was to package the suggestion that Phil and Nancy take a firmer stand with Jill in a way that made sense to them, given their concerns. Here's what I told them:

> I want you to know that I share your concern about Jill. She is obviously a very sensitive little girl who is overly concerned about how others judge her. It appears that she feels she doesn't measure up. But I've really given this situation some thought, and I question if we're not missing something crucial here. I wonder if, for some reason, all the tender loving care she has received at home and at school has backfired in a way.
>
> Let me explain. Since Jill is so intelligent, she must recognize the immense differences in how she is treated compared with her classmates or her older sister. I imagine she could be thinking that she requires special treatment because she simply can't function as well as the others. She has to wonder "What's wrong with me?" when she observes other people being handled less gingerly. Perhaps all the extra attention has inadvertently made things worse for Jill, because she really just wants to be treated like her peers, with no special considerations. That would help her feel better about herself.

As I spoke, I watched Nancy and Phil carefully to gauge their reactions. I was uncertain whether they would accept this new way of thinking about Jill and didn't want to offend them. But when I finished speaking, Nancy said, "You know, I've been wondering about that myself. In fact, I was thinking about going to school and telling her teacher to just treat Jill like a regular kid. Her teacher is very nice, but I think she has gone too far in making exceptions for Jill. Michele, you have reconfirmed what I have suspected recently." Phil nodded in agreement.

Once I saw that Nancy and Phil were on my wavelength, I continued, "It's great that you are planning to talk to Jill's teacher. In addition, I wonder what the two of you would change if you were to treat her like 'an average kid' at home in order to help raise her self-esteem." Without a moment's hesitation, Phil and Nancy rattled off a long list of what they would do. Nancy began, "Every night, when I put her to bed, we read together and then I ask her what went wrong during her day to give her the opportunity to share bad feelings. I guess I could ask her about the things that went well." Phil added that, any time Jill was quiet, they both immediately questioned her about why she was feeling so sad. As he thought about this, he recognized that he was quiet on many occasions without feeling sadness. He proposed that from now on, they not assume Jill's silence signaled sadness, and therefore not question her about her feelings.

Nancy also told me that she spent an inordinate amount of time reassuring Jill that she was smart when she got even one answer wrong on a test. But the more she reassured Jill, the more Jill put herself down. When I asked her how she might respond if her other daughter behaved similarly, she said, "That's easy. Since I know she feels confident, I would just tease her about it and say, 'Yeah, that's right. Why didn't you get a perfect score? Couldn't you do any better than that?' When I do that, we laugh and she shrugs the whole thing off. I guess I could try that with Jill."

I sent Phil and Nancy home with an assignment: "For the next week, treat Jill as if she can handle her life like an average kid and see whether this improves her self-esteem." Two or three weeks later, they announced that they didn't need to come anymore, because they had "gotten the old Jill back." She was no longer experiencing any physiological symptoms, she behaved more appropriately in school and at home, and she had started playing with her friends again. Phil brought in a photograph of Jill to show me how the "twinkle in her eyes" had returned and told me how thrilled he was to see the improvements. The teacher also called to talk about the changes she observed in Jill in school.

What's the lesson in all of this? Good solutions come in smart packages. There was a time in my career (B.S.—Before Smart) when I didn't know this lesson. Back then, when a couple such as Phil and Nancy shared their perspectives, I openly informed them that they were in error and told them what they needed to do to correct their ways. Occasionally it worked, but most of the time people got defensive. When they became defensive, I thought it incumbent upon me to "teach" them (whether they asked for it or not) the basic principles of child development that I had learned in school. But most of my clients were unimpressed with my lectures and continued to discount my suggestions. The more they disagreed, the more convinced I was that they lacked pertinent information, and so I tried again and again to enlighten them. I left many sessions exhausted and frustrated by my inability to make a dent in their problems.

Understanding the importance of careful packaging has made my life considerably easier. Instead of forcing people to see things my way, I force myself to see things their way, and then I suggest an alternative way of handling a situation based on their perspective. Once they feel understood, they are less likely to resist. It is now my assumption that most people do what they do because it is the most logical alternative given the way they see things, and I deliberately avoid approaches that, from their perspective, would seem irrational or downright dangerous.

I remember a mother whose three-year-old son had recurring nightmares about a tiger coming into his room to eat him. Each night, he awoke crying hysterically, and his mother would assure him that the tiger was only a dream and "nothing to be afraid of." Her logic went in one ear and out the other, and he remained inconsolable.

One night, out of sheer desperation, she tried a totally different approach. She emptied an old creme-rinse spray bottle and filled it with water. Then she handed the bottle to her son and said, "Stevie, this is tiger spray. It is very powerful. When you spray the tiger, it can't hurt you. Keep it by the side of your bed, and if you need it, just spray the tiger." Stevie never had the tiger nightmare again.

If you have been unsuccessfully trying to convince someone to make a change, chances are it is because you haven't listened carefully enough to their reasons for not changing. Instead of becoming more adamant in your efforts to persuade, start from the beginning and follow these steps:

1. Make certain you completely understand the other person's point of view even if you don't agree with it.
2. Identify in your own mind the target behavior (the specific behavioral change) you would like the other person to make.
3. Acknowledge the other person's position and feelings—it won't kill you. For example, say, "I see what you mean. You are telling me (repeat the person's message)," or "I can understand how you feel that way."
4. Frame the change you are suggesting so that it is consistent with that position and those feelings.

Several years ago, I was working with a couple who, after ten years of marriage, were inches from divorcing. It was a second marriage for both of them. Stu's three children from a previous marriage were grown. Marge's son, Keith, was a senior in high school, and his father had died. Part of the reason Marge had married Stu was to give Keith a father, but Stu had never fulfilled this dream; over the years, he had interacted only minimally with Keith. He believed that he was incapable of having an intimate relationship with a male child, citing as evidence the fact that he was much closer to his daughter than to his own sons. Despite his reasoning, Marge felt hurt, disappointed, and angry, so much so that, at the time they began counseling, she was fairly convinced the marriage was over.

Stu couldn't understand Marge's intense longing for a father for Keith. He felt that he was a good provider and an extremely attentive husband. He loved spending time with Marge and going on romantic weekend getaways. "If we could be alone more often," he said, "our marriage would be one of the best. But Marge always brings Keith into our marriage and puts distance between us." When I asked him what he meant by "distance," he told me that their sex life was sorely lacking. He felt that Marge refused to be physically close to him as a way of getting back at him for not having a better relationship with Keith.

From our sessions, I had a clear sense of what each of them wanted from the other and how they went about trying to get it. Marge had begun by expressing her hurt feelings to Stu, then had tried to get him to see how important it is for a boy to have a father and a male role model. When this didn't work, she tried to show Stu how he would benefit personally from overcoming his block about male-male relationships. When Stu remained unconvinced, she grew angry and let him know that he should at least be more sensitive to her needs. When this didn't work either, Marge gave up.

I decided to meet alone with Stu, whom I viewed as more willing to change. But while he professed to be very committed to making the marriage work, it had become clear to me that, if nothing improved between him and Keith, Marge was out the door. So I set about figuring out how to convince him to show more interest in Keith.

I reviewed in my own mind the arguments Marge had already tried: that it would help Keith, that it would help Stu to be a better person, that it would help Marge. I vowed not to repeat any of these ineffective strategies. Instead I asked myself, "What motivates Stu? What would he like to get out of this relationship?" I knew the answer immediately, and my approach to Stu became crystal-clear. He was deeply dissatisfied with their sexual relationship. Moreover, his belief that Marge was withholding affection because she was angry over his failure to nurture a relationship with Keith squelched any interest he might have had in doing so.

I predicted to Stu what I saw happening if nothing changed between Keith and him: Marge would leave. He agreed, but then politely repeated all of his explanations for why he couldn't change. Ignoring his response, I said, "Marge tells me that you often want to be alone with her and take her on romantic vacations. She says that you pay a great deal of attention to her, more than most husbands. You have told me that you miss the closeness with Marge that you feel when the two of you are intimate. You strike me as a real romantic."

I watched Stu closely to see if he was with me so far. "You are absolutely right. To this day, I still give her flowers on the date that we met. Marge would definitely agree that I am the more romantic of the two of us."

So far, so good, I thought. Then I continued:

For such a romantic, I'm surprised that you missed what I am about to tell you. To me it seems fairly obvious that if you were to pursue a relationship with Keith it would be like courting Marge. It would be better than a month's worth of roses. You would send her skyrocketing to the stars in terms of how she would feel about you. Your developing a relationship with Keith would consummate a dream Marge has had for years about this knight in white armor sweeping her off her feet by helping fill a void in Keith's life. She would be greatly enamored of the man who could love her son.

Again I watched Stu to see if he was understanding me. He was nodding, so I continued.

MWD: Have you ever heard the expression "If you scratch my back, I'll scratch yours?"

STU: Sure.

MWD: Well, as you begin to develop a relationship with Keith, I wonder whether Marge would feel closer to you and therefore want to be more intimate. Do you know what I mean?

STU: Yeah, I do.

MWD: Then let's spend the rest of the session figuring out what specific things you need to start doing with Keith to get Marge to notice. You can look at your new efforts with Keith as "foreplay."

Stu liked that idea and was off and running. Two weeks later, when Marge came for a session by herself, she reported that the most miraculous thing had happened: Stu was showing more interest in Keith and she was "eating it up." She felt much more optimistic about their marriage. Halfway into the session, she said, "A playfulness in our sexual relationship has returned. His kids are home from college, and everyone is wondering what Mom and Dad are doing back in the bedroom at three o'clock in the afternoon. I even found myself saying, 'Oh, darn, why does everyone have to be home? Why can't we be alone?' I haven't felt that in years!"

The moral of the story? Once Stu was presented with a package that showed him "what was in it for him" if he were to change, he was able to do so instantly, despite his supposed inability to bond with a boy.

Leading Questions

Here is another linguistic technique that will help you get the results you want.

Back in chapter seven, when we were discussing the importance of focusing on exceptions, you may recall that I asked you to identify what's different about the times when you are feeling better. Note that I didn't ask, "Are there times you feel better?" I presupposed that there *are* better times and worded my question accordingly. The syntax was no accident.

When I ask an angry mother, "Are there times when your son is co-operative?" I'm more likely to get a "not really" response than if I ask, "When is your son more cooperative?" This is what lawyers call a leading question. It establishes a premise—that her son is cooperative at times—and prompts her to scan her experiences with an eye to corroborating that premise. In therapy, the use of leading questions is an incredibly powerful tool. Those that presuppose that change is inevitable and that people have resources to solve their problems go a long way toward making those assumptions come true. Here are some examples:

"So, what's going well in your life this week?"
Presupposition: Things are going well.

"Who else in your life is noticing the improvement?"
Presupposition: There is improvement and other people are noticing.

"When you son threw a temper tantrum this week, how did you handle it more effectively than last week?"
Presupposition: You responded to the tantrum and did so in a more constructive manner than in the past.

"In what ways will you show your appreciation when your daughter puts more effort into school?"
Presupposition: Your daughter will put more effort into school and you will show appreciation.

"How will becoming punctual for work help you to feel better about yourself?"
Presupposition: You will become punctual and will feel better about yourself.

"In what ways will reasoning with your husband versus screaming at him help him to react more calmly to you?"
Presupposition: You will reason with your husband and he will respond more calmly.

"What did you do to let your boss know that his behavior was unacceptable?"
Presupposition: His behavior was unacceptable and you took some action to let him know that.

But leading questions can be extremely potent outside the therapy room as well. Salespeople use them all the time. For example, McDonald's employees ask, "What would you like to drink with that?" instead of "Do you want something to drink?" and thereby increase their chances of a beverage sale.

You can learn to use leading questions to "sell" people on changes in their behavior. Imagine, for example, that you have an employee who procrastinates a lot. Instead of demanding, "When are you going to learn to get your work done on time?" you can ask, "How will becoming more task-oriented simplify your life?" To a sick child who is reluctant to take her medicine, you can say, "After you take your medicine, do you want to watch some television?" instead of "Are you willing to take your medicine?" To a tightwad husband, ask, "Which dress do you think I should get?" rather than "Do you think I should buy this dress?"

The key to constructing leading questions is simple: Keep your questions open-ended; avoid those that allow for a "yes" or "no" response. Identify the message you wish to convey in your question and make sure the wording of the question reflects your assumption. Let's say that you want your friend to go to the health club with you more often. The message you want to deliver is that you *expect* her to be there. Stay clear of asking, "Are you going to go to the health club?"—which indicates your uncertainty that she will come. Your questions must suggest that it isn't a matter of *if* she will join you, it's simply a matter of when, where, how, or with whom. Here are some examples of the kinds of questions you could ask that would get your message across:

"Which day will be best to meet you at the club?"
"Which workout machines are you going to use on Tuesday?"

"Who are you going to get to watch your kids when you go with me to the club today?"

"Do you want to meet at the club or do you want me to pick you up?"

The techniques that follow are simply variations on leading questions.

The Illusion of Choice

As you already know, people usually balk when they feel you are making demands or giving orders, since no one likes being told what to do. So how do you suggest that someone take particular action but at the same time make the person feel the choice is his or hers?

My son, Zach, often gets so wrapped up in what he is doing in the evening that he resists when I suggest that he take a bath before bed. "Not now, Mom," and "I took one yesterday," are phrases that often echo from his bedroom. When I hear these responses, I remind myself what worked with him when he was younger. Instead of asking whether he is ready for his bath or telling him it is bath time, sure-fire precipitants of more "not now" responses, I ask whether he wants a warm bath or a cool one. He always prefers a warm bath and never questions my assumption—that *not* taking a bath is not an option. The obvious advantage of this approach is that it prevents Zach from making no choice or choosing an option with which I won't be pleased. Many parents use this technique instinctively:

"Do you want to clean your room before or after dinner?"

"Would you prefer a large or small serving of cauliflower?"

"Would you rather do the dishes or vacuum?"

"I know you have a big exam next week. Do you want to study for it all today or do half the chapter today and half tomorrow?"

"Do you want to do your homework at the dining-room table or in your room?"

"Would you rather practice the piano before or after *The Simpsons* is on?"

Get the idea? Creating choices you can live with helps children to feel in control of lives.

But this method works with adults, too. Again, McDonald's knows the principle all too well. Just pull up to the drive-through and place your order. A cheery voice repeats what you said and adds, "Do you want medium or large fries with that?" In a trancelike stupor, you say, "Medium, please." It isn't until the fries are half gone that you remember you hadn't intended to order any fries at all.

The "alternative-choice" close sales technique originated in the 1930s as the "Wheeler Which," named after Elmer Wheeler, a sales trainer who devised a means for the Walgreen Drug Company to profit from their purchase of 800 dozen eggs. Wheeler suggested to clerks that when a customer asked for a malted milk at the Walgreen fountain, the clerk should hold up two eggs, smile, and ask, "One egg or two?" Although customers had not previously even considered having eggs in their malteds, the vast majority replied "One egg." All 800 dozen eggs were sold within one week—at a profit.[2]

Here are some other examples:

"Which of these two lots would best meet your needs?" *not* "Are you interested in purchasing a lot?"

"Would you prefer my getting tickets for the theatre on Friday or would you rather just go out for dinner?" *not* "Do you want to do something on Friday?"

"I'd like to get together with you. Would you prefer meeting this week or next?" *not* "Would you be willing to get together with me?"

"I want to throw a party. Which weekend would be best?" *not* "Is it okay if we throw a party?"

"Do you think you'll stop smoking gradually or all at once?" *not* "Will you ever want to stop smoking?"

"Would it be more convenient for you to help me clean out these closets on Thursday or Friday?" *not* "Will you ever help me clean the closets?"

If you haven't tried this indirect method of influencing others, try it as an experiment and see what happens. Even if the other person is aware of the hidden assumption in your question, you are still likely to get a more cooperative response than if you put the question directly. It's worth a shot.

Where There's a Will, There's a Way

Brandy and Denny brought sixteen-year-old Robert to see me because he had cut so many classes that the principal had promised to suspend him if he cut one more. Although his parents wanted to talk about why he cut classes, what he didn't like about school, the friends he hung out with, and his bad attitude in general, I had other plans.

Instead of wondering why Robert was having trouble staying in school, a discussion that would have focused primarily on the past, I assumed that he would no longer cut class and began to help him envision his life without the problem. I did so by using leading questions that presupposed the inevitability of his changing. I demonstrated my confidence in his desire to change by using the future tense and the words "will" and "when" rather than "if" or "whether." Here is a dialogue that occurred shortly after the session began:

MWD: Which one of your teachers will be most surprised when you are attending all the time?
ROBERT: Probably my history teacher.
MWD: Really? He's gonna be shocked?

Notice that I did not ask, "Which one of your teachers *would* be most surprised *if you were* to go to school full-time?" As you review the ensuing conversation, note that, whenever possible, I continue to assume by my language that Robert *will* go to school regularly. I ask who *will* be most surprised, how his friends and relatives *will* react, and how else his life *will* change—not *whether* or *if*. And by answering my questions, Robert tacitly agrees with my presupposition that he will be in school full-time.

BRANDY: Will he know your name? (Laughter)
MWD: More shocked than your principal?
ROBERT: The principal will be surprised that I am not in his office.
MWD: Yeah, I bet.
ROBERT: My algebra teacher will freak out.

MWD: Is that right?

ROBERT: I like math, but I do not like the teacher.

MWD: (Ignoring that statement) Will your history teacher be the most surprised? (Robert nods) And then your algebra teacher? (Robert nods again) Where does the principal fit into that?

ROBERT: I don't know if he will notice for a while, 'cause there's kids in his office all the time.

MWD: He's going to miss you. (Brandy laughs)

ROBERT: (Smiling) Probably, because I'm in his office . . .

MWD: Are you going to drop in his office and say hi?

ROBERT: Probably not.

MWD: You don't like him that much, right? . . . Who else will be surprised in school that you are attending full-time?

ROBERT: I don't know, I'm sure some of the kids will wonder what's going on.

MWD: They are going to ask you, don't you think?

ROBERT: Yeah.

MWD: What kind of response are you going to give them?

ROBERT: I'll probably tell them I got in too deep.

Although my question "What kind of response are you going to give them?" encouraged Robert to develop a plan to overcome peer pressure, a better question would have been, "How will you let your friends know that you won't be cutting anymore?"

MWD: Will they give you a hard time about that?

ROBERT: They just kid around, but they won't give me a hard time.

MWD: Okay. You know, once you have been in school for a while and things continue to be on the right track, how's your life going to be different?

ROBERT: . . . I probably won't go out and party as much. I'll probably calm down a lot. When we go to birthday parties, I don't want to talk, I just kind of sit there.

MWD: You mean family stuff?

BRANDY: Yeah.

MWD: How are you going to be different there?

ROBERT: Um. We don't go there very much, and I don't see them very much, so I kind of get nervous . . . and I guess in a way I am kind of different, because my cousins are good in school and don't get into trouble a lot. Then there's me. I get into trouble all the time and I just get nervous, like they think I'm crazy or something.

MWD: So, once they start hearing about the fact that you're in school full-time, you'll feel more comfortable being with them?

ROBERT: Probably.

MWD: Who is likely to tell them that you're doing okay in school?

ROBERT: I don't know, they seem to find out.

MWD: They do? Who do you think is going to tell them? Do you think it is more likely to be your mom or dad or . . .

ROBERT: Probably Mom. (Mom laughs)

MWD: It will be Mom? She's going to brag about you, huh? . . . Who will she tell first?

ROBERT: Hopefully my uncle.

BRANDY: Oh, that's true. I was going to say Grandma, but that's true.

MWD: Yeah? Your uncle, why's that?

ROBERT: Because he is always giving me a hard time.

MWD: Then he'll be more shocked than your principal and all those other guys put together.

ROBERT: Probably.

In the next session, Robert's mother happily informed me that he attended all of his classes. In fact, he did so throughout the rest of the school year. Why the sudden change? I believe that most people really want to do well and please other people. What often stops them from turning over a new leaf is a fear of losing face. My assumption that Robert was going to attend school regularly, rather than doubt of his intentions to do so, allowed him to move forward without having to explain himself. I didn't rub his face in his prior behavior, and he apparently appreciated it. Furthermore, my unwavering confidence in his ability to improve his attendance increased his confidence in himself.

If you are trying to initiate a change in a situation involving other people, why not start asking them questions that presuppose the change is inevitable? Project into the future by beginning to wonder aloud how your lives will be different once the change has taken place. Ask, "Who will be the first to notice things are better?" "How will they let us know they've noticed?" "What exactly will change in our lives when things are better?" "What will this change enable us to do that we haven't been able to do before?" Get the idea?

Perhaps, unlike Robert's parents, you aren't interested in changing someone else; instead, you want to change yourself. When it comes to solving personal problems, the questions you ask yourself can make all the difference in the world. Certain questions lead to dead ends; others suggest solutions. The following examples will help you design the kinds of questions that will have you looking in the right direction for answers:

"When I get over my fear of flying, how will I celebrate?" *not* "Will my fear of flying always consume me?"

"What will be the first sign that things are starting to be on the right track?" *not* "Will I be able to get things on track?"

"When I lose ten pounds, who will be the first to notice?" *not* "Will I ever lose ten pounds?"

"When I pass this exam, how will I celebrate?" *not* "How can I possibly pass this exam?"

Now that you've read this chapter, are you going to start using smart talk now or wait until you finish the entire book? And how will your life be different when you do?

Chapter Thirteen

Do Nothing

SOMETHING UNUSUAL HAPPENED yesterday at my house. Since I don't allow much junk food such as candy around my house, it made perfect sense that my son, Zach, came home from a friend's birthday party delighted—he had a piece of candy in his hand. He placed it on the kitchen counter, planning to savor it the next day. His sister, however, discovered the candy and ate it without asking. When Zach noticed his candy missing the next morning, he nearly went into cardiac arrest. He cried and cried, and cried some more. Ordinarily, his tears would have been enough to send me flying upstairs to find the culprit and lecture her loudly about respecting other people's property. When I have responded this way in the past, however, she usually reacts defensively and later takes her resentment out on her brother. Not exactly the outcome I hoped for.

Yesterday I decided to do something different—nothing. I reassured Zach that I would replace his candy, but I did not go on a rampage with Danielle. She must have heard the whole commotion downstairs, and I'm sure she was very surprised to have escaped her usual lecture. What happened next was the best part. As we were leaving the house, she turned to her brother and said, "Zach, I'm sorry. I have some money and I will buy you another piece of candy at school today." Zach said, "Okay," and we left the house in peace.

Incidents like this make me wonder why I always feel so compelled to take action. I feel that, if I don't say something or do something obvious in response to a perceived wrongdoing, the problem will persist. But apparently this is not always the case. Sometimes the best thing I can do is nothing.

204 CHANGE YOUR LIFE AND EVERYONE IN IT

There are many benefits to doing nothing, actually. The first is obvious from my example. If you restrain yourself from jumping in and resolving everyone else's problems, they may just solve their problems themselves. In fact, they may even do a better job than you! Being a hyperactive problem-solver allows others to put off working things out. They don't have to think for themselves, since they know you will perform like clockwork. This doesn't promote self-sufficiency, and it gets tiring for the habitual problem-solver.

Ruth was concerned about her nine-year-old daughter, Tessie, who was being teased by other children at school. Recalling how traumatized she had felt as a child when she was teased, Ruth felt it was urgent that she step in to rescue her daughter. She immediately scheduled a meeting with the teacher and the principal to discuss the matter. However, Ruth had to go out of town on business unexpectedly and needed to reschedule the meeting. When she returned several days later, Tessie informed her that she had handled her own problem. She'd decided to ignore the nasty kids and play with the kids who were nice to her. Tessie felt a lot better about being in school.

Ruth was surprised. She had often intervened in Tessie's behalf in the past, and just assumed it was necessary to do so. At once, Ruth realized how her hastiness to jump in and solve her daughter's problems was not only unwarranted, it was deleterious. Had it not been for the fortuitous business trip, Ruth might still be solving Tessie's problems today. Instead, she learned the meaning of the saying "Less is more."

If you keep finding yourself taking the lead to resolve a given situation, try taking a deep breath and doing nothing next time it occurs. Watch what happens. When you sit back, you derail the expectation that you will solve everything. This in itself is doing something—you are sending a message that you expect others to make things better. Fixing things yourself all the time inadvertently sends the message that you believe the only person capable of fixing things is you.

There is another good reason for doing nothing. In regard to relation-
"Always express your feelings" is the worst possible
learn to pick and choose your battles. If you don't,
y five minutes, which doesn't sound like much fun.
ump on the people you love *every* time things don't
This sort of intentional overlooking is the lifeblood
aningful relationships. Obviously, it is not a good

idea to brush core issues under the rug, but it's essential to let the less important ones slide, and doing nothing initially can help you sort out which category a given conflict belongs to.

It's important to recognize that you do not always have to act on feelings of anger or antagonism. You can choose how you want to respond even when you are upset. Our emotions are powerful, but they are also changeable, and they should not control us. It is simply not true that you are "healthy" and "assertive" only if you voice how you are feeling at all times. True assertiveness has nothing to do with knee-jerk reactions to provocative situations but, rather, lies in the ability to recognize your feelings and then decide how or whether you will respond. Deciding to do nothing should be on your short list of options.

The next time you feel angry, rather than responding, you might be better off figuring out healthful ways to get rid of your anger instead. I worked with a woman who said she and her husband had an impossible time leaving work at work, because they owned a business together. Dinner table arguments about the business were the rule.

One night, she came home from work with a knot in her stomach because of a mistake her husband had made during the day. She decided to bite her tongue. I asked how she was able to do this, and she replied, "The kids have seen enough fighting. I don't want to do it anymore." I congratulated her. She proceeded to tell me that, even though she had averted an argument, she still had the knot in her stomach. Rather than suggest she confront her husband, I asked, "What did you do to get rid of your knot?" She promptly said, "I went into the barn to work. I always feel better after spending time there. My husband once asked why I spend so much time in the barn and I told him, 'I like it there. Nothing argues with me in the barn.' " She stayed there until she was calm enough to return to the house.

So, if you're wondering whether to take action in response to a provocative situation, ask yourself:

What is my ultimate goal? What are you hoping to accomplish by your actions? What would you like to see happen?

Will bringing up the issue increase the chances of achieving my goal? Envision what will happen if you respond as you plan. How will others react?

If you can't imagine good results, do nothing. Although it's hard to predict how others will react, I can tell you it will be different. Watch them carefully for telltale signs that they notice you are no longer responding in the same old way. They'll notice. I promise.

Perhaps you're wondering whether doing nothing is a helpful strategy when it comes to personal problems. Absolutely. For example, sometimes the best thing you can do for yourself if you're depressed is to allow yourself to get *really* depressed. Give yourself permission to have a good cry. Stop trying to pull yourself up by your bootstraps. Take a break from being mentally healthy. Once you stop pressuring yourself to feel better, you may find that the problem clears up.

If you're a compulsive problem-solver like me, I want to reassure you that doing nothing is really not doing nothing. Doing nothing is doing something. In fact, it is frequently the most powerful and provocative response possible, particularly when the people in your life are accustomed to your taking charge. So, compulsive problem-solvers one and all, remember: the next time you refrain from reacting spontaneously, you're not doing nothing, you're choosing not to act. And that's really something.

Chapter Fourteen

Last-Resort Techniques

I HOPE THAT you've had so much success with the techniques in the preceding chapters that you don't need to read this one. But sometimes stubborn problems with those closest to us—children and partners— require extreme solutions. If nothing you have tried until now has worked, you might consider one of the following techniques.

You may notice that these solutions are basically variations on ones you've already read about—it's just that the situations to which they are applied are more drastic. If they seem outlandish or radical, that's because they are. You should always try other, less extreme solutions first. The simpler and more direct, the better. But if all else has failed, proceed!

Stop the Chase

For those on the brink of divorce
(Variation of "Do a 180°")

Don and Rebecca have been married for eighteen years. Don knows things haven't been perfect, but he assumes all marriages have their ups and downs. Rebecca, on the other hand, feels the marriage has been a death sentence. Despite their three children and the vows they made long ago, Rebecca tells Don she wants out. Shocked, he asks her to go to counseling, but she tells him it's too late, she doesn't love him anymore. "In fact," she tells him, "I've already consulted an attorney. I want a divorce."

Don is devastated. He schedules an appointment and tearfully tells me about their marriage. It's been one month since she dropped the bomb. I ask Don what he has been doing recently to try to save his marriage. He replies:

> The last month has been hell. I've been trying everything. I've tried reasoning and pleading with her. I've reminded her that we were once happy in our marriage and that we can get that back again. "Let's try to work it out for the kids' sake," I say, but she doesn't seem to care. We've gotten in some big fights when I tell her that she is crazy or selfish. She doesn't want to hear that. There are times when I just cry, but she gets angry at me. She says I am just trying to make her feel guilty, but I'm not. I just feel sick about all of this. I admit I've been calling her too much at her work. Each time I call, I'm hoping she will come to her senses and be nicer to me. I've invited her out to dinner, sent her flowers, and even have gotten her sentimental cards. It seems, the more I show my feelings, the more she pulls back. I'm hoping this is just a phase she is going through and that she'll come out of it soon.

Although the specifics of Don's situation are unique, the patterns are not. Don fears losing Rebecca, but the more he pursues, the more she withdraws. The truth is that, if he persists, he is unquestionably going to lose Rebecca. When we are faced with the possibility of losing someone or something cherished, the natural reaction is to cling fervently. Unfortunately, the tendency to hold on tighter to that which is slipping away rarely works, and usually accelerates the distancing.

I asked Don, "Is what you're doing working?" and he said, "Obviously not." I told him, "I am not an expert on what works, but I *am* an expert on what doesn't work. I can guarantee you that, if you continue doing what you have been doing over the last few weeks, Rebecca will divorce you. I can't guarantee that what I'm about to suggest *will* work, but I know for sure what you've been doing won't."

Then Don and I put our heads together to devise a plan. I asked him,

"What could you do in the next few weeks that would shock Rebecca? What would be completely out of character, based on her view of you lately? What would you need to do to really make her wonder why you are acting so differently?"

Don thought for a minute, then said, "To begin with, if I stopped calling her at work, she would notice that right away. She would wonder what happened. Also, if I stopped telling her 'I love you' all the time. She sees me sitting around the house all weekend, waiting for her to notice me. I suppose, if I were to go ahead and make plans for myself once in a while, she would be surprised. Another thing I could do that would make a big difference is to act happier around the house. Lately, I've been so depressed that I mope around. I'm sure I'm a drag. She's got to feel bad every time she looks at me. I suppose, if I were to lighten up a bit, she would think that unusual, plus I might be more inviting to be around. Who knows?"

Don agreed to implement some of his ideas. He figured he had nothing to lose and everything to gain. Two weeks later, he came back, reporting the following:

> I stopped calling her at work immediately, and within a few days, she even called me. Granted, she just had a few questions to ask, but she would have avoided calling me entirely before all this. On Saturday, instead of waiting around to see what she had planned, I made plans with a buddy to go golfing, something I haven't done in a very long time. I could tell by the look on her face that she was surprised when I told her I would be leaving. When I returned, I was in a really great mood and she started asking me all kinds of questions about my day. That shocked me. Later that evening, she made dinner and the meal was fairly pleasant. That's a first in four weeks!
>
> More than anything else, I made a decision not to sit around being depressed anymore, and I can't help but think she realizes that, with or without her, I'm going to be okay. Maybe that scares her. All I can say is that, even though things are far from great between us, they seem somewhat better. She hasn't brought up the topic of divorce even once in the last two weeks. I'm wondering if she put the whole thing on hold.

I suspected that, if nothing else, Rebecca was having second thoughts about her departure from their marriage. Although that was a good sign, Don's work had just begun. I advised him that, no matter how tempting it might be to fall back to his old ways—calling her, telling her he loved her, and so on—he should restrain himself. I assured Don that the only reason Rebecca was waffling in her decision to leave was that he was no longer pressuring her. If he were to revert to his desperate ways again, she would resume her flight. Don understood the importance of remaining on track; his marriage depended on it.

In the next few weeks, Don was respectful and cooperative with Rebecca but didn't solicit her affection. He allowed her to make the first move. Several weeks later, she asked him out for dinner and admitted that she wasn't ready to leave their relationship: she had done a lot of thinking in the past few months and had decided to give their marriage another try. Don was ecstatic. Together they began to identify what needed to change in their marriage to make it more satisfying for both of them.

Why did stopping the chase work for Don? It is our nature to want to escape situations where we feel controlled or highly pressured by another person, even if what the other person wants is reasonable or valid. The mere fact that someone is pushing on us makes us want to pull away. As long as Don pursued Rebecca, all she focused on was the urgency of avoiding his pursuit. In so doing, she avoided thinking about what life would really be like without him. It wasn't until Don distanced himself that she was able to reflect on their years together and the sadness of leaving it all behind. Once she reminisced about their marriage and their family, leaving began to seem less desirable.

Remember the seesaw? Don had become the caretaker of their marriage. He was doing all the emoting, all the nurturing, for both of them, which left Rebecca free to do anything but. When Don relinquished his role, Rebecca automatically stepped into it. By pulling back, Don created the space for her to become more involved in mending their relationship.

Don was also right when he ventured that his moping wasn't all that appealing to Rebecca. She was in search of more happiness, not more sadness. Although Don's moodiness was completely understandable, it turned Rebecca off. Once he took steps to make himself feel better, she became intrigued. She began to imagine Don moving forward without her and wondered what his life would be like. Would he meet someone else? Would he remarry? Would he want to move away? All of a sudden, Rebecca questioned whether she was making the right decision by leaving. She concluded that she would be doing herself and her marriage a disservice by not trying to resurrect the love she had once had for Don.

Finally, Don's desperation had become predictable. Rebecca no longer paid attention to him, because what she expected from him was what she got. When Don did the unexpected, she noticed immediately, just as he had hoped. If you want to be noticed, you must do something noticeable. That's why this technique works so quickly.

Although Don and Rebecca went off into the sunset together, stopping the chase doesn't automatically create a happy ending. Sometimes the person in Rebecca's shoes is already out the door. She (or he) may have someone waiting in the wings or may just be so fed up with things that change no longer seems possible. Even when this technique doesn't succeed in restoring the marriage, however, it can restore self-esteem. People who use it describe the emptiness and desperation they felt as they pursued their partners; some people even say they felt as if they were going crazy. Stopping the chase helped them to regain their self-control: they felt serenity and sanity return to their lives. I described this technique in *Divorce Busting*, and readers found it incredibly helpful. Here's a recent letter from a reader who was glad she tried it.

Dear Ms. Weiner-Davis,

I am writing this letter to you to let you know how reading your book *Divorce Busting* is helping to save my marriage of twenty-nine years. Very recently, in fact only four weeks ago, my husband and I separated. Our separation only lasted three of those weeks in large part due to your advice. When I purchased your book my sister was with me and said I didn't need it, that it was too late; he'd moved out already, and worst of all, he moved to a woman he had been seeing for the past year. I knew there had to be something I could do and just needed to be set on the right path.

Your specific advice was to do a 180° turn around (stop the chase). I could not afford to waste any time and did just that. He had already told me that I should get on with my life and find someone who could "take care of me." A lot of our problems were brought on by financial difficulties, problems with our children, and expanding our business which had me working six or seven days a week, fourteen hours a day for the past year and the fact that our business involved a lot of socializing with single people.

Fortunately, we had to see or talk to each other each day because of our business. After my nasty reactions the first three days I knew I was getting nowhere fast. When I calmed down I was able to be civil and I decided to stop fighting with him and start fighting for him.

So I did go out dancing three nights in a row and when I saw him Monday morning at work and I had had my ego boosted by other men who danced with me, complimented me and three men actually asked for dates, I was probably glowing. And when he asked me how my weekend was, I told him. This got through to him and by that night he called me and agreed to talk the next day.

That was Tuesday, my fiftieth birthday and he came home that night. We've done more talking this past week we've been back together than we did all last year. We talked about how this happened and blamed nobody. We decided to drastically cut the hours I worked so we would have time together.

We intend . . . to make sure we stick to our plan to rediscover the fun we had together before we let the pressures of life fool us into thinking there is anything more important than the people we love.

This letter is a lot longer than I intended. I really just wanted to let you know how helpful your book was to me and to thank you for writing it.

Whether this technique allows you to keep your relationship alive or simply to revive your self-respect, it is worth a shot when things seem hopeless.

Drop the Rope

For parents with rebellious teenagers
(Variation of "Do a 180°")

Parent-child relationships are often a tug-of-war. Children pull one way, their parents pull the other. As parents pull with more force, kids pull harder in the opposite direction. This dynamic is particularly noticeable in families with teenagers. The more adults try to control them, the more teens press for freedom, and the more they press for freedom, the harder parents try to get involved in their choices.

In many families, the parents decide that whatever problem the adolescent is experiencing is due to the parents' laxness. Then what happens? The parents devise more rules to address the problem. More rules means more ways to violate them, which in turn provokes stricter surveillance and even more rules. Problems escalate quickly this way.

In my work with families, I have found that, when adults are clear about their expectations and consistent in applying the consequences of failing to meet them, most teenagers comply, however unhappily. Many parents make rules and threaten consequences but do not follow through. Lack of consistency on the parents' part is often the culprit in persistent parent-teen problems.

Before you consider taking more extreme measures, ask yourself whether you really do what you say you are going to do when it comes to your adolescent. Do you find yourself giving in when he or she argues for one more chance? Does that little voice inside your head argue with you when you are trying to set limits? Do you back off, not wanting to seem like an ogre? If you have answered yes to any of these questions, try consistency first. The bookstore is filled with parenting guides that can help.

It is possible, however, that you have tried being consistent with your teenager and still nothing has improved. You may feel as if you are always policing your children instead of enjoying them. You seem to live in a state of argument, even though whatever started the fighting seems minor compared with the way things are going lately. If your relationship with your teen is a tug-of-war, you may feel that you are at the end of your rope. Believe it or not, that's good. There are two ways to end a tug-of-war. One is to have the decidedly stronger team. The other is to drop the rope. Here's how:

Step 1: Set the stage. Schedule a meeting with your child, explaining that you have something important to tell him, but do not say more. This is a good way to build anticipation. At the prearranged time, sit down and carefully and slowly explain that you have been unhappy about the way things have been going. Tell your child that your expectations have not changed, and that the family rules remain in effect. Explain that it is your hope that your child will make valuable decisions that will enable him to become a successful person. Express your love for him as well.

Step 2: *Drop the rope.* Now comes the unusual part. Explain that you have decided that you are no longer willing to fight about the rules. You have come to the conclusion that he is old enough to make his own decisions. If he succeeds, he succeeds on his own. If he fails, he fails on his own as well. Inform him that you will not rescue him anymore. If he forgets something he needs at school, that's his problem. If he gets into trouble, he must get himself out of trouble. From this point on, if he chooses to "screw up," that's up to him.

Step 3: *Resist the temptation to discipline your child when he fails to follow the rules.* This is usually the most difficult step. Despite the hundreds of times you've said to yourself, "I give up," it is not easy to do so. Your adolescent is definitely going to test you at first to see if you meant what you said. Naturally, the form the test will take is to do the very thing that irritates you the most. You must appear to be unaffected, even if that's not how you really feel inside. Talk to your mate or a friend, go for a walk, count to one hundred, leave the house. Do whatever it takes not to respond as you usually do. If your teenager comes in after curfew, and you can manage to sound sincere rather than sarcastic, smile and ask, "Did you have a good time?" Be prepared for additional provocation—he will probably test you again very soon to see how long you'll hold out. But sometimes his behavior will correct itself rapidly. Offensive behavior loses its appeal when it no longer gets a reaction out of you—when "forbidden fruit" is no.longer forbidden.

Step 4: *Evaluate the results.* At the outset, establish a time frame for your plan and stick to it. A month is usually about the right time to read the results. If you don't give yourself enough time, your child may still be testing you, and you may incorrectly conclude that the technique isn't working. If your child's behavior has improved, you know you're on the right track, so don't pick up the rope. Once you feel certain that the positive changes have become a habit, you can experiment by providing input into your child's decisions once in a while. If he or she handles your feedback maturely, continue offering it. If not, back off again. Your child may just behave more appropriately if he or she is allowed to make autonomous decisions. On the other hand, if there has been no improvement after about a month, you can probably conclude that the technique is not working.

Some parents feel that their responsibility to minor children makes it impossible for them to stop setting limits. But your responsibility is precisely what requires you to be effective as a parent. Remember, if what you are doing isn't working, you are actually making the problem worse. Your child is so focused on removing himself from your control that avoiding you has become his primary concern. He isn't thinking about his behavior or how he affects others. Once you stop the power struggle, he can begin to focus on whether he has been acting responsibly or not.

Other parents, recognizing that their children may get worse before they get better, feel incapable of sitting back and watching them "go down the tubes." But there is nothing passive about dropping the rope. It will require all of your strength and every bit of will power you can muster. It will be one of the most powerful actions you have ever taken with your child. And knowing that there is light at the end of the tunnel will make the darkest times bearable.

Cassie was a single mom who dreaded mornings with her fifteen-year-old son, Derek. Derek disliked getting up for school, and Cassie claimed that she set her alarm one hour earlier than she had to in order to allow for their arguments over his lateness, which took a full sixty minutes every day. In the end, Derek was always late for school anyway. After several months of this, Cassie scheduled an appointment with her physician and asked for a prescription for tranquilizers. At that point, she realized that she had to do something different, because Derek was "driving her nuts."

She sat down with Derek that evening and explained that she loved him and that she still expected him to get up on time but that she was no longer going to fight with him about it. His response? "Yeah, right." She said nothing more. The next day, she got up but did not wake Derek. Instead, she did the laundry, went for a walk, and met a friend for breakfast.

When Cassie returned from breakfast, Derek was sitting in the living room watching television. She said nothing to him, and he left the room. Derek never made it to school that day. Cassie continued to resist the temptation to wake him or comment on his behavior. The second day, Derek missed two class periods but got himself to school by late morning. By the fourth day, Derek woke himself and got to school on time.

Cassie described how difficult it was to remain silent when Derek slept in and when he went to school late. She said it was the hardest thing she ever did. But since she noticed gradual improvement, she stuck with the plan. She also commented on how much more pleasant her life became when she abandoned her morning arguments with Derek. Very soon she decided she no longer needed the tranquilizers.

Tit for Tat

For parents with uncooperative children

(Variation of "Easier Done Than Said")

This last technique requires no fancy explanation. Although many parents won't admit it, and you would have trouble finding this method in most conventional parenting books, the truth is, many kids don't stop annoying their parents or breaking family rules until they get a taste of their own medicine. Lecture, philosophize, punish all you like, nothing seems to make a difference until you turn the tables and allow the child to experience what it feels like to be on the receiving end of his or her behavior. For example, if your teenager continually wakes you late at night with loud music, "accidentally" wake her up early in the morning vacuuming. If your child has the annoying habit of going through your belongings, leaving them in disarray, or destroying them, do the same thing in return. If your youngster continually forgets to do what is asked, "forget" that you promised a ride to the movies or that you granted permission for a friend to sleep over. Just say, "Sorry, I forgot," and nothing more. In his book, *Discipline: 101 Alternatives to Spanking*, Dr. Alvin Price has the following to say about this technique:

> In a way, this approach is a drastic one. It's taking the idea of logical consequences and applying it in a way the child will be sure to understand. But with some children this approach will prove necessary. They'll constantly miss your point until you can make them understand.
> The point is not to get revenge on the child. It's to help the child see he's playing a game, and that the rules of his game are all wrong. The

world won't let him play by those rules, and a loving parent shouldn't either.[1]

As with Drop the Rope, the key to success in implementing Tit for Tat is to restrain yourself from lecturing or disciplining in your usual fashion. Also, keep in mind that, if your motive is retaliation, Tit for Tat will simply exacerbate the situation. If you give in to the temptation to say, "See how it feels?" your child will undoubtedly seek revenge with even more annoying behavior. You must be pleasant but persistent. Keep in mind the reward you're giving yourself—a quick end to months or even years of emotional battles. As with all the other techniques in this book, observe the results and, if you see progress, keep it up for a while. But abandon the technique if the problem persists.

Truth be told, sometimes, no matter what you do, things will not get better. This doesn't happen very often, but it does happen. Don't despair. It may just mean that you need another perspective to help you see things in a new way. If you haven't done so already, try discussing your situation with someone you trust and respect, someone who cares about you. Make sure to choose someone who doesn't have a vested interest in a particular outcome. Perhaps you can think of someone who is dealing with a similar situation, and the two of you can put your heads together.

Hire a Shrink

If you have already sought the advice of others but nothing has worked, it may be time to consider talking with a therapist. That might seem like a strange recommendation coming from me, but it fits with my philosophy—if what you're doing isn't working, do something different. Sometimes seeking therapy is just the thing to do, and sometimes, as I discussed in chapter three, the very act of committing themselves to seeing a therapist helps people start finding solutions by themselves.

As I've made clear, however, I don't think all therapists are equal. If you decide to pursue the therapy route, you should choose a therapist who uses a down-to-earth, present- and future-oriented approach. I tend to agree with psychologist Martin Seligman, who notes in his book *Learned Optimism*:

> All successful therapy has two things in common: It is forward-looking and it requires assuming responsibility. Therapy that reviews childhood endlessly, that does not focus on how to cope in the here and now, that views a better future as incidental to undoing the past, has a century-long history of being ineffective.[2]

Although I naturally prefer SBT, it isn't the only practical method. Cognitive and behavioral therapies are also results-oriented. A word-of-mouth referral is the best way to hire a therapist, but it is also important to remember that what works for someone else might not work for you. The bottom line is that you *must* trust your own instincts. If you don't feel comfortable with whomever you choose, go somewhere else. Don't hesitate to ask questions about your therapist's background, training, and credentials. If he or she seems put off by your questions, you're probably in the wrong place. Competent therapists do not feel threatened by their clients' efforts to become informed consumers.

The American Association of Marital and Family Therapy publishes a helpful brochure entitled *A Consumer Guide to Marriage and Family Therapy*. You can obtain a copy by calling 800-374-AMFT.

Don't expect the therapist to do a personality overhaul. Before you attend your first session, decide specifically what you want to change, and articulate that clearly. The therapist should help you to establish goals, and should monitor your progress toward those goals throughout your meetings. If you haven't noticed any progress within a month, you should raise this issue with your therapist. Unless your therapist can offer an explanation with which you feel comfortable, go elsewhere. When you reach your goals, say goodbye to your therapist. Don't make therapy a way of life. Use the money you have been spending on it to go out for dinner, buy yourself new clothes, or take up skydiving. (There are at least two signs that you've been in therapy too long: when you find yourself commenting at parties, "My shrink says . . . ," or when the phrase "significant other" calls to your mind a picture of your therapist. Time to get a life.) When you think you're done, no matter what your therapist or anyone else says—you're done.

It may sound as if I'm somewhat skeptical about the value of therapy in people's lives. Not true. Remember, I'm a shrink, and I love and am proud of the work I do to help people in their lives. And I know many other therapists who are extremely dedicated, talented, and conscientious. Just make sure you find someone who is all these things. Make certain your therapist believes in you and your resources to deal with your problem. Never forget that *you* are the expert and the therapist is the consultant.

One final note: many people benefit significantly from seeking professional help. For instance, people in physically abusive relationships should not go another day without finding a solution to the violence in their lives, and the help of a professional who is familiar with such situations may be the most effective way to begin. Similarly, professional help is often a lifeline for people suffering from severe mental illness and their loved ones. This is not to say that everyone with a severe problem must seek professional help, however. Plenty of people have overcome serious problems such as substance abuse, the aftereffects of rape or sexual abuse, and eating disorders on their own.

For example, Dean, age thirty-eight, had a drinking problem that was wreaking havoc in his life. His wife was about to divorce him, his job was in jeopardy, and his health was rapidly deteriorating. Things looked pretty bleak.

One morning, Dean woke up and decided he would never, ever drink again. On his own, he took an inventory of what had worked for him when he tried to quit drinking in the past. Keeping busy after work, staying away from his "drinking buddies," taking a route home that didn't pass his favorite bar, posting a reminder on the refrigerator to help him appreciate his small steps forward, stocking the refrigerator with lots of club soda, playing golf (he was a scratch golfer) in the warm months, and skiing in winter were some of the strategies he recalled. From that day forward, he has been doing what works and, although it's never been easy, he hasn't had a drink since. That was twenty years ago. No therapy, no Alcoholics Anonymous. Just Dean.

Conversely, there are times when minor, even petty problems prevent people from moving forward in their lives without professional assistance. If a minor problem persists long enough, the effect can be devastating. I once worked with a couple whose main point of contention was whether it was acceptable or not to eat dinner in front of the television. This might not seem like a major issue to you or me, but it was to them. And their inability to find an acceptable compromise left them feeling angry much of the time. It makes good sense to seek professional help when molehills feel like mountains.

The point isn't that people should avoid therapy, but that therapy should be looked at as a problem-solving process, and it should be just that. Therapy should never take the place of solid friendships, fulfilling lives, or a belief in your own wisdom.

Chapter Fifteen

Feet, Don't Fail Me Now

BY NOW, I assume you have implemented one or more of the strategies outlined in this book. As a result, you will have noticed one of the following outcomes:

1. Things are great.
2. Progress has been made, but you are not quite where you want to be yet.
3. There has been no noticeable positive change.

Depending on the outcome, you will have different questions about what to do next. If, as a result of trying something different, your life is vastly improved, you may be asking yourself, "How do I keep these changes going?" If things are better but you still haven't reached your goal, you might wonder, "What else must I do to build on what I've accomplished so far?" Finally, if you have noticed no positive changes, you are probably eager to know how to shift your strategies to get better results.

Result 1. Your Situation Is Greatly Improved

Congratulations! You risked a change from your old ways, and it is paying off. Isn't it great to feel in control of your life? If you haven't already, pat yourself on the back. Again and again and again.

But it's important not to get overconfident and start to take these changes for granted, or guess what happens? That's right. Things go back to square one. Your life has improved because *you* have been doing something different and therefore have gotten very different results. The changes are not magic; they didn't "just happen." In order to maintain them, you must maintain the behaviors and attitudes that have generated them. It is an exquisitely simple equation.

Since the key to maintaining positive changes is to continue the changes in you, it is essential you ask yourself:

What have I been doing differently recently that has led to these positive results?

Take an inventory of the different strategies you have tried. Make a list of the methods that appear to have yielded the most dramatic results. This will tell you precisely what you need to continue doing to maintain positive changes. If you are having a hard time answering the question, it sometimes helps to ask yourself: *What would others (my boss, partner, children, friends, relatives) say I have been doing differently lately?* Try to imagine how others may be seeing you.

Sometimes when I suggest that people identify their role in improving their lives, they attribute the changes to the efforts of other people. "The reason our relationship is better is because he is kinder to me now," they might say. Remember, we usually notice the effect others have on us more than the effect we have on others. Naturally, new reactions in other people play a part, but you have helped them to respond differently by changing how you treat them. The danger in assigning all the credit to someone else is that, when things take a turn for the worse, you will not know what you can do to improve them except to sit back and wait for the other person to change. You must determine what you have done to make things better so that you know how to keep them that way.

Sometimes people attribute improvement to events beyond their control. "The reason I'm more energetic is because the weather has improved." "I'm feeling less depressed because my boyfriend called last night." When I hear statements like these, I remind people, "Surely there have been times in the past when the sun was shining but you still were lethargic. What's different about *you* now that you have allowed the sunshine to help you feel energized?" Or "In the past when your boyfriend called, your positive feelings were short-lived. What is different about you now that you have made the good feelings last?"

Don't be tempted to attribute improvements in your life solely to the new moon or a good-hair day. You have changed something significant in your behavior or attitude that has produced a more desirable outcome. And, again, unless you figure out exactly what *you* have been doing right, you won't know how to maintain positive changes over the long haul.

I can just imagine you thinking, "It will be a challenge to keep this up for any length of time." Most people feel that way, because behaving in new ways requires concentration and will power. But after a while, new behaviors generally become second nature. It's like learning how to ride a bike. After you "get it," you never have to think about the mechanics again. You just get on and ride. After you have been behaving in more productive ways for a while, continuing to do so will require little conscious effort.

This is not to say that staying on track will always be easy. It won't. There will be times when you're grouchy, tired, or simply in the mood for a good fight, and maintaining a solution-minded approach will be difficult. The important thing to remember is that the process of change consists of three steps forward and two steps back. When you slip, don't berate yourself or blame others. Just remind yourself of what has worked and start doing it again. The angrier you get at yourself for slipping, the more difficult it will be to get back on track. One thing that separates winners from losers is their ability not to take setbacks to heart. They just pick themselves up and keep going.

A second characteristic that sets winners apart from losers is that winners are good planners. They consider the possible outcomes of their actions and have contingency plans to cover all the bases. Since things are going so well for you right now, you may not think that you need to strategize what you would do if things suddenly started to deteriorate. But prevention is generally a simpler task than remediation. With that in mind, ask yourself:

What are one or two things that might happen in the next few weeks that would present a challenge to my sticking with these changes?

What event or situation might "push your buttons" and tempt you to go back to your less productive ways? For example, perhaps you know that an upcoming exam, a visit from an in-law, an important presentation at work, or an usually busy schedule with the kids will have you under a great deal of pressure, or you may be anticipating a meeting with a particular person who has the ability to get to you. Create a clear picture in your mind of situations that have provoked you to feel tense, upset, or angry in the past. Once you have envisioned the potential triggers, ask yourself:

How will I handle the situation(s) differently so that the outcome will be positive?

Begin by mentally reviewing the way you would have responded in the past. This will tell you what not to do. Then brainstorm several possible alternatives. Anything other than what you know for a fact won't work is a good start. Then decide which of these alternatives makes the most sense and commit yourself to doing it should the challenging situation arise. Anticipating and planning for the bumps in the road is more than half the battle in keeping the ball of change rolling.

Let me offer you a personal example. My husband and I can be getting along swimmingly, but, inevitably, when we prepare for an out-of-town trip, we both get tense. Over the years, I have discovered that, if I respond to his abrupt comments during this time, we argue and our arguments escalate to undesirable proportions.

Prior to leaving for a recent family vacation, I made a commitment to myself to handle our departure in a solution-oriented way, so that we would start our trip on a good note. Part of my strategy was to set the tone for a smooth departure in advance. A day before we left, I said to my husband, "I'm really looking forward to this trip." He agreed. Then I said, "I'd like to leave without screaming. What do you think about that?" He said, "Absolutely. Let's do it." But I also told myself that, no matter how short his fuse was on the day of our departure, I would ignore any provocative comments he made.

The morning of our vacation arrived. The bags were packed, the kids were dressed and ready to leave on time, the cat was fed, the doors were locked, and—without a single unpleasant word—we headed for the airport. Apparently, my request to leave peacefully worked! I didn't even have to practice ignoring him, because he never got edgy. If he had made some sarcastic comment, however, it's not that I wouldn't have felt tempted to respond. But I would have had a plan in place to help me ignore him and my urge to retaliate. Don't forget to allow for such habits of feeling, which may creep up on you and lure you into doing "more of the same." Instead of acting on them, one productive approach is to notice what you do to overcome them.[1]

I worked with a woman who was eager to rid herself of daily panic attacks. Although she made a great deal of progress in overcoming these attacks, she found that, from time to time, something triggered uncomfortable feelings that gave her the sensation she was on the verge of a panic reaction. I asked her to pay attention to what she did to overcome the uncomfortable feelings for the next several days. She reported the following:

> I was sitting in my living room and my heart started racing. Instead of assuming that I was going to experience a panic attack, I did what you suggested: I started to pay attention to what I do to calm myself down. I began talking to our parrot and he started talking to me. That distracted me and I felt better. Soon after, I picked up a sweater that my daughter left at our home and I noticed that it had her perfume on it. Since she and I are very close, the aroma of her perfume helped me feel good inside. That's when I started playing solitaire, and before I knew it, I was calm again.

Rather than focus on a feeling that in the past would have acted as a catalyst for "more of the same," it's helpful to emphasize what you now do to overcome that feeling. Make a list of all the mechanisms that help you to resist the temptation to go back to the old you. If you want to, post this list in a visible place, such as your refrigerator door (if it isn't too overloaded with notes already).

Despite your plans or your best intentions, it is not always possible to prevent backsliding. But it is possible to ready yourself to contain the slippage. You can do this by asking yourself:

What would be the first sign that things are really starting to slip? Who would be the first to notice? Then who? What would they notice me doing that would suggest I need to get back on track? What would be the best thing to do to put things back on track?

For interpersonal problems, it helps to plan in advance what each person will do if he or she notices things slipping.

For instance, I was working with a couple whose pattern was the following: When they spent time together, they got along great. When he worked long hours, she felt abandoned and angry, so she clammed up. When she got quiet, he withdrew. They would go for long periods of time not speaking to each other.

After a couple of sessions, they started spending a great deal of time together, and things were good between them. But they planned for future setbacks, agreeing that, if she noticed him spending too much time working, instead of getting angry she would tell him she missed him and wanted to spend more time with him. In the past, if her initial requests were not immediately fulfilled, she would get angry and withdraw. She agreed not to stop inviting him to be with her, until he got the message. He agreed that, instead of avoiding her when she got quiet, he would pursue her, ask her what was wrong, and initiate more communication.

The more specific your contingency plan, the quicker you will be able to nip any setbacks in the bud. If, for some reason, you fail to notice things sliding backward until you find yourself in the middle of a muddle, think back to a time when things weren't going so well in the past and ask yourself:

What did I do to make things better before?

Rather than get frustrated and decide that nothing is working, it's probably better to assume that you have just stopped doing what works. What was it that got everything going in the first place? Remember, and do that again. If for some reason your life has changed so that it isn't possible to repeat a prior solution exactly, determine how you could most closely replicate it.

A nurse found herself extremely overwrought when one of her fellow nurses became ill and was hospitalized on her unit. Just the sight of someone she knew and cared about being ill and in pain upset her disproportionately. She was, after all, a competent, seasoned caregiver who had witnessed much pain and suffering. But, confronted with the illness of her friend, she couldn't function properly at work and found herself having trouble sleeping.

In an effort to get back on track, she asked herself, "Have I ever had this difficulty before?" All of a sudden, she realized that in fact she had. Several years before, another colleague became hospitalized and died. This death had been devastating to her. Then she asked herself, "How did I handle that situation?" She remembered that her anxiety had rested on her inability to do much to keep her friend alive. Being a "helper," she found it unbearably painful to be "helpless" in this regard. Finally, she had written a letter to her friend explaining her sadness and frustration at not being able to be more helpful, and that had helped tremendously. Once she remembered this, she decided to write another such letter, and, again, it helped her to feel better.

Result 2. You Have Made Some Progress

When I ask people to describe the improvements in their lives, they are often eager to tell me about what *hasn't* improved. But it is extremely important to take an inventory of the nature and extent of your gains in order to assess what still requires work. If you proceed without a clear picture of what you've already accomplished and what you haven't, you may waste time trying to fix things that are already fixed or, conversely, overlook important issues that still need to be resolved. Therefore, ask yourself:

What's happening in my life recently that I enjoy or appreciate?

Again, be specific. Describe concretely what you or those around you have been doing that you would like to continue. Concentrate on actions rather than general attitudes. For example, "I've been appreciating that my son is straightening up his room lately," rather than "My son has been more considerate." Or "I feel good that I've been working out three times a week," rather than "I like that I've been more motivated." Make a list of everything you've noticed about changes in yourself, other people, or your situation, and try not to omit anything. You won't have to share this list with anyone, so be as generous as possible with your praise. (Some people resist acknowledging change in others for fear that they will go back to their old ways once they believe the relationship is out of danger.) Be a change detective! Then ask yourself:

In what ways have these changes helped me feel better about myself and others?

Perhaps you have noticed that, as a result of the improvements in your life, you are feeling different about yourself or other people. Maybe you are feeling more self-esteem or more confidence. Maybe you feel more relaxed and less irritable. How have these new feelings helped you stay on track? For example, if you have been feeling more self-confident, you might be less likely to misinterpret colleagues' comments. Or, if you have been feeling more loved, it may have become easier to be affectionate to your partner. In what ways have the improvements in your life made you easier or more fun to be around?

How have changes in one area affected the rest of my life?

Remember the butterfly effect? How has change snowballed in your life? Has getting along better with your partner made work more enjoyable? Has receiving more cooperation from the kids left you with more energy for yourself? Do improved relationships with co-workers make it easier for you to leave work at work and have more pleasant interactions with family members?

Who besides me has noticed the changes?

Has a friend mentioned that you seem to be smiling more? Have your kids told you that you are less grouchy? Do co-workers comment that you seem different in some way? What other feedback have you gotten that things are moving in the right direction?

These questions should give you a more vivid picture of what is working. You need to keep doing the things that have brought about these changes, and make plans for how to maintain the changes, as described in the previous section. Many people discover that, when they keep doing what works, the good times eventually crowd out the bad. But it helps to have a clear idea of what still needs work:

On a scale of 1–10, with 10 being "great" and 1 being "awful," how would I rate my situation prior to making my changes?[2]

Recall when things were at their lowest point. What was happening at that time, and how did you feel about it? Although these feelings may be clouded by whatever changes you have made, try to quantify them.

On the same scale, how do I feel about my situation since the changes?

Recognizing that your feelings may fluctuate from day to day, try to determine an average rating over the course of a week. Appraise honestly the extent of the improvement.

Given that life is never perfect, where on the scale would I need to be in order to feel satisfied?

As you think about your response, remember that we all have our ups and downs, and we can't expect our lives or the people in them to be flawless. (If you figure out a way to have it otherwise, write me—I want you to be my mentor.) Typically, people rate their worst time as a 2 or a 3. Those who think things have improved somewhat rate their present situation at about 6. When I ask them where on the scale they would need to be in order to feel satisfied, they say 8 or 9. Then I have them ask themselves:

What are one or two small things that I could do in the next week or two that would bring me up a half-point or a point?

Although you may be feeling that a momentous change in your situation is the only thing that will help you feel better, the truth is that small changes make big differences. If you set overly ambitious goals, you won't get there and you will get discouraged. The more reasonable the goal, the more attainable it is. So think small.

For instance, a woman wanted to feel better about her body. Although joining a health club helped her feel somewhat better about herself, she determined that she needed to lengthen her workout sessions by ten minutes to feel she was making progress.

Commit yourself to doing one or two small things to make your life even better next week. When you think about what you might do, be as specific as possible. Then, once you begin doing these things, keep track of all small improvements.

Sometimes people say that, in order to feel satisfied, they don't necessarily need a higher rating, but they need to feel more confident that the changes will last. They recall that past improvements never lasted very long. If this is how you feel, ask yourself:

What is the longest period I can remember during which things were going well?

Was it a week, two weeks, a month, or longer? Then ask:

What is the shortest period of time beyond this that the positive changes would need to persist in order for me to feel a bit more confident that they will last?

If you've found in the past that good times generally last for no longer than two weeks, would two and a half or three weeks persuade you that something different is happening this time? If not, how much longer would be necessary? Once you determine the length of time, get out a calendar. Mark the date that will indicate to you that the changes have lasted longer than in the past. Once you arrive at that date, celebrate. Pat yourself and other people on the back. You have turned the corner. Make certain you reward yourself in some way. After you're done celebrating, ask yourself:

What needs to happen next for me to be even more convinced the changes will last?

As you keep track of your progress, be realistic. Even in the best of situations, we have off days. Be forgiving of yourself and other people. Try to take a broad view of your situation rather than scrutinizing each and every move that is made. You will be a lot happier, and so will everyone in your path.

And now to the part of your situation that still needs improvement. Start by distinguishing the strategies that have been useful to you from those that have not. Make a list of all the strategies you have tried recently, and rate, on a 1–5 scale, how effective each has been (with 1 being "not very effective" and 5 being "extremely effective"). Any strategy receiving a 3 or above is worth continuing. Anything below a 3 should be abandoned. Reread chapters nine through twelve to get other ideas about what else you can try. If you feel stuck, ask yourself:

What wild ideas have I had about what could be done to solve this problem?[3]

Frequently, in our frustration, we conjure up zany ideas about what we could do to eliminate a problem. Unfortunately, we quickly discard these solutions as absurd. But insidiously persistent problems may require solutions that border on the preposterous. Don't veto any idea without seriously considering it. (It goes without saying, however, that, though zany ideas are fair play, hurtful or harmful ideas are not. Use good judgment.)

A mother driven to her wits' end by her teenage daughter's unwillingness to get out of bed in the morning told me that she had tried everything but nothing ever worked. When I asked what she had tried, she told me, "I've reasoned with her, I've gotten her her own alarm clock, I've tried punishing her, screaming at her, and rewarding her on days when she made an effort to get up. I've even bodily dragged her out of bed. Nothing seems to makes a difference." When I asked, "What wild ideas have you had about what could be done to solve this problem?" she replied, "I honestly thought about buying a water gun and squirting her in the morning. This way I wouldn't get so angry, and I also wouldn't argue with her, but I haven't done it because it seemed so silly." I asked if she would be willing to give it a try anyway and she said yes. When she came back for another session, she told me that she had bought the water gun but had only had to use it twice before her daughter started getting up on her own.

Result 3. There Have Been No Noticeable Positive Changes

Occasionally, people say that they have tried a number of techniques but they still feel things haven't improved at all. There are several common reasons why.

The change is camouflaged. Sometimes when I ask people how their lives have improved, they look angry and tell me emphatically that nothing has changed. It quickly becomes apparent that they are chomping at the bit to discuss an argument they had, usually not long before the appointment. The immediacy of the unpleasant interchange gives it center stage in our discussion. But once the intense feelings subside, it becomes clear that the argument has prevented them from recognizing or acknowledging the positive changes that have been happening. After they address the fight itself and find some resolution, they are able to present a more accurate picture of their lives. Before you conclude that nothing has worked, ask yourself:

Did something unpleasant happen recently that is preventing me from acknowledging the progress I have made?

Is a bad day at work coloring how you look at your relationships with your friends? Did an insult overshadow several days of pleasant interaction? Granted, there may be some things (even many things) that still disturb you about your life, but it is important to identify even the baby steps forward. If nurtured properly, they can grow into major changes.

Another reason that some people see no change in their lives is because they are expecting too much too soon. In your impatience, you may be focusing on your end goal rather than on the smaller steps you've set for yourself along the way. Be patient—change happens one step at a time.

You've only tried one new idea. Perhaps you had been used to handling a situation in a particular way, and, as a result of reading this book, you tried something new. Unfortunately, it hasn't been working. But instead of moving on to another technique, you have been clinging to your hope that, sooner or later, this one will work. Let me remind you that no single technique works all the time. Although a particular method worked for each of the people you've been reading about, you and your situation are unique. The best thing you can do if your approach isn't working is to abandon it and try something else. If you have been afraid to experiment further, let me give you a little advice.

Even more important than finding a solution to a given problem is learning how to think about developing solutions. Solution development requires that you remain open-minded about the potential of various strategies. You try something, stick with it a while, and observe the results. If it works, keep doing it. If not, try something else. It happens all too frequently that, just when you think you've discovered the perfect answer to your dilemma, it stops working. You must be flexible and allow your curiosity to guide you. So give yourself credit for having tried something new, but move on.

You haven't stuck with any single method long enough. Another reason people get bogged down in their journey to find solutions is that they jump from method to method without giving any single method ample opportunity to work. It's like channel-surfing with the remote control: you're not watching any program long enough to discover what it is about.

Without knowing the specifics of your situation, I cannot tell you how long you should stick with one method. But I can tell you that, if you think your energies have been scattered because you haven't proceeded in an organized fashion, start over, but go slowly this time. Be patient. Unless you get extremely poor results using a particular method, try it for a week or two. That should be sufficient time to assess the results. However, if something obviously backfires, stop doing it immediately.

What you've been doing is not different enough from your "more of the same." Wendy wanted more attention from her husband. For months, she verbalized her wishes to him, but it seemed that he never had enough time. He was either working or busying himself with a project around the house. When Wendy reached the end of her rope, she sought therapy.

I asked her what she had been doing to solve her marital problem, and she told me that she had tried many different approaches. "I used to constantly remind him that we weren't spending enough time together, but it never worked, so I decided to change my approach. During the last few weeks, instead of getting angry, I cried in his presence, hoping that my display of emotions would reach him. I even solicited the help of his close friend to try to influence him. Last night, I shared my feelings reasonably. This morning, when he began to read the newspaper at the breakfast table, I calmly reminded him again."

Although Wendy thought that her problem-solving strategies were diversified (she wasn't getting angry anymore), they really were variations on a single theme: pursuit. Her various efforts were all perceived by her husband as forms of chasing, nagging, or harassing him.

What could Wendy do that would be different enough to make a difference? The answer is simple: *anything but* pursue him. She could take a cue from the character Kathy Bates portrayed in the movie *Fried Green Tomatoes*, who also wants more attention from her husband. She tries talking to him, serving him his favorite meals by candlelight, taking classes in enhancing her sexuality, even greeting him naked and wrapped in cellophane, but his response is always the same. He grabs his plate of food, pops open a can of beer, seats himself in front of the television, and ignores her. It isn't until she gives up the pursuit, focuses on herself, and makes herself unavailable to him that he goes in hot pursuit of her.

One good way to figure out whether what you are doing is really different from what you had been doing is to think about how others perceive you. Is it unexpected enough to get their attention? Reread chapter nine, "Do a 180°," to get an idea whether your strategy is different enough. Be sure that nothing you're doing resembles the approaches on the following list.[4]

APPROACHES THAT USUALLY DO NOT WORK

The unsolicited lecture

- lectures and advice (especially when given "for your own good!")
- nagging
- hints
- encouragement ("Why don't you just try to . . .")
- begging/pleading/trying to justify your position
- appeals to logic or common sense
- pamphlets/newspaper articles strategically left lying around or read out loud
- the silent, long-suffering "look at how patiently and bravely I am not saying anything" approach

Taking the high moral ground by beginning your arguments with

- "If you really loved me . . ."
- "Anyone with sense . . ."
- "After all I've done . . ."
- "Look how ill/desperate/depressed I've made myself by worrying about . . ."

Self-sacrifice/denial

- continually operating to keep peace
- constantly "walking on eggshells" in order not to upset or anger others
- constantly putting the happiness of others before your own
- protecting others from the consequences of their actions
- putting your own life permanently on hold while you wait for other people to change

A word to the wise: if any of these approaches seems vaguely familiar to you, it's time to switch gears.

You are ambivalent about change. Let's face it, change isn't always easy. It takes you to new places, uncharted territory. Although you may have imagined how the future might be when things change, there are no guarantees. Even though life isn't perfect now, there's something safe and secure about it. You know what to expect and what tomorrow will bring. If you change, who really knows what the outcome might be? And maybe it takes more effort to change than you wish to exert. Things aren't great, but maybe they are not so bad after all.

It's natural for such thoughts to cross your mind. Everyone should give a great deal of consideration to whether he or she really wants to change and, if so, at what cost. Ambivalence is a common feeling when it comes to breaking comfortable habits, even when the habits are unproductive ones. If you have mixed feelings about making changes, by all means, slow down. Reconsider your goals. Unless you truly want things to be different, you will not fully commit yourself to doing what it takes to make it happen anyway. If you are unsure, ask yourself:

What might be beneficial about my situation's not changing?

I know you must be thinking, "Of course I want things to be different. What in the world could possibly be positive about staying in this rut?" But please do not dismiss this question too quickly. Even if it seems strange to you, answer it anyway. You may be surprised.

I once asked a woman who was depressed, "What might be beneficial about your being down in the dumps?" Naturally, at first she thought I was crazy, but when I encouraged her to think about the question, she replied, "When I feel down, I don't force myself to do things I don't want to do. I give myself permission to take a time out. When I feel up, I pressure myself to get lots accomplished and take care of everybody else's needs." She realized that either she had to find ways to take better care of her own needs—such as learning how to set limits on what she could comfortably do—or, recognizing the up side to feeling down, she could give herself permission to have an occasional "blue" day.

If, after thinking about the positive aspects of the so-called problem, you realize that "things ain't so bad," so be it. Leave well enough alone. It will help you admit to youself that, while things could be better, they are not worth your agonizing over them. Give yourself permission *not* to change. It can be truly freeing.

Sometimes, when people finally agree to accept themselves as they are, they realize that other people in their lives remain critical of them and continue to exert pressure on them to change. Take it from me, unless *you* are the one who is motivated to change, you will probably not be successful. You—not your spouse, friend, parent, or therapist— have to decide it is worth the effort to make things different. The decision to change comes from within. If you come to realize that the person most concerned about your situation is someone other than you, politely thank that person for his or her concern and explain that you are working on accepting yourself exactly as you are.

You haven't forgiven yourself or others. Over the many years I've done therapy, I've noticed that the single biggest roadblock to change is people's tendency to hold grudges. "I won't change unless you change first." "*You're* the problem, so why should *I* change?" "You hurt me in the past, so why should I believe that you are going to change?" "You've rejected me before, so I can't really open myself up to you." This is extremely unfortunate, because, as long as you are keeping a mental scoreboard of hurtful deeds, you cannot move forward.

Some people fail to forgive because they believe forgiving represents condoning a hurtful act. When you forgive someone, you do not necessarily approve of his or her actions. In fact, forgiving has little to do with the other person and everything to do with you. It's an act of letting go, of not allowing the suffering to control your life anymore. The longer you immerse yourself in resentment and bitterness, the longer you remain in shackles, prisoner of your own negative thoughts. You may believe that, by holding back forgiveness, you're protecting yourself, but you're not. Animosity always takes a toll, physically and emotionally. Perhaps, by not letting bygones be bygones, you are seeking revenge. However, the person you are hurting most is you.

Whether you admit it or not, as long as you are keeping score about times past, you aren't really trying to make things better. Pretend you're attempting to mend things, go through the motions if you like, but, unless you've forgiven, I can guarantee you that nothing will work. When I suspect that lack of forgiveness is an issue in the lives of the people with whom I am working, I tell them to stop wasting their time and money and come back when they are ready to let go of the past.

This does not mean I expect people to forget the past. Our experiences are valuable lessons upon which we build the rest of our lives. You will not forget that your partner had an affair, but you must forgive if you want to restore the relationship. The angry words that passed between you and your friend will not be forgotten, but there must be forgiveness if you want to feel love again. In forgiving, we give ourselves permission to empty our minds and souls of the negativity that holds us back from feeling joy.

Forgiving others is essential when it comes to resolving relationship problems, but forgiving yourself is a prerequisite to personal change. Regardless of your goal, your best intentions, your ambition, drive, and commitment, you are going to make mistakes along the way. Are you hard on yourself? Do you chastise yourself every time you get sidetracked from your goal? Do you wallow in feelings of anger and self-contempt if your actions fall short of your expectations? If so, you greatly diminish your chances of success.

Take the person who wishes to lose weight, for example. What separates the person who succeeds on a weight-loss program from the one who doesn't, has nothing to do with infallible self-control. Everyone falls off the wagon once in a while. But those who forgive themselves and get right back on track are more likely to lose weight and make sensible eating a permanent way of life than people who give in to unhealthy doses of self-reproach.

I was working with a young woman who was miserable about her body. She desperately wanted to lose weight. In our first meeting I asked her, "If you get off to a bad start with your diet in the morning, how do you turn things around later in the day?" Without a moment's hesitation, she replied, "If I overeat in the morning, I get so mad at myself, the rest of the day is shot. If I'm bad for two days in a row, I blow the rest of the week." She would also purge after work if she felt she had binged earlier in the day.

As you can see, the obstacle to this woman's losing weight was not the occasional ice-cream cone, bag of potato chips, midnight foray into the refrigerator, or trip to McDonald's. It was her *belief* that any digression from her diet, major or minor, would inevitably lead to another. The resulting contempt and self-loathing made it impossible for her simply to forgive herself and start eating sensibly again. Several months and many shed pounds later, she told me of the days that had begun less than ideally but ended well nevertheless. She also described times when she allowed herself to splurge on a few cookies or French fries but saw the slips as isolated incidents and immediately got back on track. Hearing this, I became convinced that she was well on the way to establishing sound eating habits.

Conventional wisdom suggests that people initiate personal changes only when they have hit the bottom of the barrel, when they feel so much self-disgust that they have no other choice but to restructure their lives. I suppose change happens this way for some people, but for most, lasting personal change demands a modicum of self-acceptance. Recognizing that no one is or ever will be perfect, and that the road to change is often contorted, loving yourself enough to pardon your mistakes—this is the formula for change. If you are sitting in judgment of yourself or someone else, stop. You are wasting precious time. Each moment provides a fresh opportunity to start anew.

I am reminded of this lesson each time I play golf. In the past, after each lousy shot, I would get mad at myself, first about the shot, and then about my skills as a golfer in general. The more I allowed myself to ruminate, the more these feelings affected the rest of the game (not to mention my companions). Once I gave in to my funk, my swing deteriorated with each subsequent shot.

One day, my husband pointed out that, just as I tell clients to let go of negative thoughts and give themselves permission to move on, I should view each shot as the start of a new game. I quickly learned that, to become skilled at golf, I had to practice what I preach about forgiveness. Gradually, I've learned to leave negative thoughts at the hole where I acquired them. Golf has been more enjoyable for me lately, and I've even noticed some improvement in my game.

If you are stuck and none of the above reasons sounds familiar, read on. Believe it or not, the problem may be that you're trying too hard!

Chapter Sixteen

Are You a Fix-It Addict?

SOMETIMES, NO MATTER what you do to resolve an uncomfortable situation, nothing works. It's possible that you are trying too hard to fix things. If you've found yourself thinking, "I'm doing all the work," or "Why am I the only one who cares?"—welcome to the fix-it addicts' club. Now, don't go joining Fix-It Addicts Anonymous. I don't actually mean that you have an addiction; I just mean that your habit of trying to fix the problem is consuming all of your energy. And since the problem isn't changing, you're depleting your resources to improve any other aspect of your life. It really doesn't matter *what* you have been doing; the mere fact that you are consumed with trying to solve the problem *is* the problem.

Dina and Lee had been married for eighteen years, and they had four children. Dina had good feelings about their early years together, but lately Lee's drinking had become a major problem for her. When they met, Lee drank at parties or had an occasional beer after work. Gradually, Lee's drinking increased until he was drinking every day and often had late nights out "with the boys." Dina detested that his drinking appeared to be out of control. She'd also noticed that lately, after Lee had had a drink or two, he would become verbally abusive to her.

But when Dina broached the subject of Lee's getting help, he became very defensive, insisting that his drinking was not a problem. Dina tried to point out how he had changed of late, but Lee just got angrier. Months passed and he kept drinking, until Dina felt she must try again to convince him that his behavior was wrecking his health and destroying their marriage. This time, she gave him telephone numbers of places he could go for professional help and addresses where Alcoholics Anonymous meetings were held. Lee blew his stack. "Why don't you just mind your own business?" he shouted. "I don't tell you what to eat or drink or how to run your life. Why do you think you have the right to tell me how to live mine?"

Dina couldn't decide whether she was more hurt or shocked by the intensity of his response. She loved Lee and was just trying to help him. Yes, of course, his stopping drinking would benefit her, but her primary concern was Lee. Why didn't he understand that? Thinking that he might be more open to suggestion from someone outside the family, Dina tried getting friends to talk to him. Although Lee was a bit more courteous to them, he declined their help as well.

Dina thought of practically nothing else besides her mission to get him sober. She spent less time with their children, put her friends on the back burner, stopped working out, and in general did the bare minimum to get by. She waited up for Lee and greeted him with lectures about drinking and driving. She hid his whiskey bottles and emptied his glass when he wasn't looking, hoping he would think he'd drunk enough and go to bed. When Dina realized that Lee's drinking was running her life, she decided to call me.

Although she didn't say she was depressed, she sure looked it. But she was certain that she did not want to leave the marriage. She did, however, want some suggestions about how to deal with Lee and her unhappiness over his life-style. She was quite aware that her nagging wasn't working, but didn't know what else to do. I asked her, "If a miracle happened and Lee stopped drinking tomorrow, what would you do with the time you now spend agonizing over him?" She simply could not answer the question. "I've been working so hard trying to change him, I've forgotten about my own needs. I'm clueless about what I would do if I didn't have to worry about Lee." As she said this, Dina realized that, for the past few years, she had put her life on hold. It was one thing to sacrifice your needs if the results were beneficial in some way, but no one felt better as a result of Dina's efforts.

Dina admitted she was ready to try something new. She agreed to stop trying to fix Lee and to focus on herself for a change. She would no longer reason with him, beg him, or even remind him that he had been drinking too much. When he returned from his late nights out with his friends, instead of asking twenty-one questions and lecturing him, she would simply say, "Hi, dear." Better yet, she would be fast asleep. Most important, Dina agreed to start spending more time with her children and renew contact with old friends. Just the thought of this new plan made her feel better. But I warned her that breaking old habits can be challenging and asked her to keep track of what she did to resist the temptation to fall back to them.

When Dina returned for the next session, she admitted that it was difficult to remain silent in the face of Lee's drinking, but she had somehow managed to do so. Moreover, she had noticed a new sense of relief now that she acknowledged that the only person who was going to change Lee was Lee. "Letting go," she said, "isn't easy, but, on the other hand, it's remarkably freeing." Much of our talk focused on how she was keeping herself busy, a far cry from previous sessions, when she had spoken only of Lee. In addition to spending more time with her children and friends, she started working out again and signed up for a class at the local community college. The best part is that, although she had undertaken these activities to distract herself from compulsive problem-solving, she discovered she actually enjoyed them immensely.

We met for a few more weeks, and during our last session she commented that something unusual had happened: Lee admitted that he had been drinking too much. Dina even noticed that he had cut back on his drinking at home. Late nights out were becoming less frequent, and when he did go out, he came home earlier and appeared to have had less to drink. Dina wasn't naive—she didn't assume that Lee's difficulty with alcohol was over—but she was amazed that, for the first time in his life, he had owned up to having a problem.

Dina learned an extremely important lesson. When she nagged at him, he reacted like a child, rebelling against her advice. He became as obsessed with her anger and disappointment as she had become with his drinking. Instead of being self-critical, he spent hours dreaming up ways to get Dina off of his back, and she spent just as many hours going in circles in an attempt to get through to him. In essence, her nagging distracted both of them from the self-examination that was the prerequisite for change. Once she stopped trying to fix Lee, they each had to face themselves, and neither of them liked what they saw.

"Isn't it ironic?" she commented. "All these years I had been trying to change him and nothing worked. Now I focus on myself for a change and he admits he has a problem." I understood what Dina was saying, but I didn't find it ironic at all. What I did find somewhat ironic was how strenuously she tried to get Lee to take better care of himself when she hadn't been doing such a great job of taking care of herself. Once she made a commitment to stop trying to reform his life and instead improve the quality of her own, she was unwittingly paving the way for Lee to follow suit.

So, if you are at your wits' end because nothing has worked, good. Take a vacation from trying to change things. Stop worrying for a change and focus on yourself. "Easier said than done," you say, and though that's true, the alternative is even harder in the long run. If you keep doing what you've been doing, the situation will only get worse, not to mention your mental health. Here are some ways you can kick the fix-it habit cold turkey:

Keep busy. Psychologists tell us that the best way to break an undesirable habit is to replace it with a more desirable one. For example, if you want to stop biting your nails, chew gum instead. If you have decided that fixing things isn't fixing things, take the energy that has demanded and apply it to doing other things. Ask yourself:

What would I be doing if I weren't worrying so much about (fill in the blank)?

What were you doing *before* you put your life on hold for this problem? Start doing those activities again, or take up some new ones.

For instance, if you have been unsuccessfully trying to fix an unhealthy friendship, keep yourself busy so you won't think about calling. Go for a walk, exercise, call a different friend, take up a new hobby, pick up an old one, work longer hours, play with your kids. Do anything but what you have been doing. Most people tell me that, the busier they are, the better they feel. If the pace gets too frantic, you can always cut back. But for now, keep your mind and body active. You may find yourself enjoying your life so much that you wonder, "Why didn't I do this sooner?" There will be times when you are tempted to take up your crusade. The richer your life, however, the less likely it is that you will revert to your old ways.

Learn to stop your thoughts. In addition to changing your actions by keeping busy, it helps to block negative thoughts. For example, in the past, when Dina saw Lee drinking, she told herself, "This is terrible, I need to do something about it," or "Can't he see that this is ruining our lives?" These thoughts triggered an unpleasant feeling inside her, and she felt compelled to act to change Lee. In this situation, Dina might have found it helpful to use the technique called "thought stopping."

Each time you have a thought that tugs on you to fix something, eliminate it by saying to yourself, "STOP!" Then force yourself to think about other things. Some people say that it helps to envision a big red stop sign. You might think about how fixing things has made things worse in general, or try to imagine how unproductive it would be to take action based on the thought you were having. Or think totally unrelated thoughts—where you're going out for dinner, what you need to do for work tomorrow, who you haven't called in a long time. In other words, change the channel. Don't let your thoughts control you; learn to control your thoughts.

Focus on yourself for a change. If all of your efforts have gone into changing another person but nothing has worked, it may be time to pay more attention to yourself. Remember Kathy Bates in *Fried Green Tomatoes?* The bottom line is that there is one person ultimately responsible for your happiness, and that is YOU. If your needs aren't being met in a particular relationship, and your efforts haven't managed to change the relationship, you must find another way to achieve happiness. No one else can make you happy; you must do it yourself. Furthermore, no matter how good a relationship is, no single person can satisfy all your needs all the time. Relationships can't operate in a vacuum: hobbies, interests, and friends are essential. So, if your relationship isn't going too well right now, pretend that the person with whom you are having difficulties isn't in your life. Ask yourself:

What would I do to make myself happier?

Once you are clear about your answer to this question, start doing what you can immediately. As you become more content, you might look at your situation quite differently. Change the part over which you have control—you—and watch what happens.

Accept what's unchangeable. Deb's roommate, Ann, wasn't particularly neat, which Deb found irritating. In fact, she found it downright aggravating. For months, Deb tried a variety of different strategies to get Ann to be more considerate. Ann would change a bit for a little while, but at heart she's a slob. Deb was very fond of Ann, and if it weren't for this one issue, their relationship would have been great, because Ann is a dedicated and loyal friend. At the point when I met Deb, she realized she had three choices: find a new roommate; continue living with Ann and feeling annoyed; or somehow learn to accept that Ann wasn't going to change, and focus on what was positive about their friendship. Deb chose the last.

Accepting Ann as she is wasn't easy, and Deb was not able to do it until she gave herself permission to seriously consider moving out. Once she recognized that she was not a victim or a prisoner, she decided to reject that option and accept her friend's behavior. That didn't mean that she grew to like Ann's messiness. But she made a conscious decision to overlook Ann's shortcomings in order to enjoy her good points and their friendship. "I figure that every person is a package deal. You'll appreciate some of their qualities and dislike others. I could have traded Ann in for a neater roommate, but maybe she wouldn't have been as much fun to be around. I feel better about Ann now," Deb said.

Some traits and situations defy change. When you encounter them, like Deb, you have three choices: continue to be miserable, leave, or accept the inevitable. Only you can decide which is for you. But if you decide to accept what isn't changing, reread chapter seven on identifying exceptions. It will help you to emphasize what works.

Perhaps you are not interested in changing someone else; you simply want to change something about you. Maybe it's the shape of your body, your tendency to get angry easily, your earning capacity, your fear of flying, or whatever. If you are convinced that you have done all that you can to achieve your goal but aren't making any headway, maybe the best thing you can do is to accept yourself the way you are. Learn to focus on your strengths rather than your weaknesses. Find ways to compensate for falling short of your ideal for yourself.

I once worked with a woman who had a fear of elevators. This was not the reason she was in therapy—she had come to work on her relationship with her child—but when she happened to mention her elevator phobia, being an avid "helper," I suggested several strategies for her to overcome the fear. She politely insisted that, though she was certain what I had suggested would be helpful for most people, she had long ago accepted that she would never again set foot in an elevator. She simply took the stairs. "If anyone has a problem with it, I just tell them this is how I get my exercise," she explained, and we moved on.

In case you didn't know, I'll let the cat out of the bag: no one is perfect. If you have been fighting an uphill battle trying to mold yourself into something you're not, do yourself a favor. Tell yourself that life is too short for you to be unhappy so much of the time. Imagine how your life would change if you would just accept who you are, exactly as you are. Envision how freeing it would be to feel good about yourself even if you are overweight, even if you are quick to anger, even if other people are more outgoing. You have other good attributes.

If simply accepting yourself is asking too much, at least take some time off from self-improvement. Relax, do something fun, do nothing, don't take yourself so seriously for a little while. If, at some later point, you feel compelled to get back on the self-improvement track, don't worry, you'll find lots of things to work on. In the meantime, reflect on the words of the philosopher Reinhold Niebuhr: "God, give us grace to accept with serenity the things that cannot be changed, courage to change the things which should be changed, and the wisdom to distinguish the one from the other."

Don't accept what's unchangeable. If you have been trying unsuccessfully to change a situation, another option is to leave. For example, if you have been unhappy at work for a long time and nothing you do makes a difference, stop blaming other people or yourself and start looking for another job. Certain aspects of your situation may be unchangeable. I remember when an agency where I was working started requiring a tremendous amount of paperwork. Some people moaned and groaned, others quietly complied, and still others left for greener pastures. Rather than put an inordinate amount of energy into an unwinnable fight, you may decide to reserve your energy to create a better alternative. When all else fails, parting ways can sometimes supply that alternative.

This is not to say that people should take their decisions to leave relationships or situations lightly. I'm a firm believer that most problems are resolvable (or I wouldn't have written either *Divorce Busting* or this book). But if, in your heart of hearts, you believe there is no other path to try, and the situation as it is is intolerable to you, stop prolonging the inevitable and make a change.

Make things worse. Sometimes, as strange as it may sound, people can't stop trying to fix things until the situation becomes unbearable. If you know you should stop fixing things but feel compelled to continue, you may have to consciously make things worse before you'll stop. I know this sounds like the craziest idea you've ever heard, but stick with me.

Jack scheduled an appointment because he was in turmoil over his passion for a married woman. At first their affair had sizzled—sex was great, communication was instantaneous—but that came to a quick halt when the woman sensed Jack was getting too serious about her. She did not, under any circumstance, want to leave her husband. Jack's eagerness to spend time with her started to scare her off, but she refused to cut her ties with him completely. He had become so obsessed with her that he was having difficulty sleeping at night, concentrating at work, or doing anything unrelated to thinking about her. His goal? Less anxiety.

When I asked him what he would have to do to feel more at peace with himself, he replied, "I need to stop pursuing her." I then asked, "What needs to happen before you can do that?" and he mentioned five or six very specific actions he needed to take. For example, he said, "We golf on the same league. I would have to switch leagues so I wouldn't run into her all the time," and "I'd have to look for a new job, since I'm not interested in mine anymore. If I had more challenge at work, it would take my mind off of her." We ended the session and he went home, intent on taking the steps he had mentioned.

A week later, he returned and told me he had done nothing to change his situation. In fact, he found himself calling her more often than before. He was obviously anxious and unhappy, but his plan seemed to be falling by the wayside. In thinking over why he hadn't done his "homework," I realized that, although he knew a relationship with this woman was unlikely, he was probably getting some needs met or he wouldn't continue his pursuit. I guessed that the situation would have to get worse before he would really back off.

Knowing that the woman pushed Jack away when he pursued her, I surmised the only alternative was for him to pursue her *more.* I suggested that, instead of trying to avoid this woman, he allow himself to pursue her as much as he desired. I pointed out that, over the last few months, he had restrained himself from pursuing her fully because his rational side kept telling him the chase was unhealthy for him, but it wasn't working. I told him that I assumed that giving his obsession free reign would have two possible results: either he would win her over (an unlikely outcome) or she would, in no uncertain terms, reject him (which she had not done previously).

Two weeks later, at our next session, he explained that he had pursued her without restraint the day after we last met. The result was out-and-out rejection. Since that time, he had completely turned his life around—applied for a new job, contacted old friends, and planned a vacation—and he felt tremendously relieved. Now that he had finally seen the futility of his approach, he was able to stop obsessing about the woman. It was clear that nothing he could do would win her over, and he found unrequited love a bore.

So, if you have become consumed by a situation that defies change, ask yourself: *What would have to be different in my life for me to stop trying to change things?*

Then ask yourself:

What would I have to do to increase the chances that this will happen?

If you are able to come up with a response to these questions, it means that you have not yet hit rock bottom and you are not yet prepared to let go. So stop pretending that you are. Give yourself permission to continue what you've been doing until you are absolutely convinced you're done with it. Even if well-meaning friends and relatives advise you to stop, they are not in your shoes. You won't stop until *you're* completely fed up. You can accelerate this process by letting it happen. When you're ready to change, you'll change.

Chapter Seventeen

The Beginning

THIS IS MY third book, which means it is also the third time I have written a closing chapter. I'm beginning to notice a pattern. Despite my unbelievable relief at having this enormously time-consuming task draw to an end, writing the last chapter is always a bittersweet experience for me. You see, for the last year or so, I've dedicated so much of my time and energy to writing that it has become a major focal point in my life. I have been going steady with my computer, and we're just about to break up.

Part of my sadness is due to the fact that you have been part of my life almost on a daily basis. Although we've never met, I have spent a year trying to imagine your concerns, struggles, thoughts, feelings, and triumphs. I've openly shared myself with you, in the hope that you might learn from my experiences, or just to make you laugh. We've sort of had a long-distance relationship, and now I'm pages away from saying goodbye. I have often felt that same sadness after finishing a good novel: I want the characters to live on in my life forever.

As I pondered this feeling, I recalled a conversation I had had with my daughter when she was about five or six. Danielle adores my mother, who visits frequently. One night when I was tucking Danielle in bed, she started to cry. I asked her why. She had heard an airplane fly overhead, and she told me that every time she hears an airplane she gets very sad, because airplanes take her "Omi" (her nickname for my mother) away from her. She cried for a while, and after some thought I said to her, "You know, Danielle, it's true that airplanes take your Omi away from you, but you should keep in mind that airplanes bring your Omi back, too." She really hadn't considered this, and looked somewhat relieved. "So," I said, "the next time you hear the sound of an airplane, think about it bringing Omi here." She smiled and seemed relieved and went to sleep. The story reminded me that all endings mark beginnings, too.

And now that we've both reached the end of this book, I can't help wondering what *your* new paths will be. If you were feeling defeated when you started reading this book, I sincerely hope it has rekindled your optimism, your sense of humor, and your faith in yourself. More than anything else, I urge you to trust your instincts and drop the word "dysfunctional" from your vocabulary. If you believe everything you hear on talk shows or read in magazines about human frailty, you are, as a colleague of mine likes to say, an "Adult Child of Dysfunctional Theories."

I never cease to be amazed by the way people transform their lives once they believe they can. Watching people change right before my eyes has deeply enriched my own life. I continue to be inspired by my clients every day. I have also been fortunate enough to encounter incredibly courageous and resourceful people who have overcome major challenges in their lives without professional assistance. I strongly believe that we have a great deal to learn from these people. They are an untapped resource for learning about solutions.

Take Ellie, a friend of mine, who was raped at knifepoint about twenty years ago. Although it was an intensely negative experience, she was not about to let it ruin her life. And it hasn't. She married happily and had a wonderful little boy, has a great career and lots of friends, travels extensively, and jogs by herself regularly. She would prefer that the rape hadn't happened, but she never blamed herself for it, nor has she ever thought of herself as "damaged goods."

What is it about Ellie that allowed her to retain her self-esteem despite what happened? How did she manage to keep fear from running her life? Why hasn't anger consumed her? What prevents her from regarding all men as potential rapists and sustains her remarkably healthy marriage? How has her vision of her past made it possible for her to be so resilient in the present? Why and how do people like Ellie bounce back so quickly, so soundly? We need to know. Let's stop studying failure and start studying success.

Ellie is remarkable, but she is not unique. Stories of triumph abound, but they don't often make the evening news. Apparently, good news is no news. We're told that people are more intrigued with life's harsher realities. That's unfortunate.

Recently, I happened to catch a story about a young boy who was diagnosed with cancer and about to begin chemotherapy. In anticipation of his losing his hair because of the treatment, his teacher and all the boys in his class shaved their own heads in a show of support. Weeks later, his cancer was in remission. I couldn't help thinking what a shame it was that such stories are so rarely covered. Imagine what an effect they could have on our perspectives about people and what they are capable of. The countless people who have triumphed over physical illness, poverty, abuse, loss, and emotional devastation are true experts. Let's learn from them, instead of obsessing over humanity's dark side, then running to professionals in the hope that they can cure what ails us.

The idea that experts don't necessarily have all the answers may not win any popularity contests. Remember how disappointed Dorothy and her companions were when they discovered that the so-called Wizard of Oz, their last hope for a return trip to Kansas (not to mention a heart, a brain, and courage), was really just an old man wildly waving his arms behind a screen? A tremendous amount of security is derived from believing in experts. But it's a false sense of security that in no way compares to the strength you get from knowing that you can depend on yourself. Don't forget—in the end, the old man showed Dorothy and her friends that the answers for which they were searching were within them all along. (He was a real wizard after all.)

Since I am an "expert," I realize it may seem somewhat paradoxical for me to tell you to take expert advice off of its pedestal. But this isn't paradoxical at all. What I have proposed to you in this book is just another theory, not necessarily more "correct" than any other theory. It's only a different way of seeing things. You be the judge of whether it works for you or not. It's my hope that you will absorb the ideas, then adapt them to make them your own, using what's helpful and disregarding the rest. My goal is to put the "self" back in self-help.

The messages I have brought to you are really quite simple: believe in yourself; do more of what works, less of what doesn't; and don't analyze problems to death. That's all. If nothing else, I hope this advice has simplified your life. I know it has simplified mine.

Still, I can't help but wonder how this book will affect your life. I'm curious to know how the butterfly effect will transform an idea you read into an avalanche of creative solutions. The problem is, I'll never know—unless I hear from you, that is. Nothing would be more rewarding to me than to know I've touched your life in some way. Please write to brag about your accomplishments. Send your letters to:

Michele Weiner-Davis
P.O. Box 197
Woodstock, Illinois 60098

Notes

Chapter One: Why Ask Why?

1. J. H. Weakland, R. Fisch, P. Watzlawick, and A. Bodin, "Brief Therapy: Focused Problem Resolution," *Family Process;* S. de Shazer, I. K. Berg, E. Lipchik, E. Nunnally, A. Molnar, W. C. Gingerich, and M. Weiner-Davis, "Brief Therapy: Focused Solution Development," *Family Process;* S. Fisher, "Time-limited Brief Therapy with Families: A One Year Follow-up Study," *Family Process.*

Chapter Two: Putting the Past Behind You

1. T. E. Fuller, "Oedipal Wrecks: Has a Century of Freud Bred a Country of Narcissists?," *Washington Monthly.*
2. M. Yapko, *Suggestions of Abuse: True and False Memories of Childhood Sexual Trauma.*
3. S. Glucksberg, "Symbolic Processes" in *Introduction to Psychology: A Self-Selection Textbook.*
4. R. De Monbreun and E. Craighead, "Distortion of Perception and Recall of Positive and Neutral Feedback in Depression," *Cognitive Therapy and Research.*
5. M. Yapko, *Suggestions of Abuse: True and False Memories of Childhood Sexual Trauma.*
6. M. Blau, "Adult Children Tied to the Past," *American Health.*
7. M. E. P. Seligman, *What You Can Change and What You Can't.*
8. S. & S. Wolin, *The Resilient Self: How Survivors of Troubled Families Rise Above Adversity.*
9. A. H. Rosenfeld, "Does Abuse Beget Abuse?," *Psychology Today* (1987).
10. S. de Shazer, *Clues: Investigating Solutions in Brief Therapy.*

Chapter Three: The Anatomy of Change

1. M. Weiner-Davis, S. de Shazer, and W. C. Gingerich, "Constructing the Therapeutic Solution by Building on Pretreatment Change: an Exploratory Study," *Journal of Marital and Family Therapy.*
2. J. Gurin, "Remaking Our Lives," *American Health.*
3. M. Weiner-Davis, "In Praise of Solutions," *Family Therapy Networker.*

4. P. Watzlawick, "If You Desire to See, Learn How to Act," in J. Zeig (ed.), *The Evolution of Psychotherapy*.

5. D. G. Myers, *The Pursuit of Happiness*.

6. P. J. Peters and R. H. Waterman, Jr., *In Search of Excellence: Lessons from America's Best-Run Companies*.

7. L. C. Plunkett, "Encourage Failure and You'll Spur Growth," *Executive Female*.

8. M. E. P. Seligman, *Learned Optimism: How to Change Your Mind and Your Life*.

9. R. Rosenthal and K. L. Fode, "The Effect of Experimenter Bias on the Performance of the Albino Rat," *Behavioral Sciences*.

10. M. Yapko, *When Living Hurts: Directives for Treating Depression*.

11. M. E. P. Seligman, *Learned Optimism: How to Change Your Mind and Your Life*, p. 5.

Chapter Four: The Whole Is Greater Than the Sum of Its Parts

1. W. J. Lederer and D. Jackson, *The Mirages of Marriage*.

2. G. Bateson, J. Haley, and J. Weakland, "Toward a Theory of Schizophrenia," p. 88.

Chapter Five: The Butterfly Effect

1. T. Robbins, *Unlimited Power*.

Chapter Six: If You Don't Know Where You're Going, You'll Probably End Up Somewhere Else

1. E. Lipchik and S. de Shazer, "Purposeful Sequences for Beginning the Solution-Focused Interview," in *Interviewing* edited by E. Lipchik, pp. 114–17.

2. S. de Shazer, *Keys to Solution in Brief Therapy*.

Chapter Seven: If It Works, Don't Fix It

1. M. Gold, *The Good News about Depression*.

Chapter Eight: Do Something Different

1. S. de Shazer, *Keys to Solution in Brief Therapy*.

Chapter Eleven: Easier Done Than Said

1. W. J. Lederer and D. Jackson, *The Mirages of Marriage*, pp. 98–99.

2. J. H. Bryan and N. H. Walbek, "Preaching and Practicing Generosity, Children's Actions and Reactions," *Child Development*.

Chapter Twelve: Smart Talk

1. R. Fisch, J. Weakland, and L. Segal, *The Tactics of Change: Doing Therapy Briefly*, p. 90.

2. R. Bryant, J. H. Amendt, L. Frank, and T. Kleckner, "Friendly Persuasion," *Family Therapy Networker* (July–Aug. 1990), p. 62.

Chapter Fourteen: Last-Resort Techniques

1. A. Price, *Discipline: 101 Alternatives to Spanking*, p. 93.
2. M. E. P. Seligman, *What You Can Change and What You Can't: The Complete Guide to Successful Self-Improvement*, p. 241.

Chapter Fifteen: Feet, Don't Fail Me Now

1. S. de Shazer, *Keys to Solution in Brief Therapy*, pp. 132–33.
2. E. Lipchik and S. de Shazer, "Purposeful Sequences for Beginning the Solution-Focused Interview," in *Interviewing* edited by E. Lipchik. pp. 113–14.
3. T. Heath and B. Atkinson, "Solutions Attempted and Considered: Broadening Assessment in Brief Therapy," *Journal of Strategic and Systemic Therapies*, pp. 56–57.
4. B. Cade and W. O'Hanlon, *A Brief Guide to Brief Therapy*, pp. 81–83.

Bibliography

Baker, R. *Hidden Memories*. New York: Prometheus Books, 1992.

Bateson, G., Haley, J., and Weakland, J. "Toward a Theory of Schizophrenia." *Behavioral Science*, vol. 1, 1956, pp. 251–64.

Baxter, S. "The Last Self-Help Article You'll Ever Need." *Psychology Today*, vol. 26, no. 2 (March–April 1993), p. 70.

Blau, M. "Adult Children Tied to the Past." *American Health*, July–Aug. 1990, pp. 57–65.

Blau, M. *Families Apart: Ten Keys to Successful Co-Parenting*. New York: G. P. Putnam, 1994.

Bryan, J. H., and Walbek, N. H. "Preaching and Practicing Generosity: Children's Actions and Reactions." *Child Development*, vol. 41, no. 2 (1970), pp. 329–53.

Bryant, R., Amendt, J. H., Frank, L., and Kleckner, T. "Friendly Persuasion." *Family Therapy Networker*, July–Aug. 1990, p. 62.

Burns, D. D. *Feeling Good: The New Mood Therapy*. New York: Avon Books, 1980.

Cade, B., and O'Hanlon, W. *A Brief Guide to Brief Therapy*. New York: Norton, 1993.

Cole, K. C. "Small Differences." *Science Digest*, June 1985, pp. 42–81.

Covey, S. *The Seven Habits of Highly Effective People: Powerful Lessons in Personal Change*. New York: Fireside Books, 1989.

De Monbreun, R., and Craighead, E. "Distortion of Perception and Recall of Positive and Neutral Feedback in Depression." *Cognitive Therapy and Research*, vol. 1, 1977, pp. 311–29.

de Shazer, S. *Clues: Investigating Solutions in Brief Therapy*. New York: Norton, 1988.

de Shazer, S. *Keys to Solution in Brief Therapy*. New York: Norton, 1985.

de Shazer, S., Berg, I. K., Lipchik, E., Nunnally, E., Molnar, A., Gingerich, W. C., and Weiner-Davis, M. "Brief Therapy: Focused Solution Development." *Family Process*, vol. 25, 1986, pp. 207–21.

Fisch, R., Weakland, J., and Segal, L. *The Tactics of Change: Doing Therapy Briefly*. San Francisco: Jossey-Bass, 1982.

Fisher, S. "Time-Limited Brief Therapy with Families: A One Year Follow-up Study." *Family Process*, vol. 23, 1980, pp. 121–26.

Fuller, T. E. "Oedipal Wrecks: Has a Century of Freud Bred a Country of Narcissists?" *Washington Monthly*, vol. 24, nos. 1–2 (Jan.–Feb. 1992), p. 32.

Gibbs, N. "Bringing Up Father." *Time*, June 28, 1993, p. 61.

Glucksberg, S. "Symbolic processes." *Introduction to Psychology: a Self-Selection Textbook*. Iowa: Wm. Brown, 1966.

Gold, M. *The Good News About Depression*. New York: Bantam, 1986.

Gurin, J. "Remaking Our Lives." *American Health*, vol. 9, no. 2 (March 1990), pp. 50–52.

Heath, T., and Atkinson, B. "Solutions Attempted and Considered: Broadening Assessment in Brief Therapy." *Journal of Strategic and Systemic Therapies*, vol. 8, nos. 2–3 (1989), pp. 56–57.

Hillman, J. "Is Therapy Turning Us into Children? An Interview Between James Hillman and Michael Ventura." *New Age Journal*, May–June 1992, pp. 60–141.

Kaminer, W. *I'm Dysfunctional, You're Dysfunctional*. Reading, Mass.: Addison-Wesley, 1992.

Kiser, D. As quoted in "Brief Therapy on the Couch." *Family Therapy Networker*, March–April 1990, pp. 34–35.

Kohn, A. "Make Love, Not War." *Psychology Today*, vol. 22, no. 6 (June 1988).

Lederer, W. J., and Jackson, D. *The Mirages of Marriage*. New York: Norton, 1968.

Lipchik, E., and de Shazer, S. "Purposeful Sequences for Beginning the Solution-Focused Interview." In E. Lipchik, ed., *Interviewing*. Rockville, Md.: Aspen, 1988.

McGarvey, R. "Rehearsing for Success." *Executive Female*, vol. 13, no. 1 (Jan.–Feb. 1990), p. 34.

Molnar, A., and Lindquist, B. *Changing Problem Behavior in Schools*. San Francisco: Jossey-Bass, 1989.

Myers, D. G., Ph.D. "Pursuing Happiness." *Psychology Today*, vol. 26, no. 4 (July–Aug. 1993), p. 35. Excerpted from *The Pursuit of Happiness*. New York: Avon Books, 1993.

Nichols, M. *Power of the Family*. New York: Simon & Schuster, 1988.

Niebuhr, R. "The Serenity Prayer." 1934.

Peters, P. J., and Waterman, R. H., Jr. *In Search of Excellence: Lessons from America's Best-Run Companies*. New York: Warner Books, 1982.

Plunkett, L. C. "Encourage Failure and You'll Spur Growth." *Executive Female*, vol. 16, no. 4 (July–Aug. 1993), p. 11.

Price, A. *Discipline: 101 Alternatives to Spanking*. Woodland Hills, Utah: SB Publishers, 1983.

Rieff, D. "Victims, All? Recovery, Co-dependency, and the Art of Blaming Somebody Else." *Harper's Magazine*, Oct. 1991, pp. 49–56.

Rosenfeld, A. H. "Does Abuse Beget Abuse?" *Psychology Today*, vol. 21, Aug. 1987, p. 9.

Rosenthal, R., and Fode, K. L. "The Effect of Experimenter Bias on the Performance of the Albino Rat." *Behavioral Sciences*, vol. 8, 1963, pp. 183–89.

Seligman, M. E. P. *Learned Optimism: How to Change Your Mind and Your Life*. New York: Knopf, 1990.

Seligman, M. E. P. *What You Can Change and What You Can't*. New York: Knopf, 1994.

Snyder, M. "When Belief Creates Reality." *Advances in Experimental Social Psychology*, vol. 18, 1984, pp. 260–61.

Straus, H. "The Lazarus File: When the 'Spontaneous' Cure Comes from Within?" *American Health: Fitness of Body and Mind*, vol. 8, no. 4 (May 1989), p. 67.

Toufexis, A. "When Can Memories Be Trusted?" *Time*, Oct. 28, 1991, p. 86.

Ungerleider, S. "Visions of Victory." *Psychology Today*, vol. 25, no. 4 (July–Aug. 1992).

Watts, A. *The Book: On the Taboo Against Knowing Who You Are*. New York: Vintage Books, 1972.

Watzlawick, P. "If You Desire to See, Learn How to Act." In J. Zeig (ed.), *The Evolution of Psychotherapy*. New York: Brunner/Mazel, 1987.

Weakland, J., Fisch, R., Watzlawick, P., and Bodin, A. "Brief Therapy: Focused Problem Resolution." *Family Process*, vol. 13, 1983, pp. 141–68.

Weiner-Davis, M. *Divorce Busting: A Rapid and Revolutionary Program for Staying Together*. New York: Summit, 1992.

——— "In Praise of Solutions." *Family Therapy Networker*, March–April 1990, pp. 42–48.

Weiner-Davis, M., de Shazer, S., and Gingerich, W. C. "Constructing the Therapeutic Solution by Building on Pretreatment Change: An Exploratory Study." *Journal of Marital and Family Therapy*, vol. 13, no. 4 (1987), pp. 359–63.

Wolin, S., and S. Wolin. *The Resilient Self: How Survivors of Troubled Families Rise Above Adversity*. New York: Villard Books, 1993.

Yapko, M. "The Seductions of Memory." *Family Therapy Networker*, Sept.–Oct. 1993, p. 35.

———. *Suggestions of Abuse: True and False Memories of Childhood Sexual Trauma*. New York: Simon & Schuster, 1994.

———. *When Living Hurts: Directives for Treating Depression*. New York: Brunner/Mazel, 1988.

Index

ALSO BY MICHELE WEINER DAVIS:

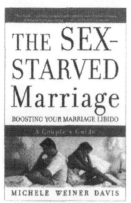
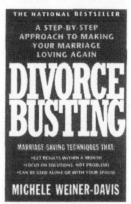
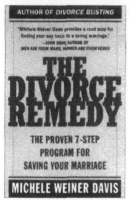